The UFO Report 1991

Other books by Timothy Good

The UFO Report 1990
Above Top Secret

THE
UFO REPORT
1991

edited by
Timothy Good

SIDGWICK & JACKSON
LONDON

First published in 1990 by Sidgwick & Jackson Ltd

Copyright © 1990 by Timothy Good
First Reprint April 1991

ISBN 0–283–06070–0 (Paperback)
0–283–06069–7 (Hardback)

Set in Linotron Times by
Rowland Phototypesetting Ltd
Bury St Edmunds, Suffolk

Printed in Great Britain by
Mackays of Chatham plc, Chatham, Kent
for Sidgwick & Jackson Ltd
1 Tavistock Chambers, Bloomsbury Way
London WC1A 2SG

Contents

Editor's Foreword

We live in exciting times. So many sightings of UFOs have been reported during 1989 and the first half of 1990 that it is difficult to keep track – and harder still to come to terms with the nature and purpose of these intrusions. Partly for this reason, I have included a world round-up of selected reports, which at least gives some idea of the massive scale of the phenomenon (see Chapter 10).

The extraordinary but by no means unprecedented incidents at Voronezh, USSR, reported world-wide and endorsed by TASS (Chapter 3), are a recent milestone in terms of coverage, yet the national media, in general, continue to ridicule these and other incidents. There are exceptions, of course. In the United States, local newspapers often contain lengthy and serious accounts of sightings. In a three-page, in-depth article in the *Little River News* (Ashdown, Arkansas), for example, editor Jim Williamson dismissed conventional explanations for the cattle mutilations that had occurred in the area in March 1989 (Chapter 9), and concluded: 'We're not qualified to offer answers on mutilations. But it's a crime, regardless of who is doing it.'[1]

It remains a sad fact of life that beliefs – whether of a political, scientific or religious nature – tend to divide rather than unite mankind. The ufological community remains divided about the nature of the UFO phenomenon, and here in Britain there has been much acrimonious debate over the cause of the Cropfield Circles, with a number of leading researchers insisting that they have nothing whatever to do with UFOs. Perhaps they don't. Yet evidence to the contrary – in some cases at least – is cited by George Wingfield (Chapter 1).

The hypothesis that some UFOs are extraterrestrial in origin continues to be unfashionable among researchers in Europe. It is believed, for example, that extraterrestrials would not conduct themselves in such a bizarre and elusive manner, neither would they be able to get here in the first place owing to the vast distances

7

involved. These objections not only presuppose a knowledge of how aliens would or would not behave, but also fail to allow for advanced alien technology – a technology that may well involve the manipulation of space and time – and mental abilities that transcend our current knowledge.

There are, however, categories of UFO experience which seem to preclude an extraterrestrial explanation. I have studied various aspects of the paranormal for many years and have had numerous personal experiences throughout my life which have left me in no doubt that our conventional view of reality is seriously flawed. So I am no philistine in these matters. But like UFOs, this is a complex and multi-disciplinary subject, as Ralph Noyes explains in his erudite article (Chapter 4), and those who pontificate on the link between UFOs and the paranormal would be well advised to study both subjects thoroughly before jumping to conclusions.

UFOs: The Gulf Breeze Sightings, by Ed and Frances Walters,[2] is undoubtedly the most important book on the subject for years, and should be read by all those who want to gain an insight into the nature of the UFO phenomenon and its interaction with human beings. The astonishing series of authentic colour photographs, together with the many shared encounters, go a long way towards establishing the objective reality of these phenomena. In 1989 I made a second visit to Gulf Breeze, and was again impressed by the integrity of the witnesses I spoke with who had seen identical crafts. And the sightings have continued in that area. (Four reports are included in Chapter 10.)

If the disturbing accounts of injuries to humans caused by UFOs in Brazil (Chapter 5), and the 'abduction' of US Navy jets in Puerto Rico (Chapter 8) are factual – and I see no reason to believe otherwise – then the attitude of governments becomes more understandable. Such reports are not without precedence, after all. Could it be that the new era of co-operation between the superpowers is due in part to the UFO intrusion? 'At our meeting in Geneva,' said Mikhail Gorbachev, referring to the 1985 summit conference, 'the US President said that if the earth faced an invasion by extraterrestrials, the United States and the Soviet Union would join forces to repel such an invasion. I shall not dispute the hypothesis, though I think it's early yet to worry about such an intrusion . . .'[3]

Finally, I am indebted to the team of distinguished contributors who have made this book possible, and to the numerous journalists, researchers, magazines, and newspapers whose reports are cited herein. My apologies for any omissions of credit. I would also like to thank Dorothee Walter for assistance at the word processor and for her photograph on the back cover (of the hardback edition) and Leslie Banks, who has flown George Wingfield, Ralph Noyes and myself so many times on photo-reconnaissance flights over the Cropfield Circles.

TIMOTHY GOOD
London
May 1990

REFERENCES
1. *Little River News*, Ashdown, Arkansas, 20 April 1989.
2. Walters, Ed and Walters, Frances: *UFOs: The Gulf Breeze Sightings*, Bantam Press, London 1990; *The Gulf Breeze Sightings*, William Morrow, New York 1990.
3. Speech at the Grand Kremlin Palace, Moscow, 16 February 1987, published in *Soviet Life* Supplement, May 1987, page 7A.

1

Ever Increasing Circles

GEORGE WINGFIELD

Educated at Eton College and Trinity College, Dublin, George
Wingfield graduated in 1966 with an M.A. Hons. degree in Natural
Sciences.

He worked briefly at the Royal Greenwich Observatory, Herst-
monceux, on stellar spectra and the Earth's magnetism, and currently works for IBM UK Ltd in the field of Systems Engineering.

George Wingfield became interested in the Corn Circles
phenomenon on 8 August 1987, after visiting Westbury, Wiltshire,
where a number of Circle formations had recently appeared. This
also led to an interest in the related subject of Ufology. He is a
Principal Field Research Officer for the recently formed Centre for
Crop Circle Studies (CCCS).

Imagine, if you will, the following scenario. By dint of sheer
genius, amazing luck, or else by having the right contacts either on
this Earth or beyond, you have uncovered the complete solution to
the mystery of the UFO phenomenon. Armed with total conviction, not to mention conclusive proof, you stride confidently on to
the stage of a lecture theatre to address a prestigious audience of
scientists, Ufologists and researchers who have assembled to hear
what you have to say. They listen with baited breath and hang on
your every word. Finally, amid rapturous applause, they come
forward one by one to congratulate you and acknowledge their
complete agreement with all you have said. At last the UFO
mystery is finally solved and understood!

There are no prizes given for spotting the deliberate mistake
here. Such a scenario can never happen and it does not require a
very deep understanding of matters ufological to see why not. The
same arguments apply equally to the Cropfield Circles, which have
rapidly become an allied subject of research due to their un-
doubted connection with the UFO phenomenon.

The first and most obvious problem which precludes any possible agreement as to the nature of the UFO phenomenon is that the majority of researchers into this subject tend to form far too narrow a view of the solution. This will range from the hardened sceptic who passionately believes that all UFOs can be explained in terms of misidentifications, hallucinations and hoaxes, to those who think only in terms of nuts-and-bolts flying saucers from extraterrestrial sources. And in between there is a whole gamut of interpretations usually held with equal conviction. This means that many books on the subject contain very little but the prejudices of the individual author and we often learn more about their psychology than the phenomenon itself.

The second problem is more subtle but even more intractable than the first. Our failure to understand the nature of the phenomenon seems clearly to be because the basic premises from which we work are flawed. Our current view of the external world as no more than a three-dimensional physical realm with a uni-directional dimension of time seems, even to physicists these days, to be inadequate. Also there is a duality present between the physical sciences and the realm of the psychic or paranormal, which is inextricably involved in these areas of knowledge. Very few researchers are able to bridge this gap and consequently there is little understanding of the phenomenon as a whole. This is the great bugbear of Ufology.

Thus, however inspired, or indeed correct, your explanation of the UFO phenomenon might be, the majority of the distinguished audience in our imagined scenario would find it unacceptable. They might politely clap, but secretly each one who disagreed with you would think, no matter what proof was offered, that you were deluded, crazy, perverse or just plain wrong – because they knew better.

Here let me hasten to add that I have no complete solutions to offer regarding UFOs, or the mystery of the Crop Circles. However, it has become increasingly impressed on many researchers that the subject of the Crop Circles is encompassed by four quite distinct areas of knowledge which often seem totally unrelated. These areas are Ufology, the physical sciences, dowsing (or 'Earth mysteries') and the realm of the psychic and metaphysical. I suggest that no solution can afford to ignore any of these four areas of knowledge, and this article seeks to justify this statement.

Already there have been howls of derision from the sceptics and armchair scientists who seldom, if ever, venture out into the fields to investigate the Circles. Let me assure them that I, too, as a science graduate, started out from their position with no previous inclination towards the mystical or paranormal. The fact that these aspects of the phenomenon are indisputably present owe nothing to my thinking on the subject, and all cereologists (as Crop Circle researchers are now called[1]) are aware of this to a greater or lesser degree. One critic of my previous article, 'The English Corn Circles in 1988' (*The UFO Report 1990*),[2] even deplored my advocacy of the need for an open mind. All I can say is that his mind would have to be totally impenetrable to all external influence if he were to deny these aspects of the subject, were he to study them at first hand. In that article I merely reported on what had been happening in the cornfields, without attempting to define a solution. Those who unwisely lay down rigid rules of behaviour for the Circles have almost always been confounded!

The UFO Connection

In *The UFO Report 1990*, I wrote at some length about the close connection between the strange UFO events at Warminster during the late 1960s and 1970s, and the subsequent appearance of Circles in the very same places only a few years later. The conclusion that the Crop Circle phenomenon somehow evolved from the Warminster happenings was also given impetus by Arthur Shuttlewood's description of a perfect Circle forming in grass at Warminster, accompanied by a high-pitched humming sound, during the early 1970s.[3]

Further evidence that connects the UFO happenings of that time with the Circles of today has now come to my attention in Arthur Shuttlewood's book, *The Flying Saucerers*.[4] American Ufologist Bryce Bond had gone to Warminster in August 1972 to interview Shuttlewood. While talking to him in a car parked near Starr Hill, a peculiar light appeared in the field in front of them. Bond wrote:

> . . . Arthur then said quietly: 'I am very glad that you are here tonight, Bryce. There in front of us is a UFO. Notice the triangle shape and coloured lights going around? That is a very good sign.' It then started to lift in a weird pattern – then just disappeared. I was flabbergasted! It was so close. While describing that one on tape for American listeners, another one popped up about 25 degrees along the horizon. This one was very brilliant white, while the other was a blaze of coloured lights. The intensity increased as it raised itself very slowly, did a little dance in the sky, then took off and disappeared. But before

it did, Arthur jumped from the car, borrowed a flashlight from someone and sent Morse code to it. It in turn sent back the same signal that Arthur flashed out. Then it flew off . . .

This episode recalls the similar response of some of the UFOs observed during the 1980s at Hessdalen, Norway, which responded to light signals flashed at them by observers. Bryce Bond next went down into a nearby hollow where three 'entities' had been seen two nights earlier. Nothing was seen by him then, but in making his way back to the cars, another strange incident occurred:

> . . . the wheat in the field next to me as I walked back up the dirt road was about waist high . . . I walked along the road very close to the fence. Suddenly I heard a noise – like something crushing the wheat down. There was no breeze blowing that night. I looked over. The moon had just come out, shining very brightly – and there, before my eyes, a large depression was being formed. The wheat was being crushed down in a counter-clockwise position. It too was shaped like a triangle and measured about twenty feet from point to point. I stood there a few moments and experienced a tremendous tingling sensation – the same sweet smell – being engulfed by warm air. Not fully understanding what had happened, I walked up the road to get Arthur . . .
>
> Speaking of the field, Arthur pointed out some landing impressions in the section fronting the farm barn: a circle about thirty feet in circumference, with another depression spotted, but this one in a long cigar shape. All the depressions, recently made and noticed, were in a counter-clockwise formation.[4]

These descriptions of events at Warminster on 26 August 1972 certainly provide an unequivocal link between the UFO phenomenon and Circles (and other shapes) which occurred in the cornfields at that time. Yet again one sees that luminous shapes seen in the sky sometimes correspond to the shapes which later appeared in the corn. In my previous article,[2] descriptions were given of lights in the sky arranged like the five on a dice; these were seen in places where quintuple Crop Circles were found in the fields, sometimes much later. Without making any judgement on the nature of these Warminster UFOs, which certainly exhibited a strong psychic interaction with the observers present in many cases, one might infer that the depressions in the wheat were produced by just the same agency as the UFOs.

A further description of an event at Warminster during the 1970s can also be related to the experiences of the Circle investigators of today. Steve Evans and Roy Fisher reported that on one occasion, as they were looking at the sky from the vantage point of Cradle

Hill, 'a forcefield seemed to move through the grass like a snake, crackling furiously like static electricity. It came straight for Roy's feet,' Evans said, 'then veered suddenly to the right. Sheep in the field were going frantic. When daylight came, we found flattened grass, as though something had landed.'[5]

The 'crackling . . . like static electricity' is something that Colin Andrews has described in the vicinity of a Circle near Kimpton, Hampshire, on 30 June 1987.

During 1989 several of the Circles were linked to UFO sightings, and in two of these events Circles were found precisely where luminous objects had descended, as described later. Others, such as sightings preceding the formation of the Husbands Bosworth, Leicestershire, Circle[6] and a sighting at an unverified Circle near Mansfield, Nottinghamshire, are omitted due to lack of space.

Quite apart from Britain, a smattering of Circle reports from Australia, Canada, the USA, and a few other countries, were received during 1989. Many of these were associated with UFO sightings. One particular case of interest was the report of a Circle in long grass at Gulf Breeze, Florida, close to where Ed Walters' bizarre series of UFO encounters occurred.[7] These encounters, together with a large number of photographs, are to be found in a significant new book, *UFOs: The Gulf Breeze Sightings*.[8]

The Circles in 1989

My previous article on the Circles of 1988 suggested that they would return again to perplex and amaze us in 1989. Indeed they did, to an extent which could never have been predicted. The Circles started to appear thick and fast from the middle of May. The first reported were found in a very large field of barley near Avebury Trusloe, where we counted no less than twenty-eight separate Circles. This was close to the thirteen Yatesbury Circles of 1988, but such a great concentration was unprecedented. There were two quintuple sets immediately adjacent in one part of the field and a separate quintuple about 250 yards away. Additionally, there were thirteen Circles varying in size between three and fourteen feet in diameter, in close proximity to these formations. These little ones became known as 'grapeshot', and had never previously been recorded. They subsequently became quite common in the Avebury and Westbury area during 1989 but were not seen elsewhere.

Curiously, these quintuple sets at Avebury Trusloe were exactly where farm worker Roy Lucas had seen 'puffs of smoke' rising from the ground in June 1988, as described in *The UFO Report 1990*. These had rapidly begun to twist and formed dense swirling columns before dispersing, but no Circles were found in the field at the time. Nearly a year later this very barley field was peppered with Circles.

More Circles appeared rapidly over the next few weeks and the predominant formation type was the double quintuple, which in previous years had only once been seen – at Silbury Hill in July 1988. Then, formation of the two quintuple sets, immediately adjacent to each other, had been nine days apart, and the overall pattern was not considered as a double. But now pairs of quintuples were found, always in the same field if not immediately adjacent, at Westbury, at Heytesbury, and also just to the north of Silbury Hill (see Plate 1:1). With the first two of these pairs it was not possible to say whether the two quintuples both formed at the same time; with the two near Silbury Hill they most definitely did not. In that case a somewhat skewed quintuple appeared first, followed some days later by a large Circle flanked on either side by two smaller ones, the whole triplet spanning about 100 yards. A BBC group which flew over these Circles between Silbury Hill and Avebury reported back that there were two quintuples in the field. The triplet had in fact 'sprouted' two extra satellite Circles and become a quintuplet.

This peculiar behaviour served only to confirm once again that the unseen agency which produces the Circles remains *in situ* before and after the corn is actually laid flat. There is no other explanation for the precise positioning of two additional satellite Circles to form a quintuplet which started off as a linear triplet. And this corresponded closely to what we were being told by dowsing expert Richard Andrews.

Further consideration of this aspect would indicate that the 'blueprint' for a formation may only develop into a visible formation of Circles of flattened corn in several stages. This caused some of us to take a fresh look at the pattern of thirteen Circles which had appeared in three separate stages at Silbury Hill in July 1988. Aerial photographs showed that one of the last Circles to appear there made a common basepoint, turning both quintuple sets into well-proportioned long-shaft crosses of the familiar Christian variety. Could this symbolism have really been intended by whatever intelligence lay behind the Circles?

The Long-shaft Crosses

If that idea seemed entirely preposterous to those unfamiliar with the Circles, it was not very long before dramatic confirmation of it was presented in a way that seemed quite unmistakable. On 2 June 1989 a new formation was found just north of Scratchbury Hill, near Warminster. From the hill above, could be seen just such a long-shaft cross, and this is shown in Plate 1:2. It consists of a quintuple set, like the five on a dice, with an extra satellite Circle in line. The left and right 'arms' and the base of the long shaft were formed by anticlockwise satellite Circles; the other Circles were swirled clockwise. On several occasions I sat on Scratchbury Hill that month looking down upon this prodigy in the barley below, pondering its significance.

A day later, a survey flight by Circles Phenomenon Research (CPR) turned up a further long-shaft cross, or crucifix, formation at North Down, very close to the position of 'Rupert's Circle' of 1988. Although similar in shape and size to the Scratchbury crucifix, three of the satellite Circles here were vestigial – a mere three feet or so in diameter – compared to the usual fourteen foot satellites, as if they had not 'fired up' properly. Such had been the case with one satellite of 'Rupert's Circle' the previous year, and this also occurred in a quintuple found later south of Silbury Hill.

Shortly after the end of the White Crow experiment (described in the next section), a third magnificent crucifix formation was found in wheat near Cherhill, Wiltshire (see Plate 1:3). Yet again, we had this unmistakably symbolic formation type, which lay just across the valley from the ancient Cherhill White Horse, carved in chalk on the hillside. I examined this formation, together with Colin Andrews and Dr Terence Meaden, and besides the usual measurements, Colin dowsed this site thoroughly. Strong dowsable reactions, similar in pattern to those found at the White Crow Circle, were evident. Quite clearly, Terence Meaden was impressed by this dowsing, and I believe that he has subsequently taken up dowsing Circle sites.

In addition to this long-shaft cross formation, whose base satellite is just slightly out of alignment, there was a small linear triplet close to the east. When I flew over the crucifix a month later, two further small Circles had appeared very close to it, to the north, demonstrating that the site, out of a very large and otherwise untouched wheat field, was still active weeks after the initial event. The original crucifix formation at Cherhill was filmed by BBC

Television from the air, and this film has since been extensively screened as a prelude to various Circles programmes.

Project White Crow

During June of 1989 the Circles Phenomenon Research (CPR) group mounted an operation known as 'White Crow', whose primary purpose was to photograph the actual process of a Crop Circle forming. The name 'White Crow' was chosen because of a familiar proposition that all crows must be assumed black until such time as one is found that is white. It was hoped that by catching a Circle actually forming, the supposition that 'all Circles are hoaxes' could be finally disproved. Nevertheless it is fair to say that no one involved believed for one moment that the Circles were all hoaxes. The only person we knew who had clung to this assumption was Mr Peverill Bruce, owner of the land in the punchbowl at Cheesefoot Head where it was intended to carry out the White Crow surveillance operation.

Since Mr Bruce had refused CPR access to this land where Circles had appeared regularly since 1981, it was proposed that the surveillance equipment should be set up on the west side of the A272 Winchester to Petersfield road, but trained on the punchbowl on the other side. About fifty of us took part in White Crow, which was principally planned and organized by Colin Andrews. The idea was to mount 24-hour-a-day surveillance of the punchbowl for eight days, starting on 10 June. Video-recording equipment was linked to both television cameras and an infrared image intensifier for night-time use.

In addition to CPR members, Professor Archie Roy of Glasgow University and Dr Adrian Lyons of Photonic Science were participants. Dr Terence Meaden also took part and installed a small weather station to record data such as windspeed and direction, cloud cover and atmospheric temperature, etc. The surveillance equipment was mounted on a tower of scaffolding overlooking the punchbowl and an adjoining vehicle contained the recording gear. We settled down to three eight-hour watches each day, manned by groups of two or three volunteers.

Just two weeks earlier on 27 May, a pair of Circles, one about fifty-three feet across and the other fourteen feet, had appeared at Cheesefoot Head, not in the punchbowl, but on the same side of the road as our surveillance gear and about a quarter of a mile further up the hill towards Petersfield. Both were swirled clock-

18

wise and both were dowsed frequently by various members of the White Crow project. In the smaller of these Circles, John Haddington recorded the now familiar tapping noises which I mentioned in my previous article on the Circles.

Despite the fact that new Circles had been reported thick and fast, especially in Wiltshire, in the four weeks preceding White Crow, nothing new was reported anywhere, so far as we knew, during the eight days of the project. Certainly no Circle appeared in the punchbowl during that time, or later during the summer, but this may have been because the crop there in 1989 was peas, in which Circles have never been recorded. Although one cannot draw conclusions from any of this, it did seem as if the 'Circle-makers' were deliberately refusing to perform for us! Nevertheless, there was a general air of optimism initially, and Dr Meaden was heard to say to a colleague that he thought 'by the end of the week we shall have this thing by the tail'. In view of what subsequently happened towards the end of June, one could be forgiven for thinking that the 'Circle-makers' had overheard this remark and reacted with an impish sense of humour.

In the early hours of 15 June a luminous object was seen over the punchbowl and recorded on the videotape. It remained visible for a short while before fading away, and it is hard to say how far away it was. Although this can be described as a UFO in so far as it was not readily identified, I can say that it occasioned little interest, since what we sought was a Circle. Though no Circle appeared in front of the cameras during the watch, we were eventually rewarded in a most unexpected manner.

The Trilling Noise

On the final evening of the White Crow project, Saturday 17 June, six of us decided that we should sit in the existing large Circle, at the top of the hill, and see whether we could make some sort of contact with whatever 'agency' caused the Circles. How this might be done was to say the least vague, but we felt that the opportunity should not be missed since we had with us that evening Rita Goold, the medium (see Plate 1:5), who might be able to establish some kind of communication. In view of all that we knew about the Circles, the psychic aspect of the phenomenon was something that could be hardly doubted any more.

Not long after midnight, Rita and her husband Steve and myself, together with Colin Andrews, Pat Delgado and Busty Taylor, walked up the road to the large Circle where we sat and tried to

19

mentally relax. It had become extremely cold after a hot and humid day and most of us were well wrapped up to keep out the chill. A nearly full moon hung in a clear but hazy sky giving excellent visibility all around. There had been a forecast on the radio news that aurora might be seen that night due to intense solar activity earlier that day, and some faint luminous streaks had been seen in the night sky.

The trilling noise started quite suddenly but in a way that made me unsure of what was happening. At first I thought that it had begun right in the centre of my head, but I soon realized that all the others could hear it too, and we looked at each other in amazement. In no time it appeared to have distanced itself from the six of us in the Circle. It was quite unlike any noise I have ever heard before, and is best compared to a high-pitched trilling or whirring which wavered slightly in tone. It was not loud as regards decibels but was totally pervasive and seemed to induce an hypnotic effect on the company. Its insect-like quality was somewhat reminiscent of large crickets or cicada in hot climates, but whatever this was, it was not the noise of a cricket.

I believe that the noise started at 12.40 a.m., though I am unsure since I did not look at my watch. It continued for a very long time. Colin at once remarked that this was the same as that he had heard two years earlier near the Circles at Kimpton near Andover. Then it had lasted but a few seconds and seemed to come as a response to his most urgent wish, indeed prayer, for some clue to the Circles mystery. He described the noise on both occasions as like an electrostatic chattering, and what we now heard did sound at times like a rapid chatter as if a tape recording was being played back at high speed.

The noise now seemed to come from the direction of a large clump of bushes in the hedge on the south-west side of the field about forty or fifty yards away (see Plate 1:6). It was very hard to estimate quite how far from us it was. Sometimes it seemed to have the quality of a rattlesnake's rattle, but to be continuous. Certainly its effect was mesmerizing. I was very conscious of a feeling of expansion inside my head, unlike a headache, but nevertheless uncomfortable. This sound affected one's senses unlike any normal sound.

Rita, meanwhile, attempted to speak with whatever unseen source was producing this weird noise. Various questions were asked, and at one stage she said: 'If you understand us, stop.' The sound did then pause for a second or two. As far as I recall, this was the only apparent definite response to her questions. The pitch and intensity of the sound did vary, and I believe that we all had the impression that it was coming closer to us. It seemed that whatever caused the sound was extremely wary of us. Slowly it approached the Circle, or, possibly, 'they' approached us. There was no certainty whether the sound had a single source or multiple ones. At one stage it seemed to have closed almost right around us and there was a definite impression that 'they' had come through the corn right up to the edge of the Circle. But I cannot say that I ever saw anything. Colin and Rita both believed that they saw something moving in the corn. Colin described this as a luminous blur, but Rita wondered whether this might be the pale-coloured head of some small, perhaps humanoid, figure. The height of the barley was about three feet, so, if this was humanoid, its stature would have had to be less than that. I believe that at least one of the others thought he saw ripples running through the corn as the sound approached. Whether or not the sound emanated from one or more entities possessing visible form, I have little doubt that all of us had the impression that it was caused by something living and intelligent, if not actually seen. It certainly did not feel as if it were made by anything mechanical.

During the time that it approached its closest, Pat and then Colin, Rita and myself walked separately to the edge of the Circle. I was surprised that I did not feel in the least bit afraid of whatever this was. There was no impression of hostility. At one stage I said, addressing our apparent but unseen visitor: 'Please will you make us a Circle.' It would appear from what was found later that this wish was granted.

At about this stage another White Crow participant, Ron Jones, entered the field, having heard the strange noise from where he had been walking up the hill on the road. He saw six figures in the Circle and directly above them in the sky a luminous object shaped like a pair of horns. Somewhat disconcerted he paused, uncertain of what was going on. This luminosity, initially as bright as the moon according to him, may of course have been part of the aurora which had been forecast. It was not seen by any of us in the Circle, but then we were preoccupied, to say the least. Whatever it was faded, and Ron then continued into the Circle.

Two others from the project also arrived at the Circle at this time, down the narrow track through the corn. I frantically waved to them to sit down, fearing that their intrusion might terminate our encounter. It was at this point that the source of the noise appeared to recede from the Circle back towards the large bush in the hedge. Nevertheless we stayed there for quite some time trying to draw it back towards us again, but without success. Prior to this, one had felt that whatever was there in the corn was on the point of making itself known to us. But the moment had gone. Finally Pat and Rita declared that we should all return to the White Crow caravan and leave our 'visitors' alone. By now we estimated that it was 2.10 a.m. If that was indeed the time when we left the Circle, it seems to be quite incredible that the experiences which I have related could have lasted as long as one hour and a half. Certainly no one present has suggested that we may have had a 'missing time' experience, but it did seem that our sense of time had been severely distorted.

We all returned to the project caravan and made coffee and discussed what had just occurred. Rita and Steve Goold (who concur that we left the Circle at 2.10 a.m.) departed to drive home to Leicester shortly after we had got back down the hill. Others who had not been up at the Circle were with us in the caravan, but little attempt was made at secrecy. Quite clearly whatever had occurred had left a deep impression on those of us who had been present.

An hour after we had come down from the Circle I suggested to Colin that we return to find out whether our 'unseen visitors' were still present. We went together with Ron Jones in Colin's car back up the road and turned down the track, stopping opposite the larger Circle. I lowered the window and listened carefully. Sure enough, the strange noise could still be heard, fainter now but quite distinct. It seemed to be located in the hedge beyond the Circle on that side of the field (south-west) to which it had previously retreated. We all got out of the car and listened. There was no mistaking that this was the same sound which we had heard before. I said that we should approach slowly and cautiously, and led the way further along the footpath and past the hedge. Almost as an afterthought, we took Colin's tape recorder which he kept switched on. Without this we would have no recorded evidence of the 'visitation'.

Once inside the next field we turned down along the hedge and made our way slowly through the corn, keeping to a tramline as much as possible. It was very hard to assess how far we were from the source of the noise, but it always seemed to be ahead of us and close to the hedge, if not in the hedge and bushes. We paused from time to time to listen. I took three or four camera shots into the darkness ahead with my automatic Canon. Once, at least, the noise ceased momentarily as if in response to the automatic flash. Nothing significant appeared on these films. At this time we had the impression that we were getting really quite close to 'them'. I say 'them' since at this stage, I believe, all three of us had the impression that the noise came from several unseen living entities, whether such a belief was justified or not. Ron, who was trailing behind, heard a terrific crackling at one point, as if the noise was right next to him in the hedge. He came running to join us under the distinct impression that he was being herded.

When we reached a wire fence some two hundred yards down the field we halted. The night sky was already lightening somewhat and the chattering sound was as distinct as ever. The noise seemed to emanate now from long grass and bushes not more than twenty or thirty yards ahead of us, but for some reason we were reluctant to go any further. Whatever this was had now been present for well over three hours and there seemed at that time no reason why it should not still be audible after it grew light. We went back up the field and got back into the car. Still the noise could be heard in the distance as we left the field again, and drove back down the hill to the caravan.

I then slept for about an hour on a recliner in the video-recording vehicle. The next time I returned to the field where the Circles were, it was fully light and the sound which we had heard earlier had ceased completely. In the field where the Circles were, various patches of rough damage to the crop had appeared from time to time throughout the week of the White Crow project. No one had given much thought to these patches, which were always assumed to have been caused by the wind, though animals or birds might have been contributory factors. On that morning, I noticed very many more such patches in the standing crop in the immediate vicinity of the larger Circle, where we had been sitting a few hours before. These had not been caused by any of us and were mostly on the west side of the Circle. I was struck by the appearance of this rough damage on a night when there had been almost no wind, but I am unable to say whether or not it might have been connected with the events which we had experienced.

I left Cheesefoot Head to drive home at around 6.00 a.m. At that time, I was quite unaware that a further ringed Circle had appeared during the night, approximately 500–600 yards from the Circle where we had first heard the noise. It was found soon after first light, within hours of our hearing the strange sound, and its situation in exactly the same direction that the sound had receded from us, seemed highly suggestive that we had been in the presence of whatever was responsible for the Circle's creation. One might also be excused for thinking that my request for a Circle, made when the 'visitors' were at their closest approach, had been specifically granted, though one could never be certain of that. This was the first Circle reported anywhere for over ten days.

White Crow Aftermath

Had the strange trilling noise only been heard on that occasion in the early hours of 18 June, I should have inclined to think that this phenomenon was a psychic one more associated with Rita Goold rather than the Circles. However, it had been heard previously by Colin Andrews in 1987, and it has now been heard several times since. The connection with the Circles is quite unmistakable. A French UFO group which camped out at Cheesefoot Head in June also heard the noise and recorded it on tape not knowing what it was.

Later in the year a BBC television crew who were filming Pat Delgado and Colin Andrews in a large ringed Circle at Beck-hampton (see cover photo) heard the trilling noise in broad daylight. It appeared to move around near the centre of this Circle and was recorded and later heard on the *Daytime Live* programme. At the time, the television camera being used (which was electronically independent of the audio system) experienced severe picture break-up, and subsequently required a complete rebuild. Again, nothing visible was observed which might have caused the trilling noise. The tape recording made at Cheesefoot Head was later analysed at Sussex University. Peak frequency of the high-pitched sound was found to be about 5.2 kilohertz, and it could not be equated with any known insect or animal noise. The Beckhampton trilling was of about 5 kilohertz frequency as well.

For what it is worth, one had the distinct impression that the trilling noise at Cheesefoot Head had originally emanated from out of the Circle where we were, or even out of us. Some sort of psychic link (of which only certain people seem capable) appears to have been required to initiate this sound. Once the link was made, it then seemed to assume an independence of its own, albeit transient, enabling it to function like an animated entity, although we saw no visible form. I should emphasize that this is only my impression. But if this transient energy is what actually causes

Circle formation, then clearly it is able to operate without human assistance.

Nevertheless, one discovers this kind of sound and such a link process described in similar terms again and again in the literature of Ufology. Especially in abduction or encounter cases, the process almost invariably requires the establishment of a link, or psychic interaction, between the person or persons who experience the event and whatever is out there in a (presumably) different continuum or dimension to our normal physical world. In the book, *UFOs: The Gulf Breeze Sightings*,[8] for example, Ed Walters describes how a hum or high-pitched sound would start up immediately prior to the appearance of the UFO and his encounter experiences. Again, in *The Tujunga Canyon Contacts*,[9] two of the girls who experienced 'UFO abduction' events describe how these were preceded by a pervasive and hypnotic high-pitched sound.

The 'Tadpole' Circle

Exactly one week after the events just described at Cheesefoot Head, Ron Jones had just gone to bed in his house near Andover when he heard the trilling noise start up. It was insistently loud so he sat up and listened. Suddenly he found himself back in that field at Cheesefoot Head where the loud crackling in the hedge had frightened him before. But this was no dream since he felt totally conscious and awake. Looking away from the hedge he saw horizontal bands of light moving up and down at eye level in a concertina-like fashion, and also rotating. What this was he was unable to imagine. Minutes later, he suddenly found himself back in bed and the noise had stopped.

How do we interpret such an experience? Quite possibly this corresponded to an out-of-body experience (or astral projection) which many people have described. Certainly his physical body could not have been instantly translated to that field. Maybe this state is indeed the one in which UFO abductee experiences occur, though paradoxically many abductees then undergo what appear to be very physical experiences.

Whatever happened to Ron Jones, it is quite remarkable that, on that very night, a new Circle appeared at Cheesefoot Head in the very place where he saw the horizontal bands of light. It was found early on 25 June within about forty yards of where the three of us had walked while making the tape recording of the mysterious trilling noise. No Circle had ever appeared in that field before. This one was about thirty feet across, swirled clockwise, and had a unique feature of the most distinctive kind. It had an eighty-five-foot long curving tail with sharp parallel sides, between which the wheat lay in a long sweep towards the Circle (Plate 1:7). Nothing like this had ever been seen previously. By virtue of its tail, it became known as 'the Tadpole', and it lay only a short way from where Dr Meaden had expressed the hope that we should soon have this thing by the tail!

Although the new tailed Circle appeared to mock Dr Meaden, it also set what was to be a booby trap for Colin Andrews and CPR. Not all that long afterwards, CPR received reports from a remote part of Powys in Wales, that mysterious circles had been found on the heather-clad hills to the west of Gladestry. Many of these had 'tails' and there were nearly one hundred, all of similar size. Unfortunately, details of these supposed Circles were given to the press before any proper investigation was carried out. I travelled to Gladestry on 30 July and walked a very long way to find the heather circles, but, as soon as I did, I could see that they bore no relation to the Crop Circles. They had been made by some kind of agricultural machinery and the tails were in fact tractor marks. But why on earth should someone make a large number of circles on a remote Welsh hillside? I made enquiries at a local farm and found that this was a grouse moor. Circular patches of heather were mown to promote new growth and facilitate feeding by young birds. On my return, I alerted CPR to this, but too late to stop one tabloid newspaper's puerile piece to the effect that CPR had been disappointed in its pursuit of little green men. Nothing is further from the truth, of course. Why is it that certain Fleet Street hacks can only visualize anomalous phenomena such as the Circles in terms of Dan Dare and ET?

Dowsing the Circles

As I have written previously, the Circles exhibit strongly dowsable patterns which persist long after the initial event which causes the corn to fall. It is also quite possible that dowsable ley energies in such a pattern are present long before a Circle is visibly formed, and that some kind of surge of ley energy precipitates the flattening of the corn. This of course is speculative, since it is not currently possible for a dowser to say whether such an energy formation in a bare field corresponds to a Circle that occurred long before or whether it might be a potential future Circle.

In general, a primary Crop Circle, rather than smaller satellite Circles, will exhibit seven concentric dowsable rings within the main floor area and at least two further concentric rings outside this in the standing crop. With a ringed Circle or a quintuple set, these outer dowsable rings will coincide with one or more visible rings or with the centres of the satellites. I must emphasize that this is a generalization which may well have many exceptions to it.

The sense of these dowsable rings is either clockwise or anti-clockwise, and the formation pattern will usually remain unchanged for perhaps weeks. Then, maybe, the sense of one (or more) of the dowsable rings is found to have reversed. What is most intriguing is that such a change will usually be found to have also occurred in other Circles as well, at any rate those in the same locality. It is as if all the Circles were interconnected.

I express this with great caution since much more work needs to be done to confirm such an effect, and it is unwise to formulate strict rules for how the Circles behave, since the Circles will almost invariably prove one wrong. Nevertheless, this persistence of a particular dowsable pattern for a time, before a switch to a different pattern, is borne out by the fact that certain (visible) formation types prevail for perhaps a few weeks before a different type takes over. This effect may be confined to, say, Wiltshire as distinct from Hampshire.

For example, in July 1988, giant quintuplet sets, of approximately 100 yards across, were the prevailing formation type occurring all in the general area of Silbury Hill. A month earlier, there had been three almost identical double-ringer Circles in Hampshire. At the beginning of the 1989 Circle season, in May, pairs of large quintuplets seemed to be the flavour of the month, occurring at Avebury Trusloe, Westbury, Heytesbury and Silbury Hill – all in Wiltshire.

Were this not enough to illustrate the crucial importance of the dowsable ley energies in Circle formation, an episode that occurred during the White Crow project will confirm it better still. Towards the end of that week, Colin Andrews re-dowsed the large Circle at Cheesefoot Head and announced that the first external ring in the standing corn had reversed: it was now clockwise. Previously the first external ring in all formations, so far as we knew, had always been anticlockwise. Colin was very excited by this development and soon after dowsed two other Circle sites, one being a 1988 Circle, no longer visible in any way, at Goodworth Clatford. Both these had changed, too.

Because the first external ring in ringed Circles had always previously been swirled visibly in the opposite direction to the Circle itself (anticlockwise), Dr Meaden had formulated a rule to this effect, stating (on a BBC-TV programme in October 1988) it to be a necessary consequence of the Law of Conservation of Angular Momentum. He was, it should be remembered, working on the basis that Circles were formed by atmospheric vortices sometimes enclosed by counter-rotating sheaths of air. Adamant that his vortex theory was correct, he published his book, *The Circles Effect and its Mysteries*,[10] in which this was re-affirmed, during June 1989.

Three days after Colin's detection of the dowsing pattern reversal at Cheesefoot Head, a new ringed Circle appeared there within hours (if not minutes) of the strange events following White Crow, described above. This Circle was swirled clockwise but with a clockwise ring as well, never previously seen. This was dramatic confirmation of what Colin had dowsed, and contradicted Dr Meaden's earlier assertion.

Later, on 29 June, a similar clockwise Circle with a clockwise outer ring was formed to the south of Silbury Hill, accompanied by several smaller Circles in the same field. In this case, a local resident observed a large luminous orange sphere descend into the field during the night. This was about 400 yards away from him, and the object appeared to bounce then hover just above the crop for a few seconds before blinking out. Its size was estimated at thirty feet in diameter and the 'bounce' seemed to flatten its lower side. Although one can say nothing about the substantiveness or otherwise of this UFO, Dr Meaden has eagerly claimed it as an example of his postulated Plasma Vortex in the process of forming a Circle. What his report in the *Journal of Meteorology*[11] fails to mention is the quite inexplicable effect of this event on the observer, whose name I am unable to mention. At the time, he drove in his car to where the luminous sphere had descended and reported that everything seemed to move in slow motion. Since then, he appears to have undergone a personality change which undoubtedly originated from this UFO sighting. Ideas and answers to all sorts of problems come into his head and he now spends much time recording these unexpected inspirations.

Whatever caused this ringed Circle at Silbury Hill, the complexity of the phenomenon is well illustrated once more. The direct association of a UFO sighting with a Circle is rare and it would be utterly simplistic to think that all Circles, such as this one, are caused by 'UFOs' settling in the cornfields. After all, what *are* UFOs? Equally, to say that all Circles are caused solely by dowsable energy on the Earth's surface ignores part of the equation, and to fully understand what actually occurs, we need to consider both the Earth mysteries and sky mysteries, which are but different aspects of the same thing.

Books on the Circles

Little more than two weeks after the ringed Circle at Silbury, a beautiful double-ringer Circle was found not far from the White Horse at Westbury. My photograph of this, taken a few days later from a helicopter, is shown in Plate 1:8. As can be seen, this Circle was accompanied by more tiny 'grapeshot' Circles, not previously seen at Westbury. Unlike any previous double-ringer, this clockwise Circle was enclosed first by a clockwise ring and outside that by a ring which was swirled anticlockwise. This served once more to confirm Colin Andrews' detection a month earlier of the reversal in the usual dowsable pattern. It also provided a further nail in the coffin of the discredited atmospheric vortex theory, despite the fact that it had now been resurrected as a 'Plasma Vortex'.

This new theory was expounded in one of two books which appeared on the subject of the Circles at just this time. In *The Circles Effect and its Mysteries*, Dr Terence Meaden proposed that the descending atmospheric vortices previously described by him in the *Journal of Meteorology* could become ionized or partially ionized, producing a plasma vortex, although no such thing had ever been observed or described previously. If we are to believe that such vortices are produced by eddies in the geostrophic wind caused by the lee effect of hills, it is extremely hard to see how this could produce the very high rotational velocities needed to cause ionization, as occurs in tornado funnels.

It is interesting to follow the development of Meaden's theories, from his initially postulated 'stationary whirlwind', by way of the 'descending atmospheric vortex', to the 'plasma vortex', which he now suggests. Regrettably no figures for angular velocities or mathematical formulae to justify the plasma vortex are offered in the book. Several anecdotal examples from the Warminster area of what might correspond to 'plasma vortices' are put forward and some of these come from Arthur Shuttlewood's chronicles of the

UFO flap in those parts during the late 1960s and the 1970s. In fact, the 'plasma vortex', as described, begins to sound very much like what ordinary folk would term as one sort of UFO, and is indeed equally mysterious. Whatever this phenomenon is, there is no reason necessarily to assume it is an 'alien spacecraft', and equally no reason to maintain that it is a more-or-less understood transient meteorological 'plasma vortex'.

In July, *Circular Evidence* by Pat Delgado and Colin Andrews[12] was published, and very soon became a bestseller. The chief reason for this, besides great media interest, was that their book contained many magnificent colour plates of the Circles, which brought home to the public for the first time exactly what we were dealing with. A lot of the credit for these photographs should go to Busty Taylor who supplied many of them and who usually piloted the aircraft used for the CPR aerial survey of the Circles.

Apart from the photographs, the subject is dealt with in a straightforward and honest manner which conveys well the curious nature of the phenomenon and yet does not seek any sensationalism. Certainly this book was the one which placed the subject in front of the public and has caused many people to think deeply about what is happening. Some critics will ascribe the unprecedented number of Circles in 1989 – a final count of about 280 – to all of the publicity which made people more aware of the Circles, and no doubt inspired at least one hoaxed formation. But cereologists were aware that this was indeed an extraordinary and genuine increase over 1988.

The Circles Spread Out

One had only to stand on top of Silbury Hill in July to appreciate that the veritable Circle explosion in Wiltshire was rather more than just a statistical fluctuation, as the meteorological devotees would have us believe. From there, roughly forty Circles could then be seen at one time, whereas there had been fifteen in the field south of the hill in 1988. In the years before 1987, there were no reports of Circles near Silbury Hill, so far as we are aware. Timothy Good was recently assured by an ex-RAF man who regularly flew from the nearby airfield at Yatesbury (now defunct) during and after the war, that he had never seen Circles in the area in those days.

Although it was not immediately apparent, the spreading out of the Circles from Wessex to other parts of England had started in July. Circles were reported from then on in Devon, Gloucestershire, Cheshire, Buckinghamshire, Hertfordshire, Essex, Suffolk, Nottinghamshire, Leicestershire, Avon, and Kent. There had of course been some Circles outside the general area of Wessex, such as in Leicestershire, in earlier years, but precious few. Doubtless some reports came now because of increased public awareness, and some reported could have been hoaxes, since CPR was unable to check out each site. A 'tailed quintuplet' set reported from near Polperro in Cornwall did indeed prove to have been a hoax. But nevertheless, this spread out of the phenomenon was a quite genuine effect. Among these reports from far and wide came news (reported below) of the first Circle which we had then heard of in Scotland.

An Eye-Witness Account

Sandy Reid from Dundee is a man who spends much time out in the country to the north-east of that town, where he observes foxes and badgers in their natural surroundings. One morning at the end of July 1989 he was walking home at about 5.30 a.m. along a hillside where he had spent some hours watching foxes playing around their earths. Dawn was just breaking and the dawn chorus was in full voice. Suddenly, all the bird-song ceased and in the quiet he became aware of a strange noise from the cornfield below. It seemed that in one part of the field, barely fifty feet from where he stood, the heads of the corn were rattling together, and the plants were swaying.

This continued for a few minutes, though there was not the slightest breath of wind. Then suddenly, within less than ten seconds, the corn went down in a perfect circle about thirty feet across. Sandy crouched motionless watching, half expecting animals such as deer to emerge from the crop. But there was none, so he went down into the Circle. The fallen crop was not swirled but had fallen in a straight line away from him, but with the corn in the far part of the Circle seeming to whiplash back towards him at an angle. The Circle had a short spur of flattened corn going out from its perimeter. For some minutes there remained the strong sense of some unseen presence.

This Circle was joined by a smaller one several days later, though Sandy did not see the second one form. Three weeks later he heard for the first time in that field a sound which appears to have been that same trilling noise we have encountered near the

31

Circles in the south of England. It may be significant that here too there are some large tumuli, a few hundred yards away from the Circle site.

From the Earth or from the Sky?

How then are we to reconcile Sandy Reid's account of a Circle forming, and other such accounts where nothing visible is seen, with the various reports of UFO activity immediately preceding Circle formation? Certainly it is impossible to establish any direct link in the sense that an observed UFO is seen at the very same time that a Circle forms. The case of the luminous orange sphere descending into a field at Silbury Hill where Circles were found the next day was mentioned earlier, and the *UFO Report 1990* describes the case of a young Marlborough woman who saw a bright object in the sky, from which a beam shone in the direction of Silbury Hill. Circles were found there about thirty hours later.

A promising case near Margate, Kent, in August 1989, when two students claimed to have seen a UFO descend into a field where Circles were found, turned out to have been a well organized hoax, which featured prominently in a local newspaper under the headline 'Aliens!'.[13] One has to expect this sort of thing, but it does not mean that other reports are all hoaxes.

Undoubtedly there is some occasional aerial component of the Circles phenomenon, but the vast majority of Circles form swiftly and elusively under cover of darkness with nothing seen at all. That in itself is all the more remarkable if one considers that Circle formations are frequently aligned with tractor 'tramlines' or other linear features. This became especially noticeable in 1990 when many of the pictogram formations found were actually centered on tramlines, which themselves appeared to be incorporated in the design. (It is hoped to describe the 1990 pictograms, two of which are illustrated here, in a further *UFO Report* article.)

This lack of randomness in the positioning of Circles becomes all the more evident when one considers the size of the giant Circles and Circle formations of 1989 and 1990. None of these has ever, to my knowledge, straddled a field boundary, path or road, and it is quite obvious that this would soon be the case if they descended from the sky with any degree of randomness whatsoever, as one might expect of, say, a 'plasma vortex'. The alternative may be that the 'blueprint' for an incipient Circle formation develops on the earth's surface prior to the visible event, the falling of the corn,

32

being triggered by some unknown force at a particular instant. This blueprint would correspond to the pattern of energy lines which are detected by the dowsers.

The Giant Circles

At the same time as the double-ringer Circle was found near Westbury in July, a very large plain circle was found in the same area near Bratton (Plate 1:10). This too was accompanied by small 'grapeshot' circles. It was, although we did not know it, to be the first of a series of giant Circles.

The next was the huge ringed Circle at Beckhampton, which has already been mentioned in connection with the trilling noise recorded there in August by a BBC TV crew. This was about 105 feet in diameter, which at that time was a quite unprecedented size. The ring is not quite as geometric as one might wish, but there is no doubt that this was a genuine Circle. Its photograph is shown on the cover of this book and in Plate 1:11. A further ringed Circle of almost identical size was found several days later near the Avebury Sanctuary. This part of the prehistoric Avebury site is said by dowsers and psychics to be the main source of ley energy emanating from the Avebury 'temples'.

On the same day, the very first triple-ringer Circle was found two miles from Lockeridge and close to the Wansdyke. This extraordinary formation had a 102-ft central Circle, a very thin anticlockwise ring, and outside this two further thin clockwise rings. Nothing like this had ever been seen before.

If that was enough for 1989, it set the precedent for 1990, when further giant ringed Circles appeared during May. Some of these had triple rings – one with four satellites actually on the middle ring. Again, the formations were of prodigious size, approximately 200 and 300 feet across. In 1990 we gave up saying 'Nothing like this has ever been seen before', which was (before going to press) applicable to each new major formation. It is hoped to describe the 1990 Circles in more detail in the next *UFO Report*.

Do the Circles Hold a Message?

Readers who have got this far will most likely be none the wiser as to the origin or the meaning of the Circles, and that is hardly surprising. But few will have missed my implication, which has run through this account, that the Circles are intelligently produced and are indeed the result of some kind of non-human intelligence. Leaving aside initially the question of what this might be, it becomes at once pertinent to ask whether the patterns and formations might hold some kind of message for humanity.

During 1989, many people began to gain some inkling of just what this message might be. The symbolism of many of the formations was hinted at in my article in *The UFO Report 1990*. In particular, the Celtic Cross formation was seen to closely resemble the symbol that is embodied in the ancient High Crosses of Ireland. In 1989, the symbolism of the long-shaft or Christian crosses appeared so compelling that it was impossible to ignore.

So what possible interpretation can one place on this? Not, in my view, that this is necessarily some cosmic commercial for Christianity, since I do not hold any particular brief for the Church. Nevertheless, these are spiritual symbols, and spirituality may well be the essence of the message. The Celtic Cross and the long-shaft cross are both mystical symbols found also in religions other than Christianity: they do not indicate any particular religion, but more the essence of what religion is about.

In August of 1989, two bizarre Circle formations were discovered a few days apart by 'Busty' Taylor, to the west of the village of Winterbourne Stoke. Each was a large Circle of 70-ft diameter in wheat, and each contained a swirl pattern, never previously seen, like a particular variety of the swastika; not, I hasten to add, in any way like the Nazi swastika, but more like the ancient mystical symbol of good luck which the Nazis hijacked and perverted.

One of these Circles is shown in Busty Taylor's diagram (Figure 1:1), and a splendid photograph may be seen in *The Crop Circle Enigma*.[14] Quite apart from the fact that the swirl pattern must put paid to any serious thoughts of atmospheric vortices as the causative agent, this swastika formation bears a close resemblance, we are told, to a particular kind of mandala. The mandala is found in oriental religious art, usually Buddhist or Hindu, and is used to represent symbolically the universe or the totality of existence. The possibility of interpretation of this particular

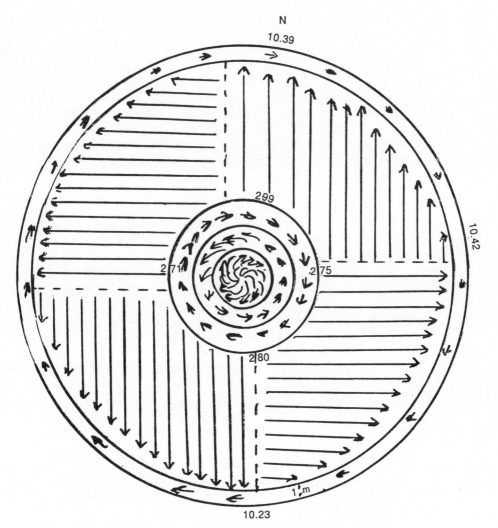

Figure 1:1. Diagram by Busty Taylor of the extraordinary 70-ft Circle he discovered near Winterbourne Stoke, Wiltshire, on 9 August 1989. (© F. C. Taylor)

Circle as a mandala is something that is still being investigated.

Figure 1:2 shows a diagram of the quintuple formation which was found near Silbury Hill in July of 1988. Two of these appeared there in close proximity. Each set had one clockwise-swirled satellite and three anticlockwise satellites, and a further quintuple

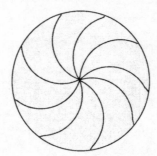

Figure 1:2. Diagram of the quintuple or 'quincunx' formation found near Silbury Hill in July 1988. The central Circle and lower satellite were swirled clockwise; the other satellites anticlockwise.

set which appeared then at nearby Beckhampton was similar, but with the swirl of the satellite reversed. Such quintuple sets are more correctly called quincunxes.

In his book on UFOs, Carl Jung describes this particular variety of quincunx with three equal and one unequal outer elements:

. . . This is a symbol of the *quinta essentia*, which is identical with the Philosophers' Stone. It is the circle divided into four with the centre, or the divinity, extended in four directions, or the four functions of consciousness with their unitary substrate, the self . . . The number 4 as the natural division of

36

the circle is a symbol of wholeness in alchemical philosophy, and it should not be forgotten that the central Christian symbol is a quarternity too, which, in the form of the long cross, even has the 3 + 1 structure.[15]

Jung's description of this kind of quincunx as the symbol of unitative consciousness, written thirty years before the Circles appeared at Silbury Hill, is indeed something to ponder, for unitative consciousness is precisely what many of the psychics and New Age people, who relate so closely to the Circles, have been talking about.

Channelled Messages

For those who are unable to discern the symbolism of the Circles – of which I have but touched the surface here – there is no way that the channelled messages of psychics and mediums, relating to the Circles, will cut any ice. This is quite understandable, for most people will see no possible connection between strange patterns in the corn and such messages of unprovable provenance.

A useful introduction to this subject is Jon Klimo's book, *Channeling*.[16] This recounts that such messages, supposedly from the dead, from non-physical beings, and from extraterrestrials, have been regularly received by a number of human channels for many years now. There is no firm proof, however, which is generally accepted of the reality of any of these beings with respect to the physical world, so acceptance of their messages – and indeed their very existence – must constitute a different level of reality which relates to consciousness, and this is based on intuition or psychic knowledge.

So what possible connection can there be with the definitely physical Crop Circles? Over the last few years, several channels have disclosed messages alleged to have come from the 'Alphas', the 'Guardians', the 'Watchers', or the 'Elohim', which relate directly to the coming of the Circles and what they represent. In *The UFO Report 1990*, I detailed some of Isabelle Kingston's channelled messages from the Watchers, which relate to Silbury Hill and the Circles found there in 1988. Since then, there have been many such communications via Isabelle and other mediums which all contain basically the same message: the coming of the New Age and the raising of human consciousness. The Circles are apparently just an outward visible sign of the 'energies' or consciousness which is being directed to Earth for this purpose.

So is there any reason to believe what the channels tell us? Since many conflicting messages of this sort have been received over the years, can it really be said to represent anything more than 'psycho-babble'? As a Circles researcher, I can only say that several verifiable predictions contained in these messages have come true, although not so far something which is precisely and instantly verifiable to the satisfaction of all. Nevertheless, there have been some remarkable instances.

Isabelle Kingston, for example, was told that there would be a 'sign' at Silbury Hill two weeks before the 1988 Circles appeared there, and she related this to several people before the event. No Circles had appeared there previously. She, and quite independently, Janet Trevisan in Malta, foretold that there would be a great increase in the number of Circles at Silbury Hill in 1989. This subsequently proved to be the case.

Both Isabelle and Janet received channelled messages – again independently – indicating that the Circles would be 'different' in 1990, with different formations and different 'physical manifestations'. This has indeed been the case up to the time of writing (June 1990), and far more so than in any previous year. There have been giant triple-ringer Circles near Devizes, Wiltshire, this month, of unprecedented size (e.g. 280-ft diameter), far larger than any Circles seen previously. And an unprecedented series of 'pictograms', consisting of Circles linked with various additional features (eg rectangles and 'keys'), began forming in May (Plates 1:14 and 1:15).

Isabelle Kingston also received messages this year indicating that there would be new Circles soon in specific places in Ireland and Scotland, where (with the exception of those reported by Sandy Reid near Dundee) Circles have never previously been reported. I have written down details of the places indicated and shall await agog the fulfilment – or otherwise – of this prediction.

Even if these predictions do come about, it is doubtful whether the sceptics would accept such evidence, however definite, preferring to think that it was contrived or faked. What is unbelievable is the dogged determination that such people have in believing that everything can be explained in terms of the physics known to us at the present time. One has only to look back 100, or 200, or 300 years to see such faith in the generally held beliefs of the day has invariably proved mistaken. But I must not blame them too much, since only a few short years ago I too was convinced that science would explain it all! The fact of the matter is that the psychic and spiritual aspect of the Circles, though hard if not impossible to grasp, is one that cannot be excluded.

One supposedly channelled message, that has at least persuaded me to listen, was received in totally unexpected circumstances. It was a hand-written anonymous letter to Colin Andrews and CPR, posted on 14 June 1989 in Rochdale, Lancashire, and marked 'Utmost urgency to read'. Inside, a note read: 'A communication by our group asked us to send this to you. Read before Saturday.' There followed two pages of doggerel, which was mainly about the White Crow project then in progress. I am unable to print this in full, but an excerpt may prove illuminating:

> Where I be is all around. Listen hard
> You'll hear my sound.
> It seems you work from back to front
> Looking for the cause of such.
> Find us first the next you'll know
> All will be clear for rings to sew.
> In your hands you have the key
> To talk to us, we are so free.
> One soul is there, they have signed in
> Who has the mind to link within.
> Your machines you have set up,
> Whate'er they cost is not enough.
> The human mind is what you need.
> To me you can't see wood for trees . . .
>
> And – I will tell you what to do.
> Get this mind and sit around
> In quiet of dark upon the ground,
> Listen hard for every sound.
> Not white of bird? But us around . . .

The letter arrived towards the end of the project and was taken to Cheesefoot Head on that Saturday (17 June), where it was discussed by a number of us there. Initially, most regarded it as some kind of hoax and thought it should be ignored. Rita Goold seemed quite clearly to be the 'one soul' referred to, but there is no reason to think that she wrote the letter.

Regardless of its authenticity, I was determined to carry out the experiment suggested in it, and persuaded the others involved to go and sit in the existing Circle not long after midnight. The rest is Circles history, and the events I have described earlier were certainly of a quite remarkable nature. If the anonymous letter, over which a question mark inevitably hangs, was indeed a channelled communication, then its interpretation of these events is even more remarkable still.

REFERENCES
1. Michell, John: 'Quarrels and Calamities of the Cereologists', *Fortean Times*, No. 53, Winter 1989/90.
2. Wingfield, George: 'The English Corn Circles in 1988', *The UFO Report 1990*, edited by Timothy Good, Sidgwick & Jackson, London 1989.
3. *Now!*, 29 August 1980.
4. Shuttlewood, Arthur: *The Flying Saucerers*, Sphere Books, London 1976, pp. 109–10.
5. Blundell, Nigel and Boar, Roger: *The World's Greatest UFO Mysteries*, Octopus Books, London 1983, pp. 131–2.
6. Goold, Rita: 'Some Notes on the Cornfield Circles at Two Sites in Leicestershire (1988 and 1989)', *Flying Saucer Review*, Vol. 35, No. 1, March 1990, pp. 10–12. (*FSR* is available from FSR Publications Ltd., P.O. Box 12, Snodland, Kent ME6 5JZ.)
7. Various articles in *FSR*, Vol. 35, No. 1, March 1990.
8. Walters, Ed and Walters, Frances: *UFOs: The Gulf Breeze Sightings*, Bantam, London 1990.
9. Druffel, Ann and Rogo, D. Scott: *The Tujunga Canyon Contacts*, Signet Books, New York 1989.
10. Meaden, George Terence: *The Circles Effect and its Mysteries*, Artetech Publishing Co., 54 Frome Road, Bradford-on-Avon BA15 1LD.
11. *The Journal of Meteorology*, Vol. 15, No. 145, January 1990.
12. Delgado, Pat and Andrews, Colin: *Circular Evidence*, Bloomsbury Press, London 1989.
13. Report by Nick Ames in *Adscene*, Canterbury, Kent, 25 August 1989.
14. *The Crop Circle Enigma*, edited by Ralph Noyes, Gateway Publications 1990. A chapter by George Wingfield is included in this book.
15. Jung, Carl: *Flying Saucers: A Modern Myth of Things Seen in the Skies*, Routledge & Kegan Paul, London 1959, p. 114.
16. Klimo, Jon: *Channeling*, Aquarian Press, Wellingborough 1988.

2

The Belgian Wave of Sightings 1989–1990

PIETER HENDRICKX

Born in Belgium in 1950, Pieter Hendrickx has been interested in UFOs for over fifteen years, and belongs to many UFO organizations, including MUFON, CUFOS, BUFORA, and Quest International, and has written many articles for various magazines, such as the *MUFON UFO Journal*. In 1986 he was honoured with a trophy for his co-operation, personal research, and international correspondence for UFO-Belgium.[10]

Pieter Hendrickx has a collection of over 500 different UFO journals from more than thirty countries.

During the first half of 1989, Ufology seemed to die a death in my country. The various UFO groups lost many members; part of a gradual decline over the years. The public lost interest in the subject and the press gave it little coverage. In October 1989, UFO-Belgium organized a meeting between researchers of the different Flemish groups, the idea being to launch a project of co-operation and to meet twice a year to exchange information. All this was done in order to arouse Belgian Ufology from its state of apathy.

Suddenly, we were given an unexpected bonus. That same month the press mentioned the Soviet landings in Voronezh, and programmes appeared on television. In November there were stories on the British Crop Field Circles in the press and on television. And then, on 29 November, came reports of some extraordinary sightings in Eupen, the French–German area of Belgium (Figure 2:1). Normally this German-speaking area gets little attention on the front pages of the daily papers, but suddenly tremendous interest was shown in Belgian UFO research by the media. Radio, television and newspaper journalists, as well as Ufologists, travelled to Eupen to interview eyewitnesses.

By the end of March 1990, the Société Belge d'Etude des Phénomènes Spatiaux (SOBEPS) had already more than 2,000 witnesses and over 500 reports. The research work is only just beginning. After the interviews, we have to evaluate all the reports and create a computer database. It is too early at the moment to explain these strange, periodical phenomena. For several reports, there are conventional explanations, such as a misidentification of an AWACS (Airborne Early Warning and Control System) aircraft, or the lights of the 'Pharao' disco in Halen. But others are so strange that a conventional solution can be ruled out.

Figure 2:1.

The first time I heard about Eupen was on BRT television news on 30 November 1989. Since then, I have collected every item of news that has been published about the sightings in Eupen and have tried to contact witnesses personally, or put them in touch with my colleagues. The extraordinary thing is that the sightings still continue, which puts them in the category of the sightings in Hessdalen, Norway. But in Hessdalen, people usually see just strange light phenomena, whereas in Eupen, people report triangular objects with three powerful searchlights and one orange-red flickering light in the middle.

Can these sightings all be due to night flights of a sophisticated ultra-light aircraft or secret test-flights of the American Lockheed F-117a Stealth fighter? If we believe the Belgian Government, the air force and the Ufologists (such as Professor Meesen, Lucien Clerebaut, Michel Bougard, Patrick VanTuyne, and Ghislain Struys), the sightings do *not* have a conventional explanation.

Sighting Reports

29 November 1989

At about 17.30, Sergeant-Majors Heinrich Nicoll and Hubert Von Montigny of the Belgian gendarmerie observed a strange light phenomenon in the small village of Kettenis. Beams of light, which came from 'a kind of dark and triangular platform', illuminated a field on the side of the road. Von Montigny reported as follows:

'We were driving our Golf GTI in the neighbourhood of Liberme Castle on the road from Eupen to Kettenis when suddenly my attention was drawn to a slow-flying object. It hung nearly 200 metres away above a field at a height of about 300 metres. It was twilight, but it was still light enough to see. Below the object, I saw three powerful searchlights directed to the ground and one orange-red flickering light. As the thing hung in the sky, the searchlights moved across the ground. When the object flew in our direction and came right over our patrol-car, we could clearly see that the object was a triangular platform.

'Then the object moved away in the direction of Eupen, flying above the vicinity of Van Hook Street . . . to Baelen, after hovering over the dam at Gileppe. The sighting lasted until 20.00, when the object completely disappeared in the direction of Spa.'

Both officers reported that they could hardly hear any noise, 'only a soft buzz, like an electric motor' and were certain it was not the sound of an aeroplane or helicopter.

In Eupen itself, other people began reporting the phenomenon. At about 17.30, a woman from Andrimont observed a triangular object with a strong light that hovered silently for five minutes before moving westward. A resident of Jalhay, however, saw a brightly lit sphere which could not have been a plane. Some witnesses reported that the object flew no higher than ten metres above rooftops. Others claimed to have seen a 'rectangle with illuminated orange portholes'.

The police followed the object as far as the dam at Gileppe, where it hung motionless for forty-five minutes before moving off again in the direction of Spa. The patrolmen alerted the air force base at Bierset, where an unidentifiable target appeared on the radar screens. The bases at Maastricht (Netherlands) and Aix-la-Chapelle were also alerted. An air force AWACS plane took off from the NATO base at Gelsenkirchen, but by the time it arrived in the Eupen area the object had disappeared.

Almost an hour later, the police officers Von Montigny and Nicoll observed a second, much larger 'triangle', which appeared to rise from behind a wood, and then watched it perform a great turn above the main E40 highway. The officers later remarked that it appeared to be 'seeking something', and judged its speed at between 60 and 70 k.p.h. They added that the object seemed to turn on its axis.

The same evening Eric Lebon saw something strange. He reported:

'At about 18.30, I left the house in search for wood for the stove. When I came back to the house, I looked at the sky for a moment

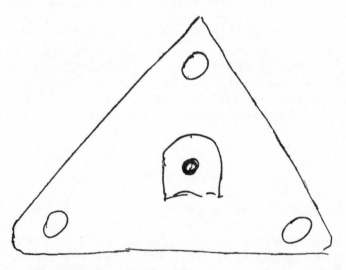

Figure 2:2. 'Between the three big searchlights we saw a red flickering light, possibly on a dome.' (Eric Lebon)

and saw something large flying. It seemed long and narrow and it flew at a height of 200 metres. As it approached, I saw three large searchlights and one red light in the middle. I immediately thought it was a military aircraft, but it flew too slowly – about 5 k.p.h.! In any case, I didn't hear any engine, just a soft whirr like a sewing-machine.

'It seemed to stop just above our garden, then it turned away and only then could I see a triangular shape with two clearly thick areas where the red-orange light was (Figure 2:2). Although it seemed like an aircraft, I saw no reflection of metal. The triangle was rather dark – perhaps black. After two minutes, it disappeared in the direction of Eupen.'

30 November 1989
On 30 November, the report of the police officers' sightings was broadcast on RTBF as well as on Belgischer Rundfunk. Immediately, the telephones of both studios became jammed as many residents in the area rang to report that they too had seen the strange object. Apart from Eupen, witness testimony came from Liège, Verviers, St Vith, and even from frontier villages of West Germany and the Netherlands.

In two areas of Liège, Citadel and the Pont d'Atlas, people reported an 'enormous shape with several searchlights and one orange, flickering light'. In Verviers, some people began talking about a 'nest of UFOs'. An AWACS plane known to have been flying in the area, however, did not report seeing anything unusual, although a 'strange lights phenomenon' was observed by a number of witnesses over the eastern cantons of Belgium. Sightings were reported to the daily paper, *Vers L'Avenir*.

At about 21.40 on 30 November, an Eupen resident contacted the local gendarmerie to report a new sighting of an object in the Baelen area. This witness saw the same type of 'triangular platform' that had been reported the previous evening.

Yet another sighting was described by a resident of Plombières:

'At about 21.20, as I was driving on the highway to Herbesthal, my attention was drawn to a strange object in the sky. It passed at low altitude across the road without any noise at all. It looked like a triangular platform. Two large lights were on the front of the object, but none behind. Unlike the observation on Wednesday evening [29 November], these lights did not illuminate the ground. The speed of the object was slow, and the sighting lasted

a little more than two minutes. I wondered if the object was an
AWACS plane, scouting the environment, but there is no flight
corridor in the vicinity of Eupen.'

According to *Vers L'Avenir*, no AWACS planes were flying in
the Eupen and Verviers area that night, nor the previous night.
However, a few days later there was a rumour that an AWACS
plane *had* actually flown in the area . . .

At about 19.00, a man in Verviers saw a kind of 'illuminated
platform'. He commented, 'I thought I was having an hallucination, but the reports of other witnesses convinced me otherwise.'

What is certain is that something highly unusual was being
observed in the skies of south-east Belgium.

Further Reports

On 1 December, front-page articles on the sightings began
appearing in the press. The Eupen daily, *Grenz Echo*, reported
that on the evening of 29 November, in the small village of
Lontzen, near Eupen, two 13-year-old boys were on their way to a
gymnastics club when they were terrified by a large, circular disk
with two bright horizontal searchlights. The disk made a sharp turn
at low altitude in the direction of the boys, who ran off in panic.
Later, they estimated the speed of the object to be about 80 k.p.h.
Only a 'soft, scraping noise' could be heard.

In a little village close to Voeren, a witness reported seeing four
or five objects and a 'ballet of lights'. In Battice, a police patrol saw
a triangular shape and a 'red ball' descend perpendicularly from it,
which then travelled away horizontally. The *Grenz Echo* reported
that one witness watched a red, flickering light below the triangle
'which pulsated like a heart'.

In Eupen, a woman saw 'a circular disk with a dome' fly over her
house. A few hours later, as she was about to drive her car, she was
'blinded' by a powerful light which came out of the sky. She said
later that both objects moved very slowly across the sky, but would
suddenly accelerate. No sound could be heard when this happened, but other witnesses reported 'a soft sound like the wind'
and 'a humming, like a ventilator'.

Sightings seemed to increase during the weekend of 2–3 December, and investigations by SOBEPS and other researchers (such
as Patrick VanTuyne) were initiated.

In the neighbourhood of Butgenbach, Luxembourg, a young

boy stood so close to a UFO that he was almost 'eye-to-eye' with it. It was late evening when a solid object approached the boy while he was close to a canal. He panicked and jumped into the canal, despite the freezing temperature, and hid for several minutes until the object went away. At precisely the same time, not far from this spot, independent witnesses claimed to have seen four or five 'machines'.

In a school in the village of Lontzen, two pupils, Christian and Andreas, had been surprised by a low-flying, triangular object with searchlights which flew over them on the previous Wednesday evening as they were playing football. Two other pupils, who saw it much closer, are still frightened by what they saw.

In Herbesthal, Henrich J. and his family encountered a strange object on 29 November.

'It was a little about 19.00 hours. We were standing beside our car when my daughter suddenly said, "Look, Daddy, what's that?", pointing across the road. Between two houses appeared a great dark triangular object with a red, a green, and a yellow light beam beneath it. They were very compact light beams . . . It flew almost at a walking pace, first over the street, then over our house, at an estimated height of fifty metres. When an aircraft flies over this low you can see the details clearly, but the strange thing was that we couldn't distinguish the body of this object. Don't ask me if it was metal or aluminium – I can't say. I saw only a dark silhouette that enclosed the lights. Others who have seen it understand me. Because you can't exactly describe what you have seen, people don't believe you.'

Although many witnesses testified to the strange sightings, the radar stations at Bierset, Maastricht (Netherlands) and Aachen (Germany) did not register any 'blips' on 29 November. However, the radar station at Glons did report 'a few strange echoes' that, according to one source, were near the Netherlands frontier. Other radar returns centred on Butgenbach and Luxembourg. Later, these echoes were officially explained away by the Belgian air force as 'atmospheric disturbances'. On 21 December, Minister of Defence Coëme stated in the Belgian parliament that the reports were not due to 'spy planes or other military experiments'.

During the weekend of 2–3 December, SOBEPS began interviewing many witnesses in each municipality of the region. Soon they amassed a dossier of 400–500 witnesses, all of whom co-

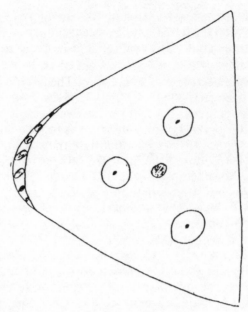

Figure 2:3. Sketch of the object seen by a trainee air force meteorologist, 3 December 1989.

operated in trying to resolve this enigma. According to the SOBEPS secretary, M. Clerebaut, only one thing was certain: 'something' had been seen in the sky (Figure 2:3) in the vicinity of Eupen which was a typical example of a UFO. 'Don't tell us that this is all a fantasy,' he said. 'I have statements of twelve policemen who saw things at a distance of less than 200 metres. We have received reports from pilots, judges, an engineer, a lieutenant-colonel, and a trainee air-force meteorologist – all serious people – who saw the thing sometimes from a distance of less than fifty metres.'

The first reaction of the media was to belittle the reports, trying to explain them away as AWACS or ultra-light aircraft. 'This is not possible,' commented the SOBEPS secretary. 'We have official statements from our Minister of Defence, Guy Coëme, and from the US Ambassador, in which they deny that any military aircraft were responsible. Thus no AWACS aircraft, nor Lockheed F-117a, nor remotely piloted vehicles were aloft. What could they be, then? Who knows, perhaps extraterrestrial visitors?'

During this same weekend (2–3 December), the owner of the 'Pharao' disco club at Halen, near Diest (Belgium), decided to promote his club with a publicity stunt, by means of a light-show in the sky, from 23.00 until 03.00 on each weekend, so that the club could easily be located. Some thirty witnesses near Halen and Diest thought they were seeing some kind of UFO, perhaps the same one that had been observed in Eupen. The following day, the Flemish press reported this. The publicity stunt was successful. Even more annoying was the fact that two weekends later (16–17 December), after several panic-stricken calls to the air force, two F-16 jets were sent over Diest to investigate the strange lights. By April 1990 we learned that the air force had sent up jets on three occasions; over Diest, Eupen, and on 23 March 1990, after a radar echo was seen over the installation at Glons, near Tungeren (Limburg). There was no trace of a UFO.

I should add that the Eupen sightings and the searchlight show at Halen (which I personally observed on Christmas Night) were two different events and bear no relation to each other. For example, there is a distance of 200 kilometres between those two areas.

UFO Fever!

On 5 December, the *Grenz Echo* began making reference to a 'UFO fever' in connection with the sightings. Each evening, UFO spotters in groups of ten or more, equipped with cameras (including video) and binoculars, came to the reservoir at Gileppe in the hope that the UFOs would return. One anxious reader asked the newspaper if there was a danger to drinking water, since many sightings had been reported near the reservoirs of Gileppe, Wesertalsperre and the lake at Butgenbach.

7 December 1989

In Mont-Rig, a woman and her daughter claimed to have observed an unusual spectacle for two hours, shortly after twilight. They saw a blue and white light which turned into 'an enormous ball covered with a mass of little twinkling lights'. It hung on the horizon for a while, then suddenly, on either side of the main lights, two luminous 'wings' opened out, after which the bottom part of the main 'body' appeared to dim. During the next fifteen seconds 'innumerable points of light seemed to escape'. After a while these lights returned to the main 'body', which then disappeared.

This colourful report tends to deviate from the other observations.

The Halen light-show

During the weekend of 9–10 December, a SOBEPS investigation team stayed at the offices of the *Grenz Echo*, where witnesses had been invited to discuss their sightings. Only twenty-nine of them bothered to turn up, however, and there were twice as many journalists present.

Meanwhile, a team of ten field investigators carried out door-to-door interviews. Witnesses also reported sightings to the police at Diest and Hasselt, as well as to the newspaper *Het Belang Van Limburg*, and to Marc Broux of UFO-Belgium. These witnesses did not report a triangular object, however, but oval-shaped lights, and we now know that this was the light-show from the 'Pharao' disco club at Halen.

Explanations

On almost a daily basis, the media came up with another theory or solution for the sightings at Eupen: A balloon, searchlights, a prototype helicopter, an AWACS plane, an ultra-light aircraft (ULM) or unknown weather phenomena. But the most popular theory was that the sightings were due to secret flights of the F-117a Stealth aircraft, based in West Germany, to test NATO radar installations in Belgium and the Netherlands.

In *La Dernière Heure*, however, General Terrason of the Belgian Air Force explained that the Americans had ridiculed the sightings until he explained to them that there had been reports by trained personnel. The general stated that the sightings could not be due to either the Stealth fighter, F-117a (Figure 2:4), nor the bomber (B-2), nor could they be due to AWACS aircraft or ULMs. None of these explanations is tenable, because the object had been reported as hovering motionless on occasions. According to General Terrason, one thing was certain: reliable witnesses had reported strange sightings.[1]

The Weywertz Sighting

One of the most extraordinary sightings that came to light during this period was that of a woman and her daughter, Evelyne, who claimed to have seen a strange object over a cemetery in the little village of Weywertz (Hoge Venen area). The witnesses were visiting the grave of the eldest daughter of the family, who had

Figure 2:4. Three views of the Lockheed F-117a, clearly different in shape from the Belgian UFO so frequently observed (Salamander Books).

been killed tragically in a car accident the previous January. The woman began:

'On Thursday, 28 November, we left the house as usual at about 19.00. At that time, there are few people around. There was no wind and the sky was clear and bright . . . Suddenly we heard a strange noise. Evelyne took me by the arm and laughingly explained that this came from the neighbour's chickens. We walked closer to the gravestone – and then we saw it. About thirty metres above the fir trees hung an object with a huge light, shining on the trees. We didn't see any beams from it, yet the trees were lit up. It was a huge, dark thing that changed shape all the time – from triangular to quadrangular, then rectangular, but always remaining a dark silhouette. You couldn't distinguish it clearly because there were lights which moved and sometimes shone into our eyes.'

Evelyne tried to dissuade her mother from looking at the object, but she seemed attracted to it, alternately putting her spectacles on and taking them off in order to try and see it more clearly. 'It isn't normal, it can't be real,' she said, and asked her daughter what she thought it was. 'I don't know, Mama, perhaps it's a UFO,' Evelyne replied. The mother asked her daughter if she thought somebody was inside. 'Mama, I don't know, I'm afraid,' Evelyne answered. Said the mother:

'I wasn't afraid, but I wanted to approach the object. I wanted to go to the fir trees in order to watch the object more closely. However, my daughter wouldn't let me go. The only fear I suddenly felt was that the object might attack us, that it could fall on us, or that somebody would shoot at it.

'Meanwhile it kept changing shape and turning over. All the time there was no noise, except a [humming or groaning] sound. The noise came from it in short bursts that seemed to coincide with the variation of shape. Also, the lights in the middle changed colour. It rotated, it turned over, it rolled . . . it was just as if we were looking at a kaleidoscope.'

Evelyne refused to stay any longer. '*Komm' doch!*', she cried. The mother continued:

'I started walking backwards with my face to the thing. Then rays came from it via the upper side – not beams like a search-light, but rays which twisted. The rays were wider at the bottom and which through twisting became a point – just like the rays of the sun as they are drawn in books for children. They were orange-white in colour, just like fire, but it wasn't fire. There was no smoke. The rays didn't stay round that thing, but shot off in the sky.

'When we left the cemetery after ten minutes, the thing – as a triangle – started to move slowly in the direction of Waimes . . . We didn't speak a word about it at home. That night, I couldn't forget the thing. Could it have been a helicopter? Or something

52

from another planet? Would it return? Was there someone in it? Perhaps it also observed us? And why did it just happen there? If my elder daughter hadn't been killed in a car accident, then perhaps we would never have seen it. All that night, I was thinking about these questions.'

The following day, the daughter felt unwell with a bad headache and had to leave school. On Wednesday evening, the mother went alone to the graveyard and stayed half an hour at the gravestone, hoping to see the flying object again. But nothing happened. On Thursday, the doctor came to see Evelyne, who was apparently suffering from low blood pressure and influenza. Her mother said:

'In my opinion, she became ill because of that thing. She had a terrible headache for four days.

'On Friday morning, we read about it in the *Grenz Echo*. I saw the heading "UFO gesichtet". We don't need publicity, but at the weekend I phoned the local correspondent of the *Grenz Echo*. I wanted to help those people who are searching for an explanation for all these UFOs. I also want to know what I saw! In our village there were people who said that we saw a hallucination or something. But how is it possible for two people at the same time to share the same hallucination? And why would we invent something like that? We were standing by the gravestone of my elder daughter, whom we loved a lot. At a moment like that, you don't start to invent crazy stories. Before, I came to the graveyard to find peace. Now, I don't dare any longer. They say that we were led by all the articles on UFOs in the journals, but people forget that we saw that thing on Tuesday – a day before all those people saw it and two days before it was published in the paper. After all, I didn't know what a UFO was, neither did I read about it.'

This is the most remarkable report of a UFO sighting in Eupen. The object was obviously not a ULM, an AWACS or an F-117a. It is a strange story, especially since it is an isolated observation that we cannot relate to the other sightings.

SOBEPS Evaluations

At a press conference on 18 December, organized by SOBEPS, a Belgian Air Force colonel denied that Stealth or other experimental

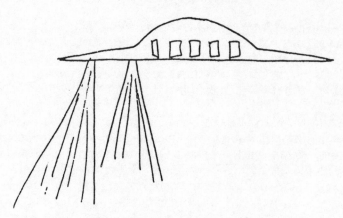

Figure 2:5. Another type of UFO observed during the Belgian wave.
(SOBEPS)

aircraft were responsible for the sightings. He argued that no aircraft can fly between five and ten kilometres per hour or hang still in the sky without any noise, 'unless it were to crash shortly afterwards', he added.

An analysis of the reports and explanations is now underway. SOBEPS did good work, but still cannot explain the sightings, although Michel Bougard believes in the ULM-hypothesis. In evaluating the reports to date, SOBEPS researchers have found the following consistent characteristics:

(1) The objects reported by the witnesses are usually described as a triangular platform with little density and a kind of dome at the top with a lot of 'portholes'.

(2) There are generally three points of light at the bottom of the object, or two searchlights on its top. It seems that the two sources of light do not work at the same time. One red-orange light is often seen in the centre of the object.

(3) The movement of the objects is noiseless, apart from the sound of a turbine ('whistling', or like the sound of an electric motor). The objects move slowly, hang motionless and then depart at a speed of between 60 and 100 kilometres per hour.

(4) The movements are unpredictable and happen all of a sudden. The intensity of the lights is related to the speed of the movement. This means that the lights and the

movement are both derived from the same source of energy.

(5)   The objects traversed the whole region, mostly following well chosen routes, not only above desolated places but also over populated areas. They do not show any sign of camouflage.

(6)   According to SOBEPS, the objects are not astronomical (e.g. Jupiter or the Moon), nor a meteorological phenomenon (e.g. noctilucent clouds or a temperature inversion), nor are they conventional aircraft.

On radio, television and in the press, Professor Meesen of SOBEPS has consistently stated his conviction that an extraterrestrial 'happening' is behind the Eupen sightings.

On 21 December the Minister of Defence, Guy Coëme, claimed in front of an audience of the Belgian *Kamer Van Volksvertegenwoordigers* (Chamber of the People's Representatives), that the government does not know what the UFOs of Eupen really are. He insisted that AWACS aircrafts were not responsible for the sightings, nor were ULMs, RPVs (remotely piloted vehicles) nor other military craft. He added that there were no F-117a aircraft operating at the time, nor any other secret aircraft. Minister Coëme said that 'it was confirmed by the US Air Force that no flights of these aircraft had occurred at that time'.

Another Shape-changing Object

Another witness to the Eupen sightings reported the following to SOBEPS researchers.

On 19 December he saw a big ball with many spots of light which changed shape from a round form to a flat triangle before splitting into two sections. From these sections twelve little spots of light emerged. After this, the object changed back into a triangle. Finally, a dark 'eye' appeared for a few seconds, before the little spots returned. When the witness observed this through binoculars, the little spots looked like the triangular object itself with three searchlights, which had often been reported by the Eupen witnesses.

Video Films Taken

On 24 December Jacqueline Druart of Nimy (near Mons) managed to take some video film on which an object is clearly visible. At about 18.45, as Mme Druart and her daughter were returning from a shopping trip, they observed a clear ball of light in the sky. 'We were only a few hundred metres from our home when we saw a point of light in the sky above Grand Large,' she reported. 'Suddenly, this light moved very fast in our direction. I just had enough time to stop the car and get my video-camera. Until then I didn't believe in all the stories the media was reporting about UFOs. But now I am sure of it!'

On that video film a round object, encircled by a black ring with a white diaphanous light around it, is visible. Afterwards, the object hung motionless in the sky, then suddenly started to rotate on its axis and shot off at tremendous speed before stopping again. The light from it became more diffuse as it gradually disappeared over the horizon. The incident lasted for two minutes.

Mme Druart is certain that what she saw was a real UFO. 'It wasn't a reflection of light, and it was too large for a star and too fast and bright for an aircraft or helicopter,' she said.

Another video film was taken on 24 December at about 17.45 in Sambreville. M. Guillaume was at home when his attention was drawn to an unusual light in the sky. After looking through his binoculars and making sure this was not a plane, he took ten minutes of video film. This shows a round white shape, with a brighter outer section, moving and rotating slowly.

Yet more films of unusual aerial objects were taken on 8, 15 and 20 February. In the last film, the object appeared as a large and intensely illuminated light that moved swiftly then suddenly climbed and disappeared. Many other witnesses reported sightings that evening.

Earth Tremors – a Connection?

Since the end of September 1989, according to *La Libre Belgique*,[2] there have been more than 300 light Earth tremors in the region between Sart-Lez-Spa and Beverce (Liège) in the Hautes Fagnes. The reservoirs of Gileppe and Robertville are situated in the 'danger zone'. But studying the graph that accompanied the article (Figure 2:6), we noticed that the period November–December 1989 was very quiet seismologically, and since there were so many

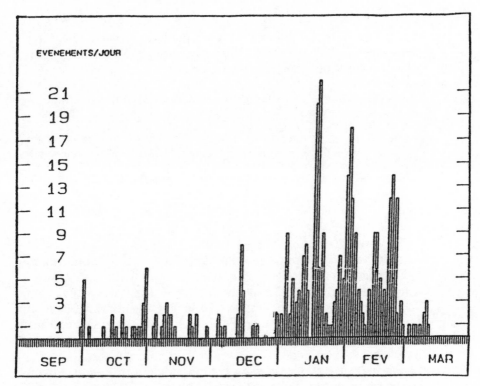

Figure 2:6. Graph showing seismological activity, which does not coincide with the peak of UFO activity in November/December 1989. (La Libre Belgique)

sightings during this period, I am unable to accept that there is a link between the seismological and UFO activity.

Brussels Film

On 27 March 1990 the air force sent up two F-16 fighters, based at Beauvechain, in an unsuccessful attempt to intercept unidentified targets that had been tracked on radar at Glons.

Then the phenomenon appeared in the nation's capital. On the night of 30–31 March, Marcel Alfarano filmed a triangular object, as large as a house, in Brussels. 'It was about 21.45, and I was watching television with my wife,' he said. 'Suddenly she saw a large, bright gold light in the sky. The object remained motionless for twenty minutes, then rose and descended. At this point we saw three large lights, shining brightly with a green colour.'

M. Alfarano immediately called the police, but a patrol car arrived too late to observe the phenomenon. A few days later, however, M. Alfarano had another sighting, and this time he was ready with a video-camera. He reported:

'Between 2.00 and 2.30 in the morning, the sky was clear and there was a full moon. From the direction of the Midi railway station two large, bright white lights came towards my house without any noise, apart from a light whistling sound. When the object came just above our roof – I even thought it was going to crash on our house – we saw a searchlight on the back and two others at the front that were part of a large, metallic-grey triangle with a kind of dome below, composed of "mounds" beneath, and there were flickering red and green lights.'

Sightings by Eighteen Policemen

At 23.00 on 30 March 1990, police officer Alain Renkin had a sighting at Ramillies. 'I was playing cards with my wife and a couple of neighbours when our attention was drawn to a light outside the house,' he reported. 'The sky was clear and full of stars. The light made irregular lateral movements and changed colours. Having convinced myself it wasn't a plane, I contacted the base at Beauvechain and asked for information about this phenomenon. Because their radar system wasn't operational, the military contacted the radar centre at Glons . . . At about 23.05, the point of light became red, and it moved off in the direction of Gembloux, gaining height.'

At about 23.08 Captain Jacques Pinson, having been informed of the report by Renkin, departed for Ramillies, together with a colleague, and was able to corroborate the sighting; he saw three points of light that formed a perfect triangle. 'It was neither an aircraft nor a star,' he affirmed.

At around 23.25, several police patrols in Jauchelette, Jodoigne and Thorembais-Les-Beguines, confirmed the presence of the lights. Five minutes later three new points of light were seen on the main triangle, forming a smaller triangle. Through binoculars, the policemen observed that each point of light looked like a sphere, divided by two 'wings'.

At 0.36, 31 March, two F-16 fighters were sent aloft by the Glons control centre to search the airspace of Brabant. The first two flights were unsuccessful, but eventually the F-16 pilots, guided by police on the ground, succeeded in circling the large, unidentified triangle. The police reported that one of the points of light became brighter at this moment, as if in reaction to the jets. (In July 1990, Colonel W. De Brouwer stated that the airforce had tracked a UFO on radar on 30 March which accelerated from 175mph to 1,125mph and altered height by more than two miles in fifteen seconds. – Ed.)

In all, eighteen policemen witnessed the strange phenomenon. 'I don't know what it was I saw, and I don't come to any conclusions,' said Captain Pinson, 'but I know that I saw it!'

Easter 1990

During the Easter weekend of 14–16 April, SOBEPS organized a massive skywatch, in co-operation with the state police, the air force, and the media. As London's *Financial Times* reported:

The Belgian air force has been on alert for three nights running . . . aircraft equipped with infrared and sophisticated electronic sensors have been patrolling the skies. Down below, the Belgian police force has kept a constant watch, helped by more than 1,000 concerned citizens. Along the border with Germany, twenty lookout posts have been set up . . .

The world's television crews camped out on a chilly Ardennes airfield to get the first pictures. But the event made rather poor viewing. Several times the UFO was 'seen' from the ground, but each time the aircraft got there too late, in one case missing the mystery intruder by just three minutes. To make matters worse, the cloud was low, the weather changeable, and the UFO tended to hover just above the rooftops, too low to be confronted by an aircraft.

The pilots, sworn to secrecy until the Defence Ministry has had time to watch the video evidence, seemed to have little to report, and could not confirm rumours of all kinds of irregular blips on their radars.

Far from declaring the operation a failure, the UFO-obsessed Belgian media appeared more convinced than ever that there is something odd hovering over the peaceful countryside of Wallonia. Scientists on the ground appear in the past few days to have produced a clear image of the object, which is said to correspond to the reports of eyewitnesses. It is a triangle 30m–50m in diameter, with red, green and white lights at the corners, ten times brighter than any star. It has a convex underbelly and makes a sharp whistling noise . . .[3]

Although it was reported that neither the aircraft nor any radar installations tracked UFOs, many witnesses contacted the air force headquarters at Bierset to report sightings. In spite of this endeavour over the Easter weekend, we are still unable to come to any conclusions regarding the origin or purpose of the mystery craft.

Further Evaluations

In evaluating the Eupen observations, we find several striking points. There exists a conformity in most of the eyewitness reports: a triangular platform with three strong searchlights, a red flickering light in the centre below the object and the rays that emerge from the 'wings' of the object. Recently there have been reports of revolving, round balls of light. There is mostly an absence of noise, except for a soft humming or whistling. The speed of the objects is very slow and they have the ability of accelerating instantly and hanging motionless in the sky for several minutes. They fly at a low altitude and their sizes vary from fifteen metres to the size of 'two football fields'.

In most cases, the objects have the same shape, but there have also been sightings of other strange-shaped objects. An interesting fact is that the UFOs prefer to show up in the south-eastern part of Belgium. Why don't Flemish people see so many UFOs? Is it because the Flemish media is not interested in publishing the sightings or is it that people think they just see a disco light-show? Of course, there are some who regard seeing a UFO as fashionable and want to participate in the sensational story of a tabloid newspaper. On the other hand, there are sightings reported from policemen, UFO-researchers, amateur astronomers, and others who certainly do not look for publicity. Yet we must still remain cautious and open-minded.

Possible Explanations

Let us take a closer look at a few of the more plausible explanations for the recent Belgian sightings.

Ultra-light Aircraft

According to several UFO researchers and UFO groups (such as CENAP of West Germany), the triangular object must be a ULM. They draw this conclusion for the following reasons: its triangular shape like a delta plane; its ability to fly three hours (an ordinary ULM can hold about twenty litres of fuel and the normal consumption is nearly eight litres per hour); and its noise like an electric motor. The average noise of a ULM motor measures sixty decibels, which can be heard when the craft flies twenty metres above the observer. When the ULM is flying at a distance of 300 metres this sound of course becomes quieter, and similar to an electric motor.

However, the speed of a ULM is sixty to sixty-five kilometres per hour. The lights on this craft are not searchlights but lights of only about forty-five watts, which cannot always be seen so clearly. For the big searchlights, as described in the reports of the triangular platform, the equipment required to power them would be too heavy for an ultra-light machine. It is also very difficult to find your way in the night or twilight with a ULM. A ULM cannot hang motionless in the sky. When the motor stops, it crashes. In my opinion ULMs are not responsible for the sightings, not only because of the powerful searchlights observed but also because of the abrupt accelerations and the high altitudes sometimes reported (e.g. on 30–31 March a UFO was tracked at over 3,000 metres).

The F-117a Fighter

Is it possible that the Americans have been flying their radar-invisible F-117a fighter, or another similar type, without warning the Belgian government and other NATO countries, thus risking a diplomatic incident? The F-117a has, of course, been operational for a number of years, and according to Hervé Gallet and Bernard Thouanel, writing in the French magazine *VSD*, six F-117a's are based at Lakenheath and Upper Heyford in England, and that some could be based at Chièvres in Belgium. They cite an interesting statement made by USAF Colonel Tom Tolin, who confirms that fifty-nine such aircraft are flying in various countries. 'Some F-117s fly over Europe during night missions, sometimes even with pilots of the Royal Air Force, but we can't say above which countries they fly.'[4]

But SOBEPS rejects the theory that the UFO sightings can be explained in this way, because of the large size of the triangular platform reported, its ability to hover motionless, and its accelerations.[5] In addition, I have referred to those cases when the flying triangle has been tracked on radar, which would not be the case if it was an F-117a.

I recently heard a rumour about a secret prototype spy plane, the Lockheed MP-18, allegedly a joint project of France and the US, that is said to be able to hover. If there is any truth to the rumour, this might possibly account for the sightings. Or is it just a rumour spread by those seeking a rational explanation for the sightings? Nevertheless, I am convinced that some of the sightings can be attributed to flights by such aircraft.

Similar Objects in Other Countries

There have been hundreds of reports of triangular-shaped UFOs throughout the world, and I have selected a few American cases for inclusion here. In October 1964 four NASA engineers sighted a fast-moving triangular-shaped craft at the Wallop's Island test site, Virginia.[6] In January 1965 there was a near collision between a huge delta-shaped object and a Lockheed Electra airliner as it approached Washington.[7] More recently, in December 1988 witnesses in Puerto Rico reported that two US Navy jets disappeared as they were pursuing a triangular UFO (see Chapter 8). And on 23 August 1989 two women in Gulf Breeze, Florida observed a silver or white delta-shaped object with an estimated diameter of seventy feet. At each apex were globes or clusters of light.[8] [*Editor's note:* I have included additional reports of triangular-shaped UFOs in the World Round-up, Chapter 10.]

Conclusions

As I write this in May 1990, the UFO 'fever' has died down and the press are no longer interested. But despite the attempts by Professor Meesen and his colleagues at the Université Libre of Brussels, who studied hundreds of reports; despite the regular observations – on an almost daily basis – by hundreds of witnesses, including police, radar operators, military personnel, UFO researchers, and amateur astronomers; and despite the official statements of the Minister of Defence and the Belgian Air Force, as well as those of the scientific community, we are still no closer to a satisfactory explanation for the extraordinary sightings over southeast Belgium. Perhaps the UFOs are really extraterrestrial, yet why are so few sightings reported from the Flemish part of my country? Is this merely due to the reactions of the Flemish media, which discourage people from reporting sightings there?

SOBEPS[9] are to be congratulated on their excellent job of tracking down and questioning hundreds of witnesses in every village, and for their co-operation with the police, the air force, the media, and Flemish researchers.[10]

One thing is certain. Something has been flying around the skies of Belgium, and the sightings have been taken extremely seriously by all the authorities. Only time will bring a solution to this mystery.

REFERENCES
1. *La Dernière Heure*, 15 December 1989.
2. *La Libre Belgique*, 15 March 1990.
3. Lucy Kellaway, *Financial Times*, 18 April 1990.
4. Hervé Gallet & Bernard Thouanel, *VSD* magazine, No. 2682, May 1990.
5. *La Province*, 8 May 1990.
6. *MUFON UFO Journal*, No. 258, October 1989.
7. Ibid., No. 261, January 1990.
8. Ibid., No. 260, December 1989.
9. SOBEPS, Avenue Paul Janson 74, 1070 Brussels.
10. UFO-Belgium, Konig Albertstraat 40, 3500 Hassett.

Editor's Note

The Lockheed F-117a (codenamed 'Senior Trend') first flew in 1981, and nearly sixty of these 'stealth' aircraft have been delivered. Referred to by its pilots as the 'Black Jet', and sometimes the 'Wobby Goblin', owing to its in-built instability, the F-117a has a wingspan of 43 ft 5 in. (13.20 m), length of 65 ft 11 in. (20.09 m), and a height of 12 ft 5 in. (3.78 m). It is powered by two 11,000 lb-thrust General Electric F-404 turbofans (minus afterburners), as used in the F/A-18 Hornet. Designed mainly for night-time operations, its official mission is 'to penetrate dense threat environments and attack high-value targets with pinpoint accuracy', and it flies at high subsonic speeds (i.e. below the speed of sound).

The unusual shape explains the secrecy surrounding the aircraft, which was intended to protect the technique known as 'faceting'; the angled flat surfaces ensuring that incoming radar energy is scattered rather than reflected back to the emitter. The highly swept wing leading edge and W-shaped trailing edge (see Figure 2:4) reduce head-on and tail-on radar reflections. The jet intakes are covered with grilles to reflect radar, which cause a distinctive high-pitched whine on approach. The engine exhausts are passed through a series of baffles and the final nozzles are wide but shallow, spreading the gases and thus reducing the infrared 'signature'. Rearward noise is a muffled rumble.

Most F-117a's are based with the 37th and 38th Tactical Fighter Wings in Nevada and California, although some operate from Europe, and it is rumoured that a squadron may be deployed at RAF Alconbury in England. It is certainly possible that some of the UFO sightings in Belgium can be attributed to one or more of these extraordinary aircraft, yet the obvious dissimilarities in shape and performance support the view that genuine UFOs have been observed in most cases, as has now been confirmed officially by the Belgian Air Force (July 1990).

(**Sources.** Doug Richardson: *Stealth Warplanes*, Salamander Books, London 1989; *Flight International*, 11–17 April 1990, 2–8 May 1990; *Air Forces Monthly*, June 1990.)

3

The UFO Landings at Voronezh

GORDON CREIGHTON

Gordon Creighton, M.A., F.R.G.S., F.R.A.S., completed his education at Cambridge University and the Ecole Libre des Sciences Politiques in Paris. He spent many years in diplomatic posts throughout the world, and subsequently served for seven years as an intelligence officer in Whitehall.

He first served as a language student attaché to HM Embassy, Peking, then at various times as HM Vice-Consul at Tientsin, HM Consul at Chungking, and First Secretary of HM Embassy, first in Peking and then at the wartime capital, Chungking. Further posts included various periods in the Far Eastern Department of the Foreign Office, London, then as HM Consul at Shanghai, Nanking, Recife (Brazil), and Consul-General at Antwerp (Belgium) and New Orleans (USA).

Gordon Creighton has studied some twenty-five languages and dialects, including Chinese, Sanskrit, Tibetan, Mongolian, Burmese, Arabic, and Russian, as well as all the major languages of Europe. He is a specialist on diplomatic and international relations in Central Asia and the Far East, on communism and worldwide communist subversion, and on relations between Russia and China.

He has also been engaged in research for HM Government on maps printed in oriental and other languages with the Permanent Committee on Geographical Names, Royal Geographical Society, Kensington.

Gordon Creighton has been interested in UFOs since the summer of 1941, when he saw one over the Far West of China, not far from Tibet, while serving in the British Embassy at Chungking. He has contributed to *Flying Saucer Review* since its establishment in 1955, and has been Editor since 1982. He has regularly produced or translated a number of books on UFOs and has taken part in over forty TV and radio programmes on the subject in various countries. He has twice given talks before the UFO Study Group of the House of Lords.

Besides a life-long study of all the main world religions, Gordon Creighton has studied parapsychology for over forty years and has witnessed many unusual experiments on five continents. He has been a member of the Society for Psychical Research (SPR) for many years.

He is also a translator of a collection of famous classical Chinese love poems dating from the Tang and Sung Dynasties (7th to 13th centuries, AD).

An announcement carried on 9 October 1989, by the semi-official Soviet News Agency TASS (always regarded throughout the world as the veritable 'mouthpiece of the Kremlin'), and repeated on the following days by the 'intelligenstia's' journal *Sovetskaya Kultura*, the youth journal *Komsomolskaya Pravda*, and several other papers, indicated that, at 6.30 p.m. on 27 September 1989 – a warm evening – an alien craft, a disk, or ball, or egg-shaped, had landed in a clearing in a park at Voronezh, a city of some 900,000 inhabitants lying about 300 miles south-east of Moscow (see Figure 3:1).

The place, Yuzhniy Park ('South Park'), is on the outskirts of the Levoberezhniy Suburb, near Mendeleev Street.

The event is claimed to have been witnessed by a number of boys and girls from the nearby School No. 33, who were playing football, and also by a considerable number of adults – possibly as many as thirty or forty – who were waiting at a nearby bus stop. According to the versions gathered by the newspaper *Sovetskaya Kultura* and by two journalists sent specially to the spot to investigate on behalf of the *Moscow News*, it seems certain that – despite the subsequent persistent efforts of the world press outside Russia to make out that *only one* landing had been alleged at Voronezh, and that its only witnesses were *children* – the truth of the matter is that UFOs were seen at or around that area many times, and by many people, at least between 21 September and 2 October. Many adult witnesses were subsequently interrogated about this by the Voronezh *Militia* (police), and they said that they had seen craft – sometimes 'banana-shaped' and bearing an illuminated emblem or sign.

Some of them also said that they had seen or encountered occupants. And these statements referred to days other than 27 September. (The principal days mentioned, other than 27 September, seem to have been 21, 23 and 29 September, and 2 October.)

The Children

Various reports seen give a variety of names of children eyewitnesses – presumably because not all of the children were interviewed by any one journalist. The names collected are: Roma Torshin (sixth form), Vasya Surin (aged 11), Denis Murzenko, Yuri Grinev, Yuri Sergachev, Roma Milkin, Volodya Startsev, Alyosha Nikonov, Oleg Chebotaryov (aged 9), Zhenyia Blinov (interviewed on TV), Yuliya Sholohova, and Lena Sarokina (aged 11).

The Approach and the Landing of the Craft

When questioned, the children stated that about 6.30 p.m. they had observed a pinkish glow approaching in the sky, on a level course, and that when it was right above them they perceived it to be a deep red, ball-shaped or egg-shaped object. (Several adult witnesses, as already noted, spoke, however, of having seen a 'banana-shaped' craft with an illuminated sign, but it is not at all clear, so far as we can see, whether this description related to 27 September or to one or other of the other days.)

The object flew around in concentric circles above the children for a while, and then vanished for a few minutes. Then it reappeared, and began to hover around them. Then it started to

Figure 3:1.

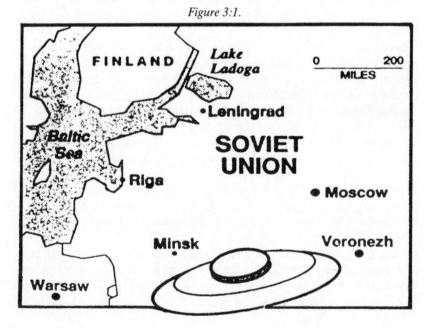

descend. When it was close to the ground, a hatch, about the size of a door, opened, and a burly silhouette appeared, more or less blocking the whole aperture. The movements of this being, which peered around, were slow. He seemed 'to have no neck', and his head was very small, described as 'like a small hemisphere set between the shoulders'. Another witness spoke of it as 'more like a knob than a head'. The being allegedly had three luminous eyes, the central one being moveable, 'swivelling around like a radar'. His nose was a mere hole, and on his breast was a shield. After looking around, he closed the hatch. Then four 'feet' came down, and the craft landed gently.

The machine is described as about thirty feet wide. But one or two reports say 'about fifteen metres long, four metres wide, and seven metres high'. (It is difficult to wed this with 'thirty feet wide'. Does this second set of measurements relate to something seen in that same park on another day, as seems likely – maybe the 'banana-shaped' machine?)

The Entities

When the deep red-coloured 'ball' had finally touched down and the hatch opened up again, the witnesses say that a total of three of the huge 'pin-headed' creatures stepped out, bringing with them what seemed to be *a robot*. Vasya Surin and other boys described the 'pin-head' beings as between three and four metres high, in silvery coloured overalls and bronze-coloured boots. One of them gave a sort of push to the 'robot', and set him moving, and then the whole party set off and strolled around the craft several times. One of the beings emitted 'sounds', which seemed to be orders, and from his breast came a beam of light that delineated on the ground a number of luminous triangles, of about 30×50 cm, which faded after a short while.

According to the *Sovetskaya Kultura* version – if we have understood it aright – at this stage both the craft and the entities flipped into invisibility for five minutes or so, and then reappeared.

Boy 'zapped'

One of the boys cried out in fear, whereupon one of the beings 'froze' him or 'paralysed' him with a glance from his glowing eyes. This particular being had a sort of 'tube', about 50 cm long, hanging at his side. (This sort of weapon has featured in several encounter reports from various parts of the world – particularly in the famous French case of Monsieur Masse at Valensole, and in some of the South American encounter cases.) The creature now pointed this 'tube' at another of the boys (aged sixteen) and 'zapped' him with a luminous beam, so that the boy vanished totally from the scene, to reappear only after the alien craft and alien beings had departed!

(Some of the press reports from Russia indicated that the parents of this boy have not permitted *any* journalist to interview him.) The London *Sunday Times* (15 October) quoted a Mr Slava Martinov, a member of the local UFO study group, as stating that in fact *most* of the children eyewitnesses had not been permitted to testify before the Independent Enquiry Commission set up by the Voronezh authorities. (See more on this below.) 'The parents all want their kids left alone,' said Martinov. However, it seems that quite a lot of the children *did* talk to journalists, and of course all of the alleged statements by children eyewitnesses given in this article are claimed to have come through the journalists who went down to Voronezh to see them.

Ground Marks left by the UFO

The reports indicate that, at the spot where the craft had stood, a circular depressed area some 60 feet wide was found, with four holes set in a rhombus pattern. Some versions said the four holes were some 15 cm in diameter and 4 cm deep. Lev Aksionov and Boris Zverev, for example, the two journalists sent from Moscow to spend two or three days in Voronezh and write a detailed report for the English and French versions of *Moscow News*, were quoted as saying the holes were 25–30 cm wide and 20–25 cm deep.

Local Official Investigation Committee Formed

Many reports described the local populace as very frightened. Within days, at the instigation of the local Parliamentary Deputy, Gennadiy Kabassin, the Mayor of Voronezh, Viktor Atlasov, and his assistant, Aleksandr Tsapin, set up an Investigation Committee, comprising scientists, criminologists, doctors, meteorologists and even local UFO investigators! The press reports made mention of two different local 'UFO investigation bodies', one being called the 'Voronezh Branch of the Alexsandr Popov Scientific and Electronic Association', and the other one being called the 'Voronezh Branch for the Study of Anomalous Phenomena'. The 'Popov Society' was heard about years ago, and a report on its activities was published. It was known in those days that its credentials sounded a bit phoney. Obviously the *real* UFO study

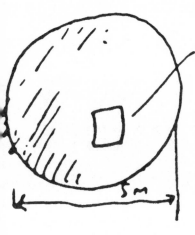

Люк "размером с дверь"

(door-sized hatch)

Figure 3:2. 'At 9 p.m. on Sept. 23, as I was returning home, I saw in the sky a round, red object with a black hatch of the size of a door. It was about 5 metres in diameter. As it landed, four legs came out, and the hatch opened and a "robot" came down the ladder.' Eyewitness Roma Torshin, Sixth-Former, School No. 33. (Sketch by Roma Torshin)

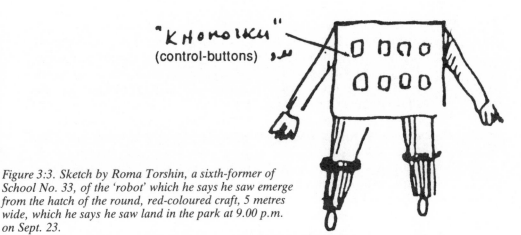

"Кнопочки"

(control-buttons)

Figure 3:3. Sketch by Roma Torshin, a sixth-former of School No. 33, of the 'robot' which he says he saw emerge from the hatch of the round, red-coloured craft, 5 metres wide, which he says he saw land in the park at 9.00 p.m. on Sept. 23.

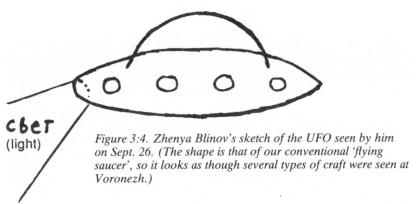

свет
(light)

Figure 3:4. Zhenya Blinov's sketch of the UFO seen by him on Sept. 26. (The shape is that of our conventional 'flying saucer', so it looks as though several types of craft were seen at Voronezh.)

Figure 3:5. Zhenya Blinov, a classmate of Roma Torshin, said that on Sept. 26, at 7.00 p.m., and at the same spot, he saw an object with portholes. Someone about 3 metres high emerged from it. 'On his head I saw two eyes and, slightly above them, a red lamp. On his breast there was a disk with three spots of different colours, and slightly below it there was a rectangle which started sticking out from the body.' (Sketch by Zhenya Blinov)

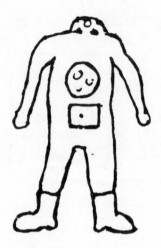

group in Voronezh is the 'Anomalous Phenomena Group'. Correspondents in Russia made known recently that for years past they have been persecuted and badgered and chivvied and driven from pillar to post by the KGB, by the university academics, and by the astronomers and intellectuals, all because they insisted on calling themselves investigators of 'NLOs' (Russian for 'UFOs'). And in the end they were obliged to call themselves investigators of 'ANOMALOUS PHENOMENA'! Evidently a rose by any other name does *not* smell as sweet.

Prominent among the Voronezh Group of 'Investigators of Anomalous Phenomena' there is a Mr Genrikh (Henry) Silanov, and many of the press reports mention him. He runs an establishment with the official-sounding title of 'Voronezh Geophysical Laboratory', but all the reports show that this is simply a private body run by Silanov. Silanov himself interrogated many of the eyewitnesses, both children and adults.

'Bio-Location' of the Site

Many of the foreign press reports on the case described how the Russians talked about '*bio-location*' having been utilized in order to confirm the precise landing site. All the American and British press agencies and journalists confessed to being baffled by this term, and complained that the Russians had given no explanation as to what it meant!

'Bio-location' is simply the Russian term for what is called in English 'dowsing'. Being second to nobody in the entire world in their knowledge of all aspects of Parapsychology and Occultism (studied intensively by the KGB in view of the tremendous possible uses in espionage, intelligence warfare, and skullduggery in general), the Russians naturally know all about dowsing. And they take it very seriously. Like a lot of things at which we profess to snigger.

According to Genrikh Silanov's statements, he and his fellow investigators used their dowsing equipment, and found that the UFO had landed precisely where the boys and other witnesses said it landed.

Magnetic and Radiation Effects

According to one of the foreign reports (seen only in the *Pensacola News Journal*, Florida, USA, 12 October 1989), a Russian aviation engineer from a nearby factory at Voronezh said that he and his colleagues examined and measured the landing site, and found there 'an intense magnetic field'.

According to the reporters Aksionov and Zverev (of *Moscow Weekly News*), two of the holes made by the feet of the craft showed far higher gamma radiation than adjacent ground. The soil around about in the park showed an average of 10–15 microroentgens per hour, whereas one of the holes registered 30 microroentgens and another gave 37 microroentgens. According to another press report seen, it was technicians from the Soviet Ministry of the Interior who discovered and measured this radioactivity.

The probable weight of the craft was stated to have been estimated as eleven tons.

The Red Sandstones

There was a tremendous hoohah in some papers about certain pieces of red sandstone allegedly found at the landing site. At first it seemed as though Genrikh Silanov himself was quoted as having said that this red stone was something never before found anywhere else on earth! Later, however, he was allegedly quoted as stating firmly that it was simply a bit of ordinary haematite such as is normal in those parts of Russia.

Britain's 'best and most famous newspaper', *Sunday Sport* (22 October) had a wonderful time with the red sandstones, announcing that these were 'alien eggs' from the Cosmos, and claiming that 'their man at Voronezh' had even brought one home to the Head Office in London; that examination of the 'egg' by British doctors and scientists had already established the presence within it of some sort of human-like embryo; and that they would soon be announcing a 'happy event' to their readers. (Since then, for some curious reason, the *Sunday Sport* seems to have 'gone off' its 'cosmic eggs', and has no doubt found something else with which to titillate us and drum up business.)

Soil Samples Taken?

In addition to the holes in the soil by the 'feet' of the alleged alien craft, investigators were reported to have found another hole (no dimensions mentioned) from which it was thought that the visitors might have taken soil samples – just as has been reported in many other UFO cases.

Statement by Lt Sergei Matveyev of the Voronezh Militia (Police)

This young policeman told investigators that he had been one of the eyewitnesses to the landing. He said that, at about 7 p.m. on 27 September 1989, he had been passing near the Park, when he suddenly saw an 'incandescent ball' pass across the sky in horizontal flight, very fast, and at an altitude of about 200 metres. He reckoned its diameter as being about 15 metres. He watched this 'ball' in flight for about 5 seconds. It was making no sound of any kind. When questioned further as to its apparent solidity, he insisted that it was definitely three-dimensional, and was no hallucination or trick of light or solar beam in the atmosphere.

Statement by a Colonel of the Voronezh Militia

Police-Colonel Ludmilla Makarova, Head of the Voronezh Department of Criminal Detection (she is consequently an official of the Soviet Ministry of the Interior) commented on the case as follows: 'I don't know what it was that happened here, but I *do* know one thing – the radioactivity at the site is very high. *Why?* No doubt because of some isotope particle. But then another question arises: Why the radioactivity inside the holes and not on the surface of the ground?'

Statement by a Soviet Nuclear Physicist

Another important Voronezh personage whose statement was published along with the others in the *Moscow Weekly News* No. 43 (22 October) was Professor Stanislav Kadmenskiy, holder of the Chair of Nuclear Physics in the University of Voronezh, and also a member of the Commission of Enquiry into the Voronezh incident.

He described how he and his colleagues had collected seventeen soil samples at the site and sent them away for analysis. Discussing the possibility that alien beings might visit our planet (which he did not appear to deem ridiculous or impossible!), his answer showed none of the hysteria displayed over this affair by our American and British press. Like Stanton Friedman he is, of course, a nuclear physicist, and therefore presumably not a total buffoon. At any rate, he merely made the remarkably interesting statement that, if a landing by a UFO at Voronezh were to be proved, then it would mean that we have something to learn about the Special Theory of Relativity, and it would indicate that there exists another sort of Physics that is at present unknown to us.

'Religious Rumours'

A rumour circulated to the effect that a priest of the Russian Orthodox Church had visited the landing site and blessed it! The story went on to say that true believers were flocking to the Voronezh Park to offer prayers there.

So the two journalists from the *Moscow Weekly News* contacted the Episcopal Office in Voronezh, and asked whether this report was true. They received a categorical denial: 'It is an act of Satan – not of God! A true Christian would never go to that place in the dark to pray.'

Consistency of Eyewitnesses' Statements

Apart from the fact that, as stated above, a number of people seem to have mentioned seeing a 'banana-shaped' object, and that more than one sighting, and possibly more than one landing, may have taken place, and on a number of days between 21 September and 3 October, the authorities and investigators at Voronezh admit that the accounts given by eyewitnesses show a remarkable degree of uniformity and agreement. This is particularly so of what the *children* said. And an odd fact which emerges, according to the two men from the *Moscow Weekly News*, is that some of the Voronezh children's descriptions and sketches of craft and aliens and 'robots' coincide to an astonishing degree with the accounts and sketches of the children who claimed to have seen landed craft and entities at the village of Konantsevo, near Kharovsk, in Vologda Oblast' (Province) in June 1989.

Indeed, when the work of translating all this year's crop of reports received directly from our Russian correspondents is done (these are investigators' reports – not press reports), we may be in a position to show that at both Voronezh and at a place near Chernushenskiy, far away in Perm Province, in Siberia, the accounts speak, at least in part, of black, square, robot-like beings, and tall beings with excessively tiny 'knobs' in place of heads. All of this will have to be studied carefully if we are to deal properly with all the weird 'poltergeistic' UFO stories received from Russia in 1989.

Statement by the Mayor of Voronezh about the Children

Discussing the eyewitnesses' accounts at Voronezh, Mayor Atlasov of that city told the two reporters from *Moscow Weekly News* that he was quite positive that the local children were telling the truth. He said he had listened very carefully both to their statement and to the taped recordings of their statements. He commented: 'I am not very young myself. And I am positive that an adult can always perceive when a child is telling the truth and when he is giving rein to his imagination. *I believe what they are saying.*'

Reports also treated seriously by other Voronezh Authorities

Vladimir A. Moisevey, Director of the Voronezh Regional Health Office, together with other City Authorities and, as stated, the TASS News Agency's staff, all treated the entire story throughout as a serious scientific phenomenon. Interviewed on the telephone by the *New York Times* on 11 October, Moisevey said that, despite all the reports of 'widespread fear' in Voronezh about the UFOs, none of the eyewitnesses had, so far, applied to his Department for any sort of medical aid or counselling. But, he went on, 'We are certainly planning to examine the children.' (He gave no explanation why no such examination had yet been undertaken, seeing that two whole weeks had already elapsed since 27 September, the day of the claimed landing in the Park.) But the children certainly were questioned at some later stage.

As regards talk of surveillance of the alleged landing site, Mr Larin, Duty Officer at the Voronezh Offices of the Soviet Ministry of the Interior, said that his own department was much too shorthanded to have extra men available for patrolling the Park, but he said that 'If they (the Aliens) appeared there again, troops would be despatched to the site'.

Of particular interest is the statement by a spokesman for the local administration of the USSR State Security Committee (i.e. the KGB), as reported in the *Moscow News* of 22 October:

Such things mustn't be taken too lightly. We must accumulate information on any abnormal phenomena, wherever they take place, and carefully study them. This is primarily a task for scientists. For the time being, at the first stage, the investigation was mainly carried out by enthusiasts. We are here to take steps – if necessary – to ensure the citizens' safety.

Statements by TASS News Agency spokesmen

Asked whether the Voronezh story could be a hoax, a genial spokesman in the TASS Moscow Office replied: 'So far as we are concerned, this is no joke. We never joke. If we start joking, we'll stop existing.'

Questioned by British journalists in London and on British television, the TASS Correspondent in London, Yuri Sidorov, said (9 October 1989): 'No. This is not April Fool's Day. We are a serious agency, and do not report things that are not true. Personally, I do not believe in flying objects, but if TASS says something, it must be so.'

Personal Statement by TASS correspondent Lebedev from Voronezh

The TASS correspondent Vladimir V. Lebedev, aged 59 and a veteran of twenty years in the TASS service, who was the man sent from Moscow to Voronezh to investigate and report on this case from the spot, told *United Press International* (report in *Los Angeles Times* of 11 October), that in Voronezh he questioned 'about ten youngsters aged twelve to thirteen', and added that he felt this large number sufficed to show that something had indeed happened there. He did not claim to have seen any UFOs or entities at Voronezh himself. He said that, in all, the Voronezh eyewitnesses had spoken to him of three landings by alien craft seen by them at Voronezh, the main one being on 27 September, and the other two on 23 September and 29 September.

In a report carried by the *New York Times* (11 October), Lebedev was quoted as saying that the three children from School No. 33 who first saw the UFO when it arrived while they were playing football were Vasya Surin, Yuliya Sholohova and Zhenya Blinov.

When Esther B. Fein, the *New York Times* representative in Moscow, telephoned Lebedev in Voronezh about the case, she reported that he 'sounded quite insulted' by the idea that anyone should treat his story of the Voronezh landing with anything but the full seriousness that he and the TASS Agency had given to it!

He went on to say that Genrikh Silanov of the Voronezh Geophysical Laboratory had asked the children, on 10 October, to sketch for him what they had seen.

Though isolated from one another, he said that several of the children had also drawn a 'banana-shaped object' and a sign which resembles the letter 'X'. Such a sign, he said, had already been reported as typical of UFOs in an article in the now defunct American magazine *Saga*.

In an article about Voronezh, in the new Spanish magazine *Mas Allá* (Special No. 9, November 1989) one of the children's drawings is published, but unfortunately too unclear for it to be reproduced here. What it clearly does show, however, is the famous and mysterious 'UMMO' sign, known by many from years ago in Spain!

What are we to make of this? These Russian children are hardly likely to have ever seen the 'UMMO' symbol anywhere, even if it had once been reproduced in *Saga* – and that is by no means certain anyway. If the Russian children, or any other witnesses, really did see the 'UMMO' sign at Voronezh, then it indicates pretty clearly that one and the same agency is behind 'UFO phenomena' in regions as far apart as Russia and Spain.

Describing the Voronezh landing site, Lebedev said: 'The traces were still to be seen. I saw holes of a clear shape, that resembled the footprints of elephants.'

Pressed by other foreign correspondents who telephoned him, Lebedev was quoted as sticking firmly to his story, while admitting that 'some exaggerations might have crept in at some stage'. He said: 'I think there is a certain amount of truth, but it is not excluded that there is also some fantasizing.' Asked to explain further what he meant by this, he replied: '[Adults] may have added certain things'. (Quoted in an article the *Los Angeles Times*, 11 October 1989.)

Reaction and Coverage by the Soviet Media

In view of the enormous size of the country and the tremendous number of newspapers and other publications, we do not know (at the time of writing) how much publicity the Voronezh landing story received *inside* the USSR.

According to one foreign report, the Soviet TV (presumably from Moscow) claimed that they had sent a team to Voronezh to investigate and that, after being there four days, had still failed to locate a single adult witness. Should this be true, it would in no way be surprising, since any adult witness coming forward might well expect to be 'in for trouble' and, as Russians prefer to do on most matters, would keep quiet.

However, it does seem that, according to an *Associated Press* report of 12 October, on the evening of 11 October Soviet TV viewers saw a fifteen-minute Vremya programme from Voronezh about the case. The two 'star' child witnesses appeared, and their sketches were shown. The boy Vasya Surin, aged eleven, said: 'We were scared. It hovered over this tree. Then the door opened, and a tall person about three metres high looked out. He didn't have a head, or shoulders either. He just had a kind of hump. *There* he had three eyes – one on each side and one in the middle.'

The children stuck to their story, while admitting that they do enjoy reading science fiction.

By the end of October, however, some negative reports began emerging from the USSR. The English edition of the Japanese newspaper, *Mainichi Daily News* of 30 October 1989, for example, reported as follows:

> Moscow (AFP-Jiji) – A Soviet scientific commission has concluded that there exists no verifiable proof of a landing by aliens last month in the town of Voronezh, in southern Russia, the commission chief said on Saturday.
>
> Sixteen radiometric analyses, nineteen checks on the ground, nine tests of micro-organisms, and twenty spectro-chemical measurements, failed to uncover 'any anomaly either in the earth or surrounding vegetation' that might indicate the landing of an unidentified flying object, the commission reported.
>
> Igor Sarotsev, vice-rector of the University of Voronezh and chairman of the commission, said that the presence of a larger-than-normal quantity of the radioactive isotope *caesium* in the area of the alleged sightings did not constitute proof of a landing.
>
> 'After Chernobyl, this kind of phenomenon has been found in many areas', said Sarotsev to the newspaper *Sovetskaya Kultura* on Saturday – referring to the April 1986 accident at the Chernobyl nuclear plant that sent a radiation cloud over Europe and killed twenty-one people.

The Soviet Scene

There has been a 'UFO problem' in Russia and the USSR just as long as there has been a 'UFO problem' in the rest of the world. We know that there are quite a number of good Russian reports that date from as far back as at least the 1980s. And in fact the third issue of *Flying Saucer Review* (July/August 1955) contained my translation of a UFO report from the prestigious Soviet scientific journal *Priroda* ('Nature'), which is published by the USSR Academy of Sciences and is the Russian counterpart of our scientific journal, *Nature*.

Ever since that date (summer of 1955), *FSR* has constantly been receiving Russian material about UFOs, by one route or another. Sometimes this material came in lengthy letters to me from my personal correspondent in Moscow, Arkadiy Tikhonov (probably long since gone from this world) or from other correspondents here and there. No doubt some of those early correspondents were writing at the instigation of, or under the control of, the USSR Academy of Sciences or one or other of the two Soviet counter-intelligence and espionage organs, the KGB and GRU. The Academy of Sciences has itself been taking *FSR* regularly ever since 1963.

In addition, there was a period, of almost a decade, when, in London, I was myself in the privileged position of seeing daily almost the whole of the principal Russian press – including many newspapers and journals not normally available to the world outside the USSR because there was (for Intelligence reasons) a Soviet ban on their 'export'.

So our link with the Soviet scene is not a new one. It has endured over many years, and it will suffice to consult our back issues to see that *FSR* has carried a long series of important articles about Ufology and UFO reports in Russia, containing more information on Russia than any other UFO investigation journal in the world has ever done.

Meanwhile, from what we at *FSR* have been able to establish, from the massive amount of material received from our own sources inside Russia (namely one of the largest Russian UFO investigation groups) and from our press coverage, both Soviet and foreign, is that the USSR has been inundated with a veritable 'flap' or 'wave' of UFO and poltergeistic phenomena throughout at least the whole of 1989, and besides 'things seen in the skies' this also includes at least a dozen good, well-vouched cases of queer entities encountered walking around on the ground.

As for the reason why 'the cat got let out of the bag' at Voronezh, we can at present merely speculate. So far, the two favourite theories in the West seem to be that either (1) some poor chap in Russia thought that 'glasnost' really meant 'glasnost', and took the bit between his teeth (in which case he is surely in the Gulag by now!), or, (2), that things have now got so bad in poor old

Mother Russia that someone at the top decided to try for a while to take Ivan's mind off the growing queues and dwindling food supplies by releasing a story about UFOs and UFO occupants!

4

Abduction:
The Terror That Comes . . .

RALPH NOYES

A former navigator in the Royal Air Force and subsequently a civil
servant in the British Ministry of Defence for nearly thirty years,
Ralph Noyes is the author of *A Secret Property* (Quartet Books,
1985) which deals largely with UFOs, including – in fictionalized
form – the Rendlesham case of 1980. In *The UFO Report 1990* he
recorded his current views about these remarkable events.

He has published a number of articles about the mysterious circles
which have been appearing in British cornfields and elsewhere since
1980, and he is editor of a new book on the subject, *The Crop Circle
Enigma* (Gateway Publications, 1990). He is also Honorary Secretary to the recently formed Centre for Crop Circle Studies
(CCCS).

Ralph Noyes became the Honorary Secretary to the Society for
Psychical Research (SPR) in 1990. His following article reflects some
of the insights which he feels that his membership of the SPR has
given him. But he stresses that he speaks for himself alone: the SPR
(perhaps wisely!) always declines to express any corporate view.

Because this paper is written for those who have seriously studied
the subject, the word 'Abduction' in its title is enough to tell you
what kind of ground I want to cover. If I were writing for
anthropologists, or psychical researchers, or psychiatrists, or the
Police Federation, or the tabloid press, I would have to start with
some tricky attempts at definition. 'Abduction' covers a multitude
of sins: all of them are unpleasant, but only a few of them are
strange.

Readers of this volume will, of course, assume – and rightly –
that I shall be concerned with the kinds of experience reported by
Betty and Barney Hill, Betty Andreasson, and the many others
whose stories are examined in books by Budd Hopkins,[1,2] Philip

Klass,[3] Jenny Randles,[4] John Rimmer,[5] John Spencer,[6] Whitley Strieber's first-hand accounts of his own experiences,[7,8] and the many other comparable volumes and articles which are now too numerous to mention here. I will merely list a few references which may not yet be widely enough known.

This freedom to begin a paper without precisely defining its subject matter is a great convenience, but I believe it also conceals a great peril. I shall be suggesting that the use of the catchword 'Abduction' to identify this field of enquiry may possibly be handy but also begs important questions at the outset. Its uncritical use may possibly have muddied our discussions and prejudged their outcome. I shall be suggesting a more neutral term (even if without much hope of seeing it adopted!).

Much of the literature of UFO Abductions, which is what I shall continue to call them for the time being, turns on a debate about whether the experiences are 'real' or 'imaginary'. I shall be suggesting that these terms, which force us to put occurrences into one of two mutually exclusive boxes, are as confusing and unhelpful in the UFO Abductions field as I think they have proved to be in cryptozoology, folklore studies, and psychical research. They divert our attention from the facts and lead to sterile polemics about the meaning of words. I shall propose different terms which might prove more useful.

The second part of my title is drawn from an outstanding but too little known work by David Hufford, a professor in the social sciences at Pennsylvania University: *The Terror that Comes in the Night – An Experience-centred Study of Supernatural Assault Traditions*.[9] Those who have read it will recognize that much of the rest of this paper is based on Hufford's insights and methods in his own very distinct field of enquiry – the study of those terrifying visitations, accompanied by paralysis and dread and occurring in the waking state, which pass by the name of 'The Old Hag' in Newfoundland but occur with surprising frequency under other names in all societies yet studied.

UFO Abductions – Are they Unique?

Whatever else they may be, UFO Abductions are reported interactions between human beings and beings of another sort. It may help us if we try to relate these reports to accounts of similar interactions which our species has often claimed with other entities of a non-human kind.

Such comparisons have, of course, been made before, notably with the Celtic 'fairy faith' in Jacques Vallee's *Passport to Magonia*[10] and *Dimensions*.[11] But the parallels he draws, suggestive though they are, often seem strained and unconvincing. His suggestion, for example, that UFO Abduction, with its alarming elements of capture and surgery, is a modern version of the gentle fairy beguilement of mortal man into the enchantments of fairyland leaves competent folklorists unimpressed: the comparison is interesting but the differences are at least as striking. The same could be said for the fanciful parallels which are sometimes drawn between flying saucers and fairy mounds or mushrooms, or between fairy rings in grass and the multitude of circular ground disturbances which are sometimes identified as UFO nests or traces.

I think we need much more more scholarly rigour than has yet been brought to bear on these interesting comparisons, and that the Little People are far from being the only population of non-human entities at which we should look. The following is a sketch of how our field of inquiry might be widened and made more exact.

Human Interactions with Strange Beings

Throughout history and in all societies for which we have records, there is a wealth of reports from individuals claiming interaction with beings far stranger than ourselves. The literature is vast, but an excellent survey, anyway of our humanoid or human-seeming visitors, is given in two noteworthy books by Hilary Evans: *Visions, Apparitions, Alien Visitors*[12] and *Gods, Spirits, Cosmic Guardians*.[13] I would merely want to add to Hilary Evans' extensive catalogue of our 'humanish' intruders the long tally of the many other kinds of strange being – far from human in their attributes – for which we have at least as much testimony: the Black Dogs of folklore, the Surrey Pumas of cryptozoology, the lake monsters, the sea-serpents, the 'manimals', the 'birdmen', the scaly monstrosities from black lagoons, the ghouls, the djinns, the demons, the angels, the vampires and werewolves, the poltergeists, the elementals . . . You name them; and if you name them 'Legion' I shall not be too surprised.

'Strange' needs some definition. The platypus must have seemed exceedingly 'strange' to the first Europeans who met it, and they probably had some difficulty in persuading stay-at-home zoologists to accept their reports. Snakes and spiders continue to seem 'strange' to me: they are clearly a different kind of flesh and I find it hard to be on fellow terms with them; indeed, I usually stand on a chair. Anybody who looks at a drop of pond water through the microscope for the first time will probably need some human comfort and a cup of tea after the 'strange' nature of what he's seen. Our remarkable planet teems with 'strange' – though very material – entities; the invented aliens and monsters of science fiction are often downright bourgeois by comparison.

But by 'strange' in the context of the present article I mean not merely 'bizarre' or 'unfamiliar' (which our reported visitors often are) but also such things as disobeying natural law, as we understand it; carrying on in a manner which tends to upset good physicists; seeming to be a good deal less substantial than most of the objects of our daily experience; manifesting only briefly; rarely leaving durable and unambiguous traces of their visitations.

Many of the reported interactions between humankind (male or female) and these stranger entities take the form of wholly 'inward' experiences. The subject tells us that gods or monsters have come to him (masculine used only for convenience) in a dream, or that something of the sort has gripped his imagination unbidden in the waking state, or that he has heard a voice 'inside his head'. He is clear that the experience is 'contained within himself' (or, if he happens to be a trance medium, those present report that whatever was going on, it went on within him). No claim is made by the subject that anything became manifest outside the confines of his body's boundaries. If he speaks of 'seeing', it is clear that he means 'seeing with the mind's eye'.

These 'inward' experiences are often of great interest. Sometimes remarkable claims are made for them of the kind worth scientific study in psychical research – for example, that they foretell the future, or reflect distant events unknowable to the subject by conventional means, or are communications from the dead or from 'other realms'. But I mention them in this paper mainly to distinguish them clearly from my prime subject, the reported *encounters* with strange beings.

The Reported Encounters

In contrast with the dreams, imaginings and inward visions are the experiences reported to us as manifesting *outside* the boundaries of the subject's body. The subject has become, according to his report, not merely a subject but a *witness* – and sometimes a witness who is involved, willingly or otherwise, in 'outward' events. He tells us that he has come face to face with a strange entity, he has heard it, he has touched it, sometimes he has even smelled or tasted it. And in the more dramatic of these encounters he engages with, or is engaged by, his transient visitor.

It is possible that there is a close relationship between these 'outward', and often very tangible, encounters and the 'inward' experiences mentioned above. The two things quite often happen to the same people on different occasions, and the subject matter of the two different experiences is often the same or similar: people who see UFOs or meet strange entities frequently dream of them as well, or receive messages from them which come 'directly into the head'. (And sometimes the dream or the message precedes the encounter.) But whatever the relationship may be between 'inward' experience on the one hand and 'outward' encounters on the other, *the two are quite distinct* anyway, as the subject tells us.

'As the subject tells us' is, of course, a crucial point. It is usually *reports* which we find ourselves examining when we try to be dispassionate students of these matters. Unless you happen to be lucky enough (or unlucky enough) to have undergone your own 'outward' encounter with a strange being, there is little you can bring by way of sympathetic attention to what the subject tells you except to listen to his story and to use your judgement. The only point I wish to make is that having asked some shrewd questions and judged accordingly, you will find that reports fall into two groups: stories of 'inward' experience, and stories of what the subject felt – *knew* – was an 'outward' encounter. And he isn't usually in much doubt about it, himself.

In the rest of this article, I shall be considering these reported encounters. And for the most part I shall, as a matter of convenience, be dropping the word 'reported'. If you think this begs important questions, I will ask you to wait for my conclusions.

Are the Encounters with Strange Beings 'Real'?

I have made the distinction, between 'inward' and 'outward' experiences because of a strong – though, in my view, mistaken – tendency of the commentators in every age to confuse the two and to assimilate the one to the other. There has been, in consequence, a great deal of futile argument about whether the 'inward' or the 'outward' is the more 'real'. And the confusion has sometimes resulted in avoidable human suffering.

The witch-finders of the Renaissance were determined to take every statement wrung from their unfortunate victims as evidence of 'real' and 'outward' events. The dream and fantasies of some wretched soul, his or her 'inward' experiences, were taken as 'outward reality'. If he or she (usually she) confessed to attending a Sabbat and engaging in activities which *The News of the World* would now report mainly for Sunday morning titillation, the inquisitors took the report at face value. Except by a few brave souls who risked a charge of heresy, no serious attempt was made to consider whether there might be a sustainable distinction be-tween dreams and imaginings on the one hand and 'outward' encounters on the other. We have, in consequence, been denied the chance of considering how much of this rich (though terrible) material truly reflected 'outward' encounters with non-humankind rather than the dreams and fantasies dragged out by the interrogators.

The fashion of the establishment in our own times is to adopt the opposite stance. Every 'outward' experience which fails to obey the laws of Newtonian physics is ascribed to something wholly 'inward' to the subject, who is likely to be described as a 'patient' rather than a witness if he presses his story. The subject is assumed to have had a dream and to be unable to tell whether he is awake or asleep; or he is 'diagnosed' as suffering from hallucinations. And attempts are made to find a medical condition which accounts for his unfortunate state.

It is characteristic, for example, that a recent survey of hallucination by two very well qualified clinicians, Peter Slade and Richard Bentall[14], defines its subject matter as being 'any percept-like experience which . . . occurs *in the absence of an appropriate stimulus . . .*' (my emphasis) but never discusses what an 'appropriate' stimulus might be. They therefore beg the question from the outset whether there is ever an 'outward' something which might, on some occasions, account for a subject's report of encountering strange entities.

This commonsense stance is perhaps understandable on the part of two clinical psychologists who have to treat much 'inward' suffering on the part of people who present themselves as ill; but it dogmatically closes the door to any serious study of whole realms of experience reported by witnesses who, though possibly terrified and sometimes 'changed' by their encounters, are not manifestly ill, as judged by any objective standard, and who know that they were not dreaming.

From the witch-finders and the clinicians, therefore, we get no help with the question which heads this section. For the first, all encounters with strange beings are 'real' if they fit doctrinal prejudices; for the second, all such encounters are 'unreal'. In place of 'real' and 'unreal' I suggest we adopt a different kind of classification, using two separate pairs of terms and applying them separately.

Whenever we are told of an interaction between a subject and a strange entity (using 'strange' as I have suggested earlier), let us in future ask two questions:

(1) Was the experience an 'inward' or an 'outward' one, *according to what the subject tells us* (provided we can be reasonably sure that he is not lying or ill – both of them matters for which there are reasonably objective tests)?

(2) If the experience was an 'outward' one, was it 'more material' or 'less material', as judged by any *independent* evidence we can get; for example, a ground trace or other damage to the environment? (The question of 'materiality' needs further comment. I shall be returning to it later.)

I claim no particular novelty for this approach; good investigators have always instinctively used something of the sort. But I believe that its determined and conscious use would save us at least some of the sterile argumentation which haunts the question, 'But was it real?' and it would, above all, avoid the preconceptions of both the witch-finders and the clinicians.

But there is, of course, a more troublesome meaning to that question, 'Was it real?'. When we are told of a particularly bizarre experience – the most urgent current instance is the UFO Abduction – it is a natural instinct of common sense to ask, 'But did it *really* happen? Was the victim *really* taken to that domed chamber and subjected to fearsome indignities? What in the world – the *real* world – took place?'

The debate which then ensues is usually doomed to muddle. Sooner or later, the protagonists on the one side, convinced that an occurrence was not 'all in the imagination', but often finding that they lack decisive evidence of a happening in the 'real' world, begin to talk about different 'levels' of 'reality', some of which are more 'real' than the rest (and other such linguistic nonsense), while their sceptical opponents jeer at such notions and refuse to accord 'reality' to anything which fails to leave lasting material traces of a very pedestrian nature (and often seek to evade such evidence even when well attested). If the arguments are pushed further, both sides fall into the bottomless pit of metaphysical polemics.

I believe that all this can be side-stepped, anyway provisionally, if we stick to the principles of inquiry suggested above. It is certainly the case that David Hufford, following similar principles, was able to reach remarkable conclusions about a phenomenon which is not much less alarming and puzzling than UFO Abduction. There is much to be learned from his methods; and the experience he was studying may well be a distant relative of the UFO Abduction experience.

The Terror that Comes in the Night

Studying folklore in Newfoundland, Hufford stumbled across a tradition that some people are sometimes visited, usually privately and usually in their bedrooms, by an alarming kind of entity. One of his early informants described it very briefly like this: 'You are dreaming and you feel as if someone is holding you down. You can do nothing, only cry out. People believe that you will die if you are not awakened.' Newfoundlanders call this experience 'The Old Hag'.

Most social scientists would have been content to note this tradition, to collect a few stories from informants (whether first-hand or not), to dismiss the experience as a form of bad dream coloured by the local folklore, and to consider solely what psycho-social significance this rather laughable superstition might have for the Newfoundland community. But Hufford, unique among his colleagues at that time, thought it might be worth considering whether something objective lay behind 'The Old Hag' tradition. He began to collect first-hand accounts and to look for common features in the wealth of confusing detail they presented. Un-troubled by any tiresome preoccupations about the 'reality' or otherwise of what he was studying, and wholly without any precon-ceived ideas into which he wished to cram the data, Hufford conducted over several years one of the most fruitful investigations we have yet had into the field of what is often called 'the super-natural'. Extending his studies from Newfoundland to the United States, and subsequently examining material reported from many other societies, he discovered what appears to be a wide-spread phenomenon.

It is impossible to do justice in a short article to the richness and meticulous nature of Hufford's study: the book should be read in full by anybody who aspires to investigate matters of this kind. I can merely hope to do three things – to describe the 'core' experience which Hufford finally identified and the findings he reached; to give you the flavour of the material he was examining; and to draw some possible conclusions for our own studies.

First, *the material*. The following are some brief excerpts from a few of the first-hand accounts which Hufford collected on tape.

(1)   . . . I tried to scream . . . But I couldn't get any sound out . . . it was like [someone] pressing down on my chest . . . I could just see this . . . white mask . . . it kind of had a funny face on it [with] black dots and a red kind of crooked mouth . . . I thought, Lord, it must be a Martian or something!

(2)   . . . the door slammed and I kinda opened my eyes. I was awake . . . I couldn't move . . . there was a murky presence there . . . this was *evil* . . . it approached towards the bed . . . it started to envelop the bed . . . I couldn't really make out a face . . . but I could see two holes that would seem . . . to be eyes.

(3)   . . . I heard a 'snurfling' sound . . . I just felt an incredible weight on my chest . . . And somebody put their hand up against my throat . . . I remember looking at something that looked like an ape . . . it was dark and it had red eyes . . . They glowed . . .

(4)   . . . I finally woke [from a series of brief and bizarre dreams while dozing in the afternoon in the university library]. I had the impression I could hear someone coming . . . I could hear the footsteps . . . [Then] I heard a female voice . . . It said, 'You knew that I would come'. [Sensations of pressure and paralysis are described] . . . I was trying to move . . . trying to scream . . . I opened my eyes . . . but all I could see was the library, and the books and the stacks . . . that's how I really knew I was awake . . . the pressure was still there. And I said, 'God, this is an incubus' . . . It surprised me that I was rational about it.

(5)   . . . I was awakened by this laughter . . . this real hysterical, cackling laughter . . . I heard this rustling on the stairs. And then I smelled this really foul odour. [Other incidents follow of the kind already indicated.]

(6)   . . . All of a sudden I saw this person coming out of the
door [the closed door of the bedroom] walking towards me
. . . the person was coming from far away in that space . . .
like if you saw someone up the hall they look smaller, and
as they walk towards you they get bigger . . . [But the
witness is clear that the door was closed and that she could
not see the hall. She is also vehemently sure that she was
awake.]

From a wealth of first-hand material of this kind Hufford
identified a core-experience with four essential features. Unless all
four were present he considered that the witness was reporting
something else, possibly quite as important, but certainly of another kind. The four primary features were that the subject
claimed (1) to be awake, (2) to see his surroundings in their usual
form, (3) to feel dread, often mounting to terror, (4) to be
paralysed (though often with some ambiguity about whether the
subject was literally unable to move or was merely too terrified to
try). If all four were present, Hufford accepted that the core-
experience had occurred. He named this experience 'The Old Hag'
by reference to his initial fieldwork in Newfoundland, but he
insisted that this was merely a matter of convenience and that no
implications should be read into this choice of a handy label.

Hufford also found many *secondary features*, that is to say
features which occurred in some but not all cases and which he
therefore considered were not essential to a diagnosis that 'The
Old Hag' experience had occurred. Sometimes, for example, an
entity was seen but not otherwise sensed; sometimes it was felt,
smelled, even tasted, without being seen; sometimes there was
merely the 'sense of a presence' (always described as unpleasant
and often as 'evil'). Many but not all subjects reported 'inward'
tinglings and sometimes strong 'outward' vibrations, e.g. of the
bed (using 'inward' and 'outward' in the sense I have suggested
earlier in this article). There was often a strong sense of pressure
on the subject's body, sometimes amounting to near-suffocation.
Not infrequently there were sounds of something approaching at
the onset of the experience: sharp footsteps (even in carpeted
rooms); or shuffling noises as of feet being dragged on a soft
surface (even on bare floors); or unpleasant sounds of breathing
(described by one subject as 'snurfling'). Occasionally there were
strong and always unpleasant odours. Hufford's book contains
many other such powerful details; they will keep you up all night if

you read him (and not necessarily from intellectual curiosity alone!).

Extending his studies to the United States and examining the folklore of other countries, Hufford discovered that 'The Old Hag' is a world-wide and age-old human experience which goes by different names in different places and at different times. He was also able to demonstrate beyond much doubt that the core-experience (his syndrome of four essential features) happens to people who are ignorant of any 'supernatural assault' traditions except in the most superficial manner (e.g. by reading popular 'ghost' fiction).

Contrary to most social scientists, who treat reports of the 'supernatural' as dreams or hallucinations or friend-of-a-friend stories whose content is determined by local folklore traditions, Hufford was able to conclude by the use of his meticulous methods that there is at least one form of encounter with strange beings. 'The Old Hag' experience, which is certainly *not* a dream (as all of us very readily understand what it means to be dreaming), is *not* a superstitious imagining, and very probably *causes*, rather than is caused by, certain of the folklore traditions of 'supernatural' assault. (Hufford is, of course, too competent an anthropologist to suppose that the content of any particular folklore tradition is caused *solely* by 'The Old Hag'; other psycho-social factors always come into the picture; folklore is complex. But these are technicalities which need not concern us here.)

What is 'The Old Hag'?

After a careful review of the little we yet know about the characteristics of sleeping, waking, dreaming, hypnagogic imagery, and intermediate states, Hufford leans a little in the direction of seeking a physiological factor as being at least the trigger for 'The Old Hag' experience (though he is emphatic, on good evidence, that nothing pathological is involved). He speculates that vivid material which would normally remain unconscious or make its appearance in a dream briefly intrudes into the waking state. This interesting idea, which has antecedents in the literature of both psychical research and conventional psychology, could, I believe, prove very fruitful, and I will come back to it in my concluding section. Let us just note at this point that Hufford does not suppose that his speculation 'explains away' 'The Old Hag'. He is definite that physiological triggers can never explain the *content* of an experience and he remains commendably open on the nature of what occurs when waking consciousness is invaded by bizarre and usually unperceived material. It is worth quoting from his concluding remarks:

> Many readers of this book will . . . respond to what I have reported in terms of its usefulness in reducing apparently super-natural events to physical [physiological] explanations; other readers will be concerned with whether my findings can be used in arguing for a reality beyond the physical. Looking back over what I have presented, I feel that there are some grounds for each argument . . . On the other hand, the explanation of the contents of that state ['The Old Hag'] appears more difficult now than when I began.

Hufford is possibly here teetering on the brink of the metaphysical abyss which always yawns when 'reality' comes into a sentence. But it is the first time in the whole book at which he does so. And because he has not allowed this semantic trap to divert him at any earlier stage from a rigorous study of the facts, he has been able to record two further pieces of information which are probably of crucial importance but might well have escaped the attention of a less impartial investigator.

The first of these facts is that in several of Hufford's cases people other than the subject *volunteered* the information (he did not seek it) that they, too, from elsewhere in the same house, had heard sounds reported by the witness – footsteps, 'snurfling', vigorous 'vibration' of the witness's bed, other noises reminiscent of poltergeist occurrences. It is much to his credit that Hufford left this testimony on record: the temptation to suppress it must have been considerable, given that he was writing primarily for sceptical peers in the social sciences community and that nothing was strictly required of him except to get a record of the first-person narrative of the victim.

The second important point is that in a few of Hufford's cases there was an independent witness to 'The Old Hag' attack. What is reported by these observers is that the victim had his eyes wide open and was clearly in a state of acute dread – *but that nothing else was detected by the observer.*

Is 'The Old Hag' a UFO Abductor?

Well, clearly not. There are far too many differences between the two experiences to enable us to assimilate the one to the other. Allowing fully for a general sloppiness of approach on the part of many Ufologists, coupled with a strong wish by some of them to cram the data into preconceived notions and to use such dubious techniques as hypnotic regression, we get a sufficiently clear picture of the average UFO Abduction to note the following differences (to mention only a few):

Old Hag	UFO Abduction
Never more than one entity.	Nearly always more than one entity.
Entity often invisible.	Entities always visible.
Onset always indoors.	Onset usually out of doors.
Victim paralysed throughout.	Paralysis only part of time.
Victim always in terror.	Victim often 'tranquillized'.
Victim not 'operated upon'.	Victim undergoes 'operation'.

But these obvious differences must not blind us to some very striking similarities. In several cases of UFO Abduction, as in 'The Old Hag' experience, we have an independent observer who watched the victim and saw nothing himself. Both kinds of experience are normally limited in duration. [Although Travis Walton, for example, was allegedly abducted for five days, the initial encounter having been observed by six witnesses. *Ed.*] Neither is more than tenuously 'material' in any lasting and unambiguous manner: We get those brief sounds and footsteps with 'The Old Hag' and perhaps a 'landing trace' or malfunctioning equipment after an Abduction; but there is never a photograph of the entities or a durable artefact or decisive evidence of lasting bodily damage to the victim other than can be ascribed to the 'conversion' symptoms of classical 'hysteria'. (However, although I cannot assess the evidence myself, in Chapter 5, Bob Pratt reports that serious damage to individuals at times ensues, as does Jacques Vallee in his recent book, *Confrontations*.[15]) In both types of experience, a wide range of different entities is reported.

Despite a tendency towards 'convergence' on a greyish dwarf in the Abduction cases in recent years, great variation exists in the literature. See, for example, Peter Hough's *The Development of UFO Occupants*[16] and Joshua Strickland's entertainingly illustrated *Extra-Terrestrials on Earth*,[17] both of which list so large a range of strange beings in UFO cases that we seem, as Peter Hough puts it, to be in the presence of 'a huge confidence trick on a grand theatrical scale'. See also Mark Moravec's *The UFO-Anthropoid Catalogue*,[18] which devotes itself exclusively to the many close encounters which have at least a tenuous link with UFO sightings but in which the entities are giant 'manimals' of the Yeti and Bigfoot kind. Let us recall the large headless figure with batlike wings emerging from a strip of woodland in which a UFO had just landed in November 1963 near Hythe in Kent, and which terrorized no fewer than four witnesses. For comparison, 'The Old Hag', when visible, ranges from a hairy ape with glowing eyes to a clown-masked pseudo-Martian by way of several other forms, including one which the witness described as a 'small collapsed elephant' (an absurdity which did nothing to reduce his over-powering sense of dread).

I believe that these similarities decisively place 'The Old Hag' and the UFO Abduction in the category of Encounters with Strange Beings as I have defined 'encounter' and 'strange' earlier in this article. Both are bizarre and frightening, both very notably disobey the laws of Newtonian physics, neither leaves much evidence of its occurrence (anyway of a kind likely to convince those who are determined to place it all 'in the imagination'), and neither can be related to anything comparable in our daily experience. Their nearest analogues are dreams, though both are credibly reported as occurring in the waking state.

Both 'The Old Hag' and the UFO Abduction therefore seem to me to belong to the genus which folklore calls 'supernatural assault'. And thanks to Hufford, we can now take 'supernatural assault' as something which actually occurs, whether or not we dislike (as I do) the implications of that question-begging term, 'supernatural'.

But in putting 'The Old Hag' and the UFO Abductors in the same genus, I am clear that they belong to different species, just as the genus Brassica contains the markedly different species, cabbages and oilseed-rape. I have indicated some of the distinguishing features above. It is, in fact, Ufologists who have tended to muddle the two together! Time and again you will have seen accounts of 'Bedroom Visitors' which the enthusiastic author identifies as visitation by UFO entities. Many of these household intruders could probably be classified as belonging to the species of 'Old Hag', if only the investigators had given us as meticulous an account as Hufford provides. But they are certainly something different. Let us try to be good naturalists in future: we shall get nowhere by muddling cabbages and rape.

So What is 'Supernatural Assault'?

From time to time humans encounter strange beings – and not merely in their dreams. Sometimes these entities seem benign (the Virgin Mary, the humanish blondies of the early contactees, the 'saints' who advised Joan of Arc); sometimes they come near to seeming 'evil' ('The Old Hag', the UFO Abductors, the smelly and red-eyed 'manimals'); and they always behave bizarrely, anyway by human standards (and what other standards can we use?). They seldom manifest for long but they sometimes achieve a degree of fleeting materiality. (I am not personally convinced of those reports relating to solid entities having been recovered and examined.) They usually manifest to only one witness at a time, who – if somebody else is present – exhibits nothing except wide-eyed terror (or, in benign cases, wide-eyed adoration or wonder); but we also have plenty of multiple-witness cases in which everybody present seems to have seen much the same thing.

How should we explain these things? I begin by rejecting the hypothesis that UFO entities, whether or not engaged in Abduction, belong to a separate class of occurrences from the rest of the great legion of strange beings. The currently fashionable UFO Abductors, the greyish dwarves, certainly possess their own distinctive features of appearance and behaviour; but every other member of the great legion also has its own particular characteristics, and at least some of these other strange beings seem happy to emerge from UFOs when it suits them. What unites them all is their brevity, bizarreness, relative insubstantialty and non-compliance with everyday regularities. In these crucial respects I cannot distinguish our UFO visitors from the many other kinds of transient which trouble our species. Perhaps you can . . . But if not, you will share my view that we need a single hypothesis which will do as much justice to trolls, imps, 'manimals', 'Old Hags', poltergeists, djinns, demons, and all the rest, as to dwarves with a taste for kitchen-table surgery and a remarkable aptitude for the swift get-away.

One unifying hypothesis might be that they are all visitants from other planetary systems (a simple extension of the Extraterrestrial Hypothesis). If so, we can only marvel at the variety of the fauna, the peculiarity of its behaviour and its ability to materialize and dematerialize at will.

A more fruitful hypothesis in my view – anyway in the sense that it offers a programme of methodical research – is that there are forms of energy around our planet which are usually undetectable by the human senses or by present instrumentation but which manifest from time to time in conditions which we don't understand. A variety of such guesses has been put forward in recent years, notably by Paul Devereux, for example in his *Earth Lights Revelation*,[19] and by Hilary Evans in his BOLs (Balls of Light) hypothesis.[20,21] These two ingenious exponents offer two different kinds of guess. Devereux and his colleagues are searching for a form of energy (probably generated by or related to such geological factors as tectonic strain) which is entirely 'mindless' but can produce remarkable visions in the human witness as well as material effects in the environment. Evans, on the other hand, if I have understood him, considers the possibility of an 'energetic entity' which possesses at least a low degree of intelligence, and is capable of taking many forms and sometimes interacts with humans.

These are attractive ideas: we can study them methodically and do some intelligent field work. Some progress, though tantalizingly slow, is in fact being made towards validating some elements of each of them. Both can, moreover, be combined to some extent with the interesting idea, drawn from psychical research and established beyond doubt for anybody who keeps a receptive mind, that humans (and perhaps other animals) are capable of producing physical effects on the environment by nonconventional means (psychokinesis). Conceivably, the human subject interacts with Hilary Evans' BOLs or with Devereux's mindless energy-forms to give them the particular 'shape' and behaviour which they exhibit on different occasions. And it might readily follow from this guess that the 'inward' preoccupations of the subject and the folklore of his community would play a large part in this process of 'shaping'.

But serious difficulties remain for guesses of this sort. We have to remember, for example, those cases of 'The Old Hag' and UFO Abduction in which an independent witness saw nothing taking place except the prone and paralytic terror of the subject. And the bizarre nature and great variety of the 'outwardly' perceived entities is hard to explain even if we grant them the degree of independent and intelligent existence which the B O Ls hypothesis would allow. Moreoever, the appeal to folklore as a conditioning factor is not very convincing. I cannot, myself, resist the feeling that folklore, though it is always elaborated by social factors, contains the residual traces of 'outward' events which people have actually experienced from time to time and that it is not in itself the cause of these experiences. I think that David Hufford might possibly agree.

If we reject the hypothesis of visitation by extraterrestrial entities and hold in suspense, pending further research, the hypothesis of earth-bound 'energy-forms', nothing much is left to us except the strange ideas – often asserted with great confidence, though also with much quarrelsome disagreement among themselves – by the enormous range of occult groups. These occult traditions are at least as old as our encounters with strange beings; perhaps they contain some core of truth.

Do our strange visitants come from the 'Astral Level', or 'Other Planes of Reality', or 'Different Realms of Existence', or whatever comparable term is currently in use among those who claim to understand them? I listen with respect to the people who use such concepts: they often sound as if they know more about these matters than psychiatrists, regression-hypnotists or self-appointed back-street abductionists. If ever troubled by a strange being, myself, I shall consult sympathetic souls of that kind – benign occultists or a well-accredited shaman – rather than my medical practitioner or any Ufologist.

But there is great difficulty in making usable sense of all those ill-defined 'planes', 'levels' and 'realms', which sound as if they ought to be something spatial but cannot be related in any coherent manner to the daily materiality we inhabit. A cogent analysis of the 'Astral', together with its 'planes' and 'levels', is given in Dr Susan Blackmore's *Beyond the Body*[22]; I doubt that anybody who reads it carefully will be in any doubt that the 'Astral', as presented to us by the occultists, is as incoherent and unusable a concept as the old-fashioned Christian heaven, or the Summerland of the Spiritualists, or the Bhuddist Nirvana – a matter of faith rather than a tool of understanding, a possible comfort to the imagination (perhaps even a preview of what is to come!), but of little use in explaining the strange events which undoubtedly occur from time to time in the bounded and material world of our common experience.

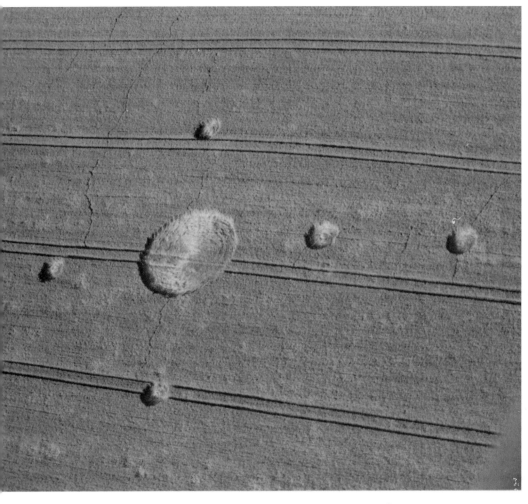

Plate 1:1.   The long-shaft cross formation near Cherhill, Wiltshire, June 1989.
(© F. C. Taylor)

*Plate 1:2.   Colin Andrews (left) with Dr Terence Meaden, during
the 'White Crow' project, June 1989. (© George Wingfield)*

Plate 1:3.   Circles to the north of Silbury Hill, Wiltshire, July 1989. (© George Wingfield)

Plate 1:4.   Long-shaft cross formation at Scratchbury Hill, Warminster, Wiltshire, June 1989. (© Colin Andrews)

Plate 1:5.   Rita Goold, the medium, during the 'White Crow' project. (© George Wingfield)

Plate 1:6.   Gloria and Michael Wingfield standing in the 'White Crow' Circle at Cheesefoot Head, Hampshire. The 'trilling' noise approached the Circle from the clump of bushes in the background, and later receded in that direction. (© George Wingfield)

Plate 1:7. *'Tadpole' Circle near Cheesefoot Head, Hampshire, July 1989. The 'tail' is visible coming from the top left of the circle. The other trail marks where made by human visitors!*

Plate 1:8. The double-ringer Circle near Westbury, Wiltshire, July 1989. (© George Wingfield)

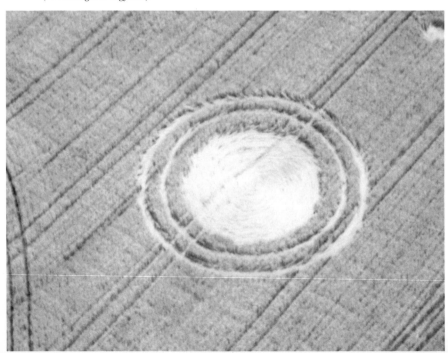

Plate 1:9.   Giant Circle near Bratton, Wiltshire, July 1989. (© George Wingfield)

Plate 1:10.   Circle near Margate, Kent, which is reported to have been hoaxed together with a UFO sighting. (August 1989) (© Malcolm Ganderton)

Some interesting attempts have, however, been made in psychical research to make usable sense of the 'Astral' and of 'Other Realms'. In a notable essay published in 1966, *Survival and the Idea of 'Another World'*,[23] Professor H. H. Price, entirely suspending his judgement on whether we 'survive' or not, makes luminous sense of the concept of 'Another World'. The paper must be read in full to follow his arguments. But, in brief, Price demonstrates that it is perfectly reasonable to suppose that we may inhabit two worlds *simultaneously*, the world of our common experience, governed by physical law, and another *space* (quite as 'real') which differs in its properties and obeys other laws. He says – and I believe this can be confirmed by introspection as well as from many published accounts – 'that a continuous dream-life goes on throughout our waking hours, and that just occasionally we may catch a glimpse of it . . . This would amount to saying that we *can* live in two worlds at once, and occasionally we do.' There is an obvious parallel with David Hufford's hunch that 'The Old Hag' experience may represent the temporary intrusion of our dream-life into waking consciousness – with the difference that Price's view would allow as much 'reality' to dreams as to the everyday.

Ideas of a similar kind have recently been carried a good deal further by Dr John Smythies. In a paper published in 1988, *Minds and Higher Dimensions*,[24] Smythies offers an ingenious model, based on current post-Newtonian physics, which makes coherent sense of the possibility that we may be inhabiting two worlds at once and points the way to testing this hypothesis. Smythies' 'second space' – the world which we probably glimpse in dreams and hypnagogic imagery – has plenty of scope for bizarre (as well as benign) events and for the occurrence of sequences of events which relate more closely to the 'inward' sequences of dreams and the imagination than to the 'outward' regularities of our daily world. And they would be just as 'real'.

It would not need much elaboration of Smythies' model to accommodate some occasional small overlap between the 'two worlds', resulting in the eruption of 'second world' events into our familiar Newtonian space. Sometimes they would achieve a degree of materiality. And they would always be conditioned by the human subject (who, by definition, stands at the intersection of the 'two worlds'). The subject's fears and fancies might well be the decisive 'shapers' of the occurrence.

So what is 'supernatural assault'? I have tried to identify three kinds of answer. First, we are the helpless hosts of a menagerie of strange visitors from other planetary systems. Second, we have around this planet a protean 'energy-form' (or a range of 'energy-forms') which may or may not be intelligent and which may or may not be 'shaped' by human psychokinesis. Third, we perhaps inhabit two worlds at once and sometimes they briefly interact.

Given these choices, I wouldn't blame anybody who opted for the comforting simplicity of extraterrestrial visitation! I would merely ask those who do so to be less selective in future about the great variety of entities they need to account for. If I lean somewhat towards the other two guesses, it is mainly because they offer more scope for the great Legion and also because they can be systematically researched.

What Comfort can we give to the Witness?

In a recent article in the *MUFON UFO Journal*,[25] Dr Rima E. Laibow, MD, makes a powerful plea for the considerate and expert treatment of those who have been engaged in strange encounters. She and her colleagues have identified a condition which they call 'Anomalous Trauma'. They relate it closely to the UFO Abduction experience. In February 1990 they held, in Virginia, the second of their two conferences to date under the title of TREAT II. (TREAT stands for 'Treatment and Research on Experienced Anomalous Trauma'.)

We should all applaud this initiative (regretting that some notable 'back-street abductionists' declined to attend the conference). It is heartening that well-qualified people are taking these matters seriously. I may well seek a consultation with Dr Laibow if I encounter strange beings (though I shall ask if I can bring my shaman with me).

I was unable to get to TREAT II and I await its proceedings at the time of writing. At this stage I can merely add my own (largely armchair) impressions of the current state of the art:

(a) However one assesses the evidence, relatively few humans have come to serious *physical* damage as a result of a strange encounter. (Animals may be more vulnerable.)

(b) Some people have certainly crazed their wits and their lives by taking too literally what our visitors tell us. See, for example, *When Prophecy Fails* by Leon Festinger *et al.*[26]

Time and again throughout human history we poor humans have received messages from strange entities which end by doing us no good unless we apply a good deal of human shrewdness to them.

(c) Strange beings, whether they 'channel' to us 'inwardly' or present themselves 'outwardly', come to us in a great variety of forms and under many different names. We need to keep our wits about us.

(d) But we probably ignore at our peril the hard core of what they seem to tell us (however jokily and vaguely). The Abduction 'scenario', for example, possibly reflects our own deep unease about current trends in genetic engineering, just as the 'mystery airship' wave of the 1890s may have reflected fears of what might soon be coming to us from the all-too-human skies.

(e) And we certainly need a bit of comfort when we've come face to face with them.

I must end as I began. UFO Abductions certainly occur; the question of whether they are 'real' or not tends to lead into a semantic muddle. They are 'outward' experiences for the subject and they sometimes affect the environment. But they seem to be merely one form of 'supernatural assault' among many others, even if of a particularly sensational and extended kind. Rejecting the term 'supernatural', I would prefer to put them for the time being into a class which we might call, quite neutrally, STROBEs (constructed, with more hope than faith, from *S*trange *TR*ransient *O*utward *B*iomorphic *E*ntities). I leave it to others to invent a more attractive term. But I hope they will find something which embraces the full range of the great Legion with which we have to deal.

REFERENCES
1. Hopkins, Budd: *Missing Time: A Documented Study of UFO Abductions*, Richard Marek Publishers, New York 1981.
2. Hopkins, Budd: *Intruders: The Incredible Visitations at Copley Woods*, Random House, New York 1987.
3. Klass, Philip J.: *UFO Abductions: A Dangerous Game*, Prometheus, Buffalo, NY 1988.

4. Randles, Jenny: *Abduction*, Robert Hale, London 1988.
5. Rimmer, John: *The Evidence for Alien Abductions*, Aquarian Press, Wellingborough, Northamptonshire 1984.
6. Spencer, John: *Perspectives: A Radical Examination of the Abduction Phenomenon*, Macdonald, London 1989.
7. Strieber, Whitley: *Communion: A True Story*, Century Hutchinson, London 1987.
8. Strieber, Whitley: *Transformation: The Breakthrough*, Century Hutchinson, London 1988.
9. Hufford, David J.: *The Terror that Comes in the Night*, University of Pennsylvania Press, Philadelphia 1982.
10. Vallee, Jacques: *Passport to Magonia: From Folklore to Flying Saucers*, Henry Regnery, Chicago 1969.
11. Vallee, Jacques: *Dimensions: A Casebook of Alien Contact*, Contemporary Books, Chicago 1988.
12. Evans, Hilary: *Visions, Apparitions, Alien Visitors*, Aquarian Press, Wellingborough, Northamptonshire 1986.
13. Evans, Hilary: *Gods, Spirits, Cosmic Guardians*, Aquarian Press, 1987.
14. Slade, Peter D. and Bentall, Richard P.: *Sensory Deception*, Croom Helm, London 1988.
15. Vallee, Jacques: *Confrontations: A Scientist's Search for Alien Contact*, Ballantine Books, New York 1990.
16. Hough, Peter: 'The Development of UFO Occupants', *Phenomenon*, edited by Hilary Evans and John Spencer, Futura, London 1988.
17. Strickland, Joshua: *Extra-Terrestrials on Earth*, Granada, London 1983.
18. Moravec, Mark: *The UFO-Anthropoid Catalogue*, Australian Centre for UFO Studies, P.O. Box 728, Lane Cove, NSW, Australia 1980.
19. Devereux, Paul, *et al.*: *Earth Lights Revelation*, Blandford, London 1989.
20. Evans, Hilary: 'BOLs', *The Probe Report*, Vol. 3, No. 1, July 1982.
21. Evans, Hilary: *BOLIDE*; an on-going series of reprints relating to the BOLs phenomenon, privately published by Hilary Evans since the mid-1980s.
22. Blackmore, Dr Susan: *Beyond the Body*, Paladin, London 1983.
23. Price, H. H.: 'Survival and the Idea of "Another World"', *Brain and Mind*, edited by J. R. Smythies, Routledge & Kegan Paul, London 1966.
24. Smythies, J. R.: 'Minds and Higher Dimensions', *Journal of the Society for Psychical Research*, Vol. 55, No. 812. (Publications of the Society are available from 1 Adam & Eve Mews, London W8 6UG.)
25. Laibow, Rima E.: 'Therapist and Investigator: A Definition of Roles', *MUFON UFO Journal*, No. 261, January 1990. (The Journal is available from 103 Oldtowne Road, Seguin, Texas 78155-4099, USA.)
26. Festinger, Leon, *et al.*: *When Prophecy Fails*, Harper & Row, New York 1956.

Editor's Note

For the most exhaustive study of the abduction phenomenon to date, I recommend *UFO Abductions: The Measure of a Mystery* by Thomas E. Bullard Ph.D. This two-volume work is published by the Fund for UFO Research, Inc., P.O. Box 277, Mount Rainier, Maryland 20712, USA.

5

Disturbing Encounters in North-East Brazil

BOB PRATT

Bob Pratt has worked as an editor and reporter on many daily newspapers and national magazines in the United States for nearly forty years, and is currently a magazine editor.

He first became interested in the UFO phenomenon in early 1975 and subsequently investigated hundreds of cases in Argentina, Bolivia, Brazil, Canada, Chile, Mexico, Peru, the Philippines, Puerto Rico, the United States, and Uruguay. He has personally interviewed about 1,400 witnesses.

Bob Pratt is particularly interested in Brazilian cases, owing to the preponderance of traumatic incidents which seem to occur in that country. He has made seven trips to Brazil and plans to return there in 1991.

During the past fifteen years, I have investigated hundreds of UFO cases in ten countries in South America, North America and Asia, and nowhere have I found cases more fascinating – or more frightening – than in north-eastern Brazil.

From the states of Paraíba and Rio Grande do Norte on the east to Pará on the west, UFOs have been terrorizing people for at least ten years. They have injured some people and, I believe, killed a few.

Millions of people around the world believe UFOs are real. Many of them also believe the occupants of UFOs are kindly, benevolent beings who have come here from other worlds to help us or save us from ourselves. Wherever they come from, some UFO beings *may* be kind and well-intentioned, but others definitely are not. If a UFO were to land in my backyard, I certainly would not run out and embrace it. Instead, I would be very wary – and with good reason.

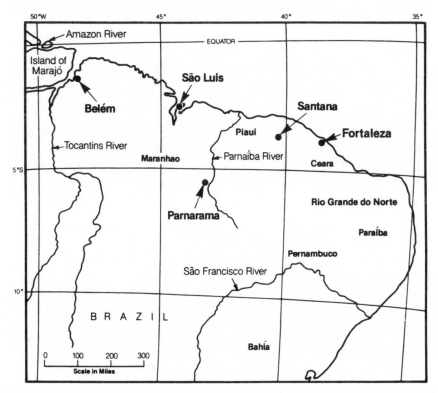

Figure 5:1. Detail of north-east Brazil. (Ballantine Books)

There is a dark side to the phenomenon that cannot be ignored. Too often in north-eastern Brazil the phenomenon has appeared to be malevolent. It does not seem to care that human beings are traumatized or injured – or worse – in encounters.

Whether any of this is intentional, we have no way of knowing. But if the phenomenon *does* represent a superior intelligence, as most of us believe, then it has to know what it is doing to people. And contrary to what true believers claim, these 'space brothers' do not always act in the spirit of brotherly love.

Assaults by Light Beams

In the small town of Pećem on the Atlantic coast west of Fortaleza lives a farm worker nicknamed Chico Gama, now in his mid-50s. For thirty years, Chico Gama fished at a nearby beach to help feed his family. But he doesn't go there any more. He doesn't even go fishing any more, because he is afraid to.

Late one night in February 1981, Chico Gama went to the beach with his fishing net. It was a clear, moonlit night. Around 2 a.m., a beam of red light suddenly struck him from above. Looking up, he saw that the red light was coming from a round object with a purplish hue around it that was hovering above him. He was terrified. Dropping his net, he scrambled across the sand dunes and into a grove of trees. The object followed him and he hid at the foot of a nearby tree.

For the next *three* hours, Chico Gama was persecuted by this object. About every five minutes, it shone its red beam down at him for a while and then shut it off. A few minutes later, the red light would again probe his hiding place. Each time he could hear a faint buzzing sound, and each time it left him chilled and shivering. As the night wore on, Chico Gama became weaker and weaker, and he struggled to stay awake.

When dawn arrived, the object simply vanished. He did not actually see it leave. He ran home and promptly hid under his bed. His family eventually coaxed him out and he tearfully told them what had happened.

Within hours he became sick. Two days after the incident, the skin on his arms and back began to peel off in fine layers, as if he had been sunburned. For a long time after the incident he suffered from fierce headaches, and for about a month perspired profusely, regardless of the weather.

This case was originally investigated by José Jean Alencar, a Fortaleza attorney and an excellent UFO investigator. Jean took me to see Chico Gama in September 1986, more than five years after the incident happened.

Chico Gama was still a nervous, frightened man. He spoke in a shrill, excited voice as he told me his story. His grown daughters told us that he has never gone fishing since that night, will not go outside at night, and is scared to stay by himself, even in the daytime. And he still hides under his bed occasionally.

Chico Gama's experience is extraordinary – as nearly all UFO encounters are – but what made this one so unusual was the UFO's persistence in trying to flush him out of his hiding place for three hours. That is a long time for a close encounter of such a terrifying nature.

Chico Gama is not the only one who has been assaulted by a beam of red light from UFOs.

Beams of Light penetrate Houses

Red beams have been reported quite a few times by people living in the village of Colares and a dozen neighbouring villages at the mouth of the Amazon River just north of Belém. Sightings were so common in this area between July 1977 and November 1978 that the Brazilian Air Force conducted an official on-site investigation that lasted for a month. The officer (now a colonel) in charge of the official investigation told me that he and his team of investigators not only interviewed many witnesses but also saw UFOs a number of times and took many photographs.

I have been to Colares twice. In 1979, the supervisor of the electricity plant told me that many villagers had seen UFOs high in the sky at night, shining red beams of light down on the houses in Colares. He said the red beams were seen *inside* about fifteen houses. The beams would penetrate the roofs of the houses and circle around inside, as if searching for something. This terrified the people inside, and they would jump out of the way to avoid the light beams. However, three people were burned when the red light touched them.

None of the people who were burned was in Colares the first time I was there, but when I returned in 1981 I found one of the victims, a woman named Claudiomira. This is what she told me:

She was asleep in her house one night in September 1978 when a beam of light passed over her face. It woke her up and she saw a *green* beam of light which quickly changed to a reddish colour. This light hit her three times on the upper right side of her chest, burning her and leaving three little pinpoint scars in a triangle, which she showed me. When the light burned her, she screamed and it disappeared. For many days after the incident she suffered from headaches, fever and extreme thirst.

Multiple-Witness Sightings

The year that the Colares area wave began, 1977, was an unbelievably busy year for UFO encounters throughout South America and North America and possibly everywhere in the world.

I personally know of hundreds of sightings that occurred in 1977 in the United States, Uruguay, Argentina, Chile, and Brazil – especially in Brazil. I spent almost the entire month of December 1978 investigating an unusual case in São Luis, in the state of

Maranhão. In doing so, I discovered that UFOs had been seen virtually every night during April, May, June, and July of 1977 in the area around the small city of Pinheiro, which is roughly 100 kilometres west of São Luis.

The mayor of Pinheiro, a businessman named Manoel Paiva, estimated that as many as 50,000 people in the Pinheiro region had seen the UFO during those months. Most of them saw what appeared to be a big ball of fire that would come and hover 300 to 400 metres above the town. Some people said it hurt their eyes when they looked at it, and their eyes were irritated for days afterward. Some people said it made them sick.

There was no set time for the UFO to appear – it came at all hours of the night. Sometimes the object would come and hover and then suddenly shoot straight out into space and be lost among the stars, just another pinpoint of light. And sometimes, Mayor Paiva said, it would come straight back down and hover over the city again.

Injuries

People were afraid to go out at night, since they did not know what might happen to them. A number of people fishing in canoes and boats said they were chased by the ball of fire, and some fishermen and farmers claimed they had been burned or injured by the UFO.

The injuries usually occurred when a UFO suddenly appeared without warning in the night sky just over their heads. The UFO nearly always seemed to be attracted by a light of any kind; the flash of a match, the glow of a cigarette, a flashlight or lantern, or anything that gave off light. The UFO would suddenly appear in a blinding flash of light, the fisherman or farmer would run in fright, and the UFO would chase them.

Some men said their skin felt like it had been burned. The next day their skin would be red, and a few days later it would peel like sunburn.

Further frightening Encounters

Most fishermen were so fearful of what the UFOs might do to them that they refused to go fishing for months at a time. Many were even afraid to go out into their backyards at night.

Mayor Paiva related a number of incidents to me involving the UFOs. In one, twenty-six men were building fences on a farm six kilometres from Pinheiro. One of the men went off to catch some fish for supper, and while doing so an object like a huge fireball suddenly appeared just above him. In panic, he ran back to the camp. The fireball followed him and was seen by everyone. It gave off a bluish light that lit up the area for about a kilometre around, frightening all the horses and cows. The fireball remained for about half-an-hour then disappeared.

The workers were so afraid that the next day they moved their camp to another site, where they made a crude scarecrow out of a piece of wood and put a kerosene lamp on top of it. They wanted to see if the strange object would come back, and hid in the woods to watch.

Late that night, the object suddenly appeared without warning, very close to the lamp. The light from the UFO was so bright that the men could not make out its shape. After about forty-five minutes it disappeared. Subsequently, many of the men returned home because they were too afraid to work there any-more.

Another encounter occurred on a farm where all the workers lived and slept in one building. One night one of the men went fishing not too far from the building, and suddenly a big bright light came just above him. He ran back to the building as fast as he could and the light followed him. From the safety of the building, he and the others watched as the UFO went slowly around and around the building for twenty minutes before finally going away.

I spent three days in the Pinheiro area and heard many stories like this. However, I was able to find only one man, João, who said he had been burned by a UFO. He lived in São Bento, a small village a half hour's drive south-east of Pinheiro. João told me that he and two other men were fishing in a boat at about 1 a.m. when a ball of fire appeared in the sky. It was red in the centre and greenish-blue on the outside, and lit up a large area as it moved from west to east, passing close to the boat. João was sitting nearest to the UFO as it went by and felt a lot of heat from it, and for three days his back felt like it had been burned. The other two men were unharmed. However, neither they nor João would go fishing for a month, and João would not even go outside his house at night.

Similar encounters occurred along the Amazon River in 1979 and 1980. In 1981 I visited the village of Guajara, which is located about three hours west of Santarém by motor launch. Fishermen there told me they had been seeing UFOs on the average of once a week for two years but had not seen anything since May, two months before my visit.

What they nearly always saw was a large ball of fire, usually moving through the night sky to the east toward an area of the Tápajos River reportedly called the Devil's Graveyard. The Tápajos is as much as fifteen kilometres wide in some places, and very deep. Local legend claims UFOs have often been seen going into and out of the river.

These fishermen of Guajara said the UFOs would sometimes come very close and chase them. The men would build a fire on the beach late at night to cook their fish, and a UFO would come without warning and shine a light down on them. In their panic to get away, some men became tangled up in their nets, destroying them. What made such encounters especially bad for these men was that they would always run into the jungle to escape, and they were afraid of stepping on poisonous snakes in the dark.

The fishermen were all afraid the UFO would take them away, and for a long time many of them refused to fish at night. They called the UFO the 'chupa-chupa', and believed it sucked the blood out of its victims. I could never get anyone to adequately explain why they believed this was so, but I had heard similar stories elsewhere, particularly in Colares, north of Belém, and in the small city of Monte Alegre, about 100 kilometres north-east of Santarém.

One of the common themes that runs through nearly all of these stories is that many people believe very strongly that they had been chased by a UFO. Perhaps they were. Certainly UFOs *appear* to be interested in or curious about their 'victims'. However, it may be that the UFOs were not really chasing them, but perhaps following them, for whatever reasons. UFOs that are able to zip out into space and return to Earth in a matter of seconds have no difficulty in capturing someone – if that is their intention.

Abductions

Dozens of people in the Pinheiro area believe UFOs have chased them, but I was able to find only one man who believes he was actually abducted. He is a prosperous chicken farmer named José Benedito Bogea, who lives six kilometres south of Pinheiro. About 1 a.m. on 10 July 1977, he started walking into town to catch a bus to São Luis. It was very dark and he used a flashlight to see where he was going. Suddenly a bright greenish-blue light appeared in the sky and chased him for about 200 metres. It then went on ahead of him, circled back and hovered over a nearby bush. He could see that it was a V-shaped object.

Benedito then made the mistake of raising his flashlight and shining the light toward the object. Almost instantly a bright light flashed back at him from the UFO and Benedito was knocked to the ground. His body tingled as if he had had an electrical shock, and he passed out.

Benedito believes many strange things happened to him that night, and it is an unusual story. Very briefly, he woke up to find people staring at him. They studied him silently for a while, and then he was allowed to wander about the city. He believes he was there for several hours, and all of this remains so vivid in his mind that to this day he is certain it was not a dream. Eventually, he went to sleep again.

The next time he woke up, it was 8 a.m., seven hours after the UFO 'zapped' him. He soon began to feel terrible pain in his kidneys, spine and his entire right side, and thought he was going to die. For eight days, he had no appetite and for many weeks had to use a cane because he was unable to stand on his right leg, nor could he hold anything in his right hand for a long time. It was two months before he was well enough to return to work.

Abduction Attempts

Whatever UFOs may be, they appear to represent a technology far in advance of ours. But they can also be quite crude. What happened to a tall, rugged old man called Januncio is a case in point. Januncio is the nickname of Francisco Henrique De Sousa, the owner of a 500-hectare cotton ranch south-east of Santa Cruz in the state of Rio Grande do Norte. Thirteen other families lived on the ranch and worked for him.

Januncio was seventy-eight years old when I talked with him in late January 1979. His strange encounter took place one evening a few weeks earlier. He had visited some friends who lived five kilometres away and was walking home in the dark. About halfway he paused to light a cigarette. Less than a minute later a brightly lit object suddenly appeared from nowhere in the sky and stopped just several metres above his head. It was shaped like a silo or a cylinder standing upright and made no sound.

Januncio was startled and frightened, and stood rooted in his tracks. Then a door slid silently open on the bottom of the UFO, and Januncio could see a man and a woman sitting in seats. They seemed motionless, as if they were robots. When the door opened, light flooded out, engulfing Janúncio. It was hot and he felt himself being pulled upward by an invisible force. Fearing for his life, he grabbed a small palm tree and wrapped his arms and legs around it.

His ordeal had just begun. Even though he held on to the tree as tightly as possible, he was still pulled upward for about half a metre. Then he would slide back down, only to be pulled upward again. This happened five times, with his arms and legs gripping the tree. Janúncio's chest felt like it was being scraped raw, and he was crying, more out of fear than pain. Drops of a hot liquid like melted wax then began falling on his arms, possibly in an attempt to get him to let go of the tree. But even though the hot liquid burned his arms and hurt, Janúncio clung to the tree as tightly as ever. Finally, the UFO beings gave up, the door closed and the object shot straight up into the sky and vanished. Only then did Janúncio let go of the tree and collapse on the ground.

Janúncio's wife told me he was very scared when he came home that night, because he thought they were going to take him away. He was sick for two days after the encounter, and was unable to eat. He said he had several small burns on his arms, and his chest was almost raw, but these wounds had healed by the time I talked with him. When Janúncio finished telling me his story, he sat silent for a long time, staring off into space. Then he sighed, smiled sadly, and said: 'I don't go out at night any more. I'm afraid it will come back.'

Two weeks after his encounter, another abduction attempt occurred on a farm forty kilometres west of Janúncio's ranch. In this case, a small slender woman of forty-five named Francisca says she was levitated into the air on a beam of light from a UFO. The incident occurred when she was walking home late one evening with her thirteen-year-old daughter Josefa, after visiting neighbours. Francisca's small, simple home is perched on the side of a long, sloping hill. She and her daughter were about 200 metres from the house when a very bright light suddenly appeared over the top of the hill beyond the house.

The light quickly grew in size, coming closer and closer. To Francisca it looked like a fire in the sky, and as it drew closer it looked to her much like an opened umbrella shining very brightly. Francisca does not know what it was, but throughout the interview she always called it 'The Animal'. When it got within 50 to 100 metres, it shot a beam of light down towards them. Francisca shouted at her daughter to run home as fast as she could. Josefa begged her mother to run too, but Francisca found herself caught in the beam of light and could not move. She started to rise off the ground in the light. Josefa grabbed her and pulled her down a little, but the force of the light was too strong and Francisca told her to save herself, and the girl ran. Francisca continued rising and felt a strong wind blowing and could see her shadow on the ground. She felt as if she was in a tornado, but there was no noise, no dust – nothing but the light.

Francisca believes she rose as high as twenty metres above the ground and was moving toward the object. She was crying all the time and praying to God for help, believing she was going to be taken away for ever. After being drawn about forty metres toward the object, the noiseless wind stopped and Francisca was lowered to the ground, hysterical but unhurt. Her body was tingling all over, and she was trembling with fear. The object swung back and forth in an arc for several seconds, then left. Francisca was so frightened she did not even see which way it went.

Her body was numb for two days and she had severe headaches for a week. She had recovered by the time I spoke with her, but became almost hysterical as she told me about her terrible experience.

As unusual as these two abduction attempts were, neither was quite as bizarre as one that occurred later that year, not far away. In this attempt, the victim was a 76-year-old man named Antonio who lived near the small village of Santo Antonio, which lies south of Natal and about eighty kilometres south-east of Januncio's ranch.

Antonio had an encounter on his farm early one Saturday night in November 1979. It was getting dark and Antonio, a widower, was working in his garden when he saw a light flying toward him. He was frightened. UFOs had been seen in the area for some time and he had heard that they had taken some people away. He began hurrying towards his house, but after only a few metres the object shone a light down on him. Someone had once told Antonio that if a flying saucer comes near you, the best thing to do is to lie down on the ground. What the rationale for this is I do not know, but that is what he did. A moment later, as he lay face down, the UFO came down very close and hovered just above him.

Within seconds, Antonio was yanked up off the ground about half a metre. Something like a rope with four hooks at the end was dangling from the UFO and apparently one of the hooks had caught the back of his shirt near the waist, so that he was hanging face down. Grabbing a plant with his left hand, he hung on tightly to keep from being pulled up any higher. Then, shielding his eyes from the light with his right hand, he looked up and could see two women and a man through a window in the object. Both women appeared to have yellow skin and neither was very attractive – at least to Antonio. All he could see of the man was boots and a beard.

Antonio hung there for what seemed a long time. He could hear the three of them talking, and at one point heard one of the women say very clearly: 'Here is a nice old man we can take with us to our earth.'

This terrified Antonio beyond imagination. He was so badly frightened at that moment that tears came to his eyes when he told us about it. At least twenty neighbours were in the room with us during the interview, and he was not ashamed of the tears.

Antonio said he was too afraid to shout for help. He hung there for perhaps fifteen minutes, when suddenly his shirt tore away from the hook and he dropped to the ground. When he looked up, he saw the object spin around three or four times before going away. He described it as brown, about the size of a Volkswagen, with a small red light on the back.

Antonio was very sick for about a week. He stopped working on another farm because he could not get home before nightfall, and no longer goes outside after dark. He, too, was afraid the flying saucer would come back.

Antonio was not the only one in that area who was afraid of UFOs. The village priest of Santo Antonio told us that 500 people lived in the nearby village of Cajazeiras and all of them had been afraid to go out at night for five to six months because of the UFOs.

Another Abduction

The fear of UFOs that year (1979) also affected life in the small town of Lajes, which is situated north-west of Santa Cruz and about 100 kilometres west of Natal, where UFOs were seen so often that the night schools had to close for two months because people were afraid to go out at night. The objects had harassed people in their cars, and everyone knew that a farmer had been abducted. That farmer was Leonel Dos Santos, then in his forties. I met Leonel in the sheriff's office in Lajes the day after I talked with Antonio. Rogerio Freitas was one of the first to investigate this case, and he took me to see Leonel. Rogerio, a university student in Natal at that time, is today a businessman and a bank official.

Leonel, it turned out, never saw the UFO that changed his life –
if it was a UFO. If it was not a UFO, then an equally baffling
phenomenon is competing for attention.

Leonel's life changed on 27 July 1979. Early that morning, he
and two friends went into the woods on Leonel's farm to cut down
some trees to build a small house. At 7 a.m., his friends stopped to
eat some food. Leonel was not hungry, so he walked on ahead.

A short time later, he was standing in the middle of a dry river
bed studying the trees when a shadow covered the ground around
him. This struck him as odd and when he looked up, he passed out.
He never saw what caused the shadow.

The next thing Leonel remembers is waking up in a place that
was not familiar to him. He looked at his watch and was surprised
to see it was 11 a.m. Four hours had passed, and he had no
recollection of what had happened.

Leonel felt unwell. His mouth was very dry, and felt like cotton.
He began walking and after a while came to some railroad tracks,
then realized he was on a neighbour's farm. He followed the tracks
back to his own farm, where his friends had been looking for him
all morning. They had seen his footprints in the river bed, but the
tracks went only so far and then stopped. It looked as if something
had scraped the ground. His machete was sticking in the sand
nearby. There were no footprints leading away from the spot.

Leonel soon began to feel a dull pain in his right leg. When he
got home that evening he was feeling worse, and asked his wife to
examine his body. She found a small puncture wound on the back
of his right hip, as if he had been injected with something. The
mark went away eight to ten days later. Leonel was also partially
deaf for one month after the incident, and had chest pains for
about forty-five days.

Six months later we talked to Leonel and found him lethargic
and melancholic. His right leg still hurt, and he had not felt well
since this had happened.

Close Encounter

A somewhat similar incident had occurred less than a year
earlier. This time the victim was a young man, Francisco, who
underwent a personality change after his experience. He lived and
worked at the Bom Fin mines, thirty kilometres south-east of
Lajes.

Francisco vanished for an entire day and does not know what

happened to him. When Rogerio Freitas and I met him, he did not want to talk about his experience, and almost everything we learned came from his father and his friends.

About 7 a.m. one Tuesday morning in September 1978, Francisco left home and went off to work in the mines. He had a small snack of bread and sugar cakes in his pocket. Normally he always came home for lunch but this day he did not. His father, José, became worried and started looking for him. José had no luck and soon ten other men from the village were also looking for Francisco, but they never found him.

About 8 p.m. that night, Francisco came walking into the village. At the same time, a flying saucer rose up from behind a hill in the direction where Francisco had come from. Francisco's father said the UFO was bright red and made no noise. It flew right over their house, within 100 metres of him and others who were watching, then flew away.

Everybody asked Francisco where he had been but he was unable to remember. When he got to the door of his father's house he simply fell forward on to the floor. The food was still in his pocket.

For eight days Francisco's tongue seemed paralysed. He had no feeling in it and could not speak clearly. During this time he was unable to eat anything except a little juice and water. He also did not want anyone to come near him or talk to him. According to one of his friends, Francisco never drank much before the UFO incident but afterwards began drinking every night after getting home from work.

Just one month before Francisco's experience, a teenage girl named Raimunda, who lives a few kilometres south of Lajes, was knocked down by a beam of light from a UFO. The girl's parents and more than a dozen neighbours witnessed the incident, and told us they thought the UFO was trying to take her away. However, she was walking with a girl-friend who managed to grab her and drag her into a nearby house.

Another Traumatic Encounter

One of the strangest injury cases in the north-east occurred in the town of Penalva in north-central Maranhão, nearly 200 kilometres south-west of São Luis. A sixteen-year-old boy named Luis disappeared on Good Friday, 24 March 1978. His mother searched for him but never found him. At 7 p.m. on the following Monday –

eighty-one hours after Luis disappeared – a fisherman heard a shout for help and found Luis lying in the forest, dazed and unable to stand up.

The fisherman carried Luis to his boat, took him across the small lake to the edge of the town, and with the help of a neighbour carried him to his mother's home. At her request, they then carried him to the small local hospital.

Doctors baffled

Dr Linda Macieira examined Luis but she was unable to determine what was wrong with him. 'Luis,' she told us, 'was completely dumb and had muscle contractions, like he was paralysed.' She thought at first that he was on drugs but found out that this was not the case.

Four of his teeth were missing. Two had simply been broken off, and one had been extracted completely. All four were still bleeding. Luis also had a full head of hair before this happened, but when Dr Macieira examined him he appeared to be bald. At first she thought his head had been shaved. On closer examination, however, she discovered that his hair had been burned off. The scalp was not burned, but the tops of his ears were, very slightly, like sunburn.

Luis seemed to be paralysed. Dr Macieira tried to move his arms and legs but could not. She pricked his arms and legs with a sharp pin to test his reactions, but there were none at all. He went nine days without eating or drinking anything, and had to be fed intravenously. He spent three days without going to the bathroom and had to be catheterized.

Dr Macieira examined his whole body and found no marks on him at all; no cuts, scratches, or bruises. His breathing was normal and he had no unusual breath or body odour. The doctor had no idea what had happened to him. Several days later, Luis was flown to a large hospital in São Luis, where more than half a dozen doctors tried to find out what was wrong with him. They never did.

Luis began to come out of his paralysis on his third day in the São Luis hospital. He was still unable to talk but managed to persuade a nurse to bring him paper and pencil. Then he began to write about the strange encounter he says he had with a UFO.

A Strange Trip

Luis said he was gathering guava fruit just inside the forest at noon on Good Friday when he heard a loud sound like a car horn above him, which scared him. He looked up and saw a light, brighter than the sun, just above the trees. It hurt his eyes and he looked away. Suddenly, something made him fall flat on his back and he could not move anything except his eyes. He lay there for some time and then began to rise into the air, although he was unable to see or feel anything touching him to make him move upward, which he marvelled at when he told us about it.

As he rose, he could see a round object above the trees, with what looked like four round balls on the bottom, one of which was lighted. In a few seconds he floated up level with the object, moved sidewards into it through a window, then fell softly to the floor.

Inside the craft were three small people, only a metre tall. They were moving around, and paid no attention to Luis. He could not see their faces, which were covered by helmets and visors. They talked in loud voices that did not sound human, and he was unable to understand them.

Soon there was a rumbling sound like a noisy machine and he could feel the object moving. Luis said he was taken to a strange land with no trees, no lakes, no birds: it was just a field with tall grass. He could see no sky, only darkness above him.

Luis said he floated out of the object and came to rest on a flat stone or table. The UFO beings put a tube in his nose, which did not hurt, then put what he thought was a transparent ball in his mouth. He felt liquid going down his throat, and passed out. He remembers nothing from that moment until he began coming out of his paralysed condition about a week later in the São Luis hospital.

Luis wrote out his story on paper for the nurses and also drew crude sketches of the object and the three beings. When he could speak again, he told the same story, again and again.

Neurological and Psychological Examination

None of the doctors could determine what had happened to him. One of them was a neurologist, Antonio Saldanho, who vividly remembered the case when I interviewed him nearly a year later. 'I thought it was a *very* strange case because in my examination I couldn't find any abnormal responses,' Dr Saldanho told me. 'Luis was in a state as if he was scared, frightened. He couldn't talk . . . He was a "locked-in" patient. He was awake, his eyes were open, fixed, like a fixed stare, but he wasn't able to talk and he didn't respond to verbal commands such as simple requests like "Open your mouth" or "Close your eyes".'

Dr Saldanho believed that something had badly scared Luis, but as a neurologist, he was unable to explain what was wrong with him. He was certain, however, that there was no way Luis could have faked his symptoms. 'Something,' he said, 'had shocked the boy. It was a very strange case. I have never seen anything like it.'

Two psychiatrists also examined Luis. The first, Dr Renato Bacelar, tried to break Luis' story about the UFO a number of times but failed. Dr Bacelar told me that Luis repeated the story without variation each time, and concluded that Luis could be telling the truth. The other psychiatrist, Dr Bacelar Viana, told me there was no doubt in his mind that Luis believed the story he was telling.

Luis recovered completely and the only after-effect of the encounter is that he now feels he is more intelligent than he was before.

Shocking Encounter

The victim in another case, also named Luis, was not so lucky. Luis Fernandes Barros, now in his late sixties, was once a prosperous businessman and rancher in Quixadá, in the state of Ceará. For fourteen years now, Luis has been totally helpless, needing the care of a full-time nurse. He is a man able to say only three words, who reacts to nothing and recognizes only his wife.

This sad state of affairs began on the morning of 23 April 1976. At 7 a.m. that day, a vaquero found Luis sitting dazed in a two-wheel carriage behind a donkey, several kilometres from his ranch home. The vaquero took him home, and when Luis became coherent later in the day he explained that about two hours before daybreak a big lighted object came down and hovered over him and the donkey. A door opened on the bottom of the object and a beam of light was projected down on to them. He did not know what happened after that.

Luis soon became very sick. He suffered from nausea, diarrhoea, headaches, and vomiting. His wife, Teresina, took him into Quixadá to have Dr Antonio Moreira Megalhes examine him. Dr Megalhes, then forty, had known Luis for most of his life. He listened to Luis' story about the UFO and then gave him some medicine. This did not help, however, so Dr Megalhes sent him to Fortaleza to see a psychiatrist. Teresina took Luis to Fortaleza, and they stayed there for two months, during which time Luis was examined by twelve psychiatrists and psychologists. The only conclusion any of them could come to was that he was suffering from a brain lesion.

Long before the end of his stay in Fortaleza, Luis stopped telling his story about the UFO because nobody believed him except his wife and Dr Megalhes. By this time too, Luis' speech was beginning to deteriorate, and three months after the incident occurred his hair turned white. By the end of six months, he had lost all his mental faculties and had regressed to the age of a one-year-old child.

Ever since then, the only words he says are 'mamae', 'medo' and 'da'. He reacts to no stimuli, except that when someone takes a photo of him with a strobe light, as I did, he screams when he sees the flash.

Reginaldo Athayde, of Fortaleza, was the first researcher to investigate this case. Reginaldo, his fellow investigator Jean Alencar and I went to Quixadá and talked to Dr Megalhes and Teresina Barros, who told us the story of Luis Barros. We then went to the Barros home, where Luis was being watched over by a nurse. He sits all day long in a chair, staring, occasionally moving his eyes but apparently seeing nothing. Dr Megalhes showed us that Luis still had control over his arms and legs and had not suffered a stroke.

It is possible that some unknown medical problem caused Luis' condition. But the donkey that was pulling his carriage that morning in April 1976 was also affected by whatever happened. Teresina, Luis' wife, told us that the donkey was in a stupor for about a week after the incident, but then apparently recovered without any serious after-effects.

What happened to Luis is tragic, but at least he is alive and maybe someday will recover. Others have not been as fortunate.

In the United States in the last few years, abductions have become very much the 'in' thing among Ufologists. I have worked on more than half a dozen abduction cases, and I have been impressed by the witnesses. But whether abductions are real or not, I do not know, and I do not think we yet understand their significance. Abductions seem to me to be some kind of a mind game, with few people ever really hurt in the way Luis Barros and other people have been in north-eastern Brazil.

What is more significant to me than abductions are those encounters that leave the witness injured or dead. To me, *the ultimate UFO experience must be death*. I cannot imagine anything more significant than that. Deaths have occurred. I cannot prove that anyone has been actually killed *by* a UFO, but in four cases that I have investigated, people have died. Whether these deaths were deliberate or accidental is impossible to say.

Miscarriage caused by a UFO?

One death – that of an unborn child – could probably be ruled unintentional. That death resulted from an encounter which took place on a Monday afternoon in April 1982, near the beach east of Pecém. Pecém, it will be recalled, is the village on the coast west of Fortaleza where Chico Gama was persecuted by a purple-hued UFO in 1981.

The 1982 case was also first investigated by Jean Alencar, who took me to Pecém in 1986 to talk to two women who were involved in it. Their names are Merces, who was thirty-four years old when I talked to her, and Neuma, who was twenty-eight. On that April afternoon in 1982, they and Neuma's elder sister, Maria, and two children were searching for firewood in the sand dunes east of Pecém. Both Maria and Merces were pregnant.

It was late in the afternoon. The sun had gone down but they could still see clearly. As they were hunting for wood, one of the children shouted, 'Mama, look, a bright star over there!' Everyone turned to look and suddenly a big orange light like a fireball appeared above their heads. They were frightened and ran, throwing away the wood they had gathered because it was slowing them down. They ran a long way, at least 500 metres, before reaching some coconut trees, where they could hide. All the time they were running from the UFO, it followed them right behind, and they thought it was chasing them. Once they reached the grove of trees, it passed on over them and went out of sight.

By the time they got home, all five were sick and nauseated, and they had headaches for more than a week. Nine days after the incident, Maria, who was two months pregnant, lost her baby. Shortly after that, Merces, who was in her seventh month of pregnancy, gave premature birth to a baby she named Kelvia. She is a sweet, good-natured child who smiles a lot and chatters a little. However, she has never learned to walk and has heart problems.

You could argue that any pregnant woman who runs 500 metres risks losing her baby, but if the UFO had not frightened those women and chased them, they would never have run and perhaps both would have had normal, healthy children today. So, in that sense, the death of an unborn baby and the premature birth of a child who may never walk can, I believe, be blamed on a UFO.

Further Injuries and some Deaths

In two other separate but strangely related cases, two men died and three were burned. Both incidents occurred on Crab Island, a swampy, mosquito-infested, uninhabited island in the Bay of São Marcos thirty kilometres south of São Luis.

The first incident was brought to my attention by Irene Granchi, whose son had learned about it on a visit to São Luis. It occurred on the night of 25 April 1977. A day or two earlier, four men sailed from São Luis to Crab Island. They took their boat inside the island on one of its rivers, tied up at a bank and went to work cutting down trees. The trees, when trimmed of limbs and branches, make poles three or four metres long, which they were to take back to São Luis to sell.

Three of the men were brothers and the other a cousin. One of the brothers was a farmer, and this was his first trip to Crab Island. The other three had gone there at least 100 times before. Each time they would cut wood, stack it on the bank and go to sleep, routinely wake up when the tide came in, load their wood and sail back to São Luis on the outgoing tide.

On this particular night they ate at about 6 p.m. and went to sleep, intending to wake up about midnight, load the wood and sail back to São Luis. They left a lighted lantern hanging on a nail in the cabin, a light which could be seen from the outside through the hatch and a rear window in the cabin.

Something strange and still unexplained happened that night. The tide came in, the river gradually filled with water, the boat floated once again and gently rocked with the flow of the water. Over the hours the tide reversed, the water flowed back out and the boat settled into the mud again.

No one woke up until six the next morning. The first to awaken was Apolinario, who heard his cousin Auleriano calling for help and found him lying in the cargo section in the front of the boat. His back was badly burned. While all this was going on, Apolinario had heard someone moaning in the cabin at the back of the boat. He went back there and found his older brother Firmino delirious and even more seriously burned.

In going back and forth between the two burned men, Apolinario kept ducking under the hammock of his younger brother, 22-

year-old Cachope, who appeared to be asleep. After finding the second man badly burned, Apolinario felt he needed help. He went to Cachope's hammock to awaken him, but to his horror discovered Cachope was dead.

Apolinario was the only one not harmed, although several years later he gradually lost the full use of his right arm without any apparent reason. As it was, he had the difficult task of sailing the boat back to São Luis all by himself, a boat that normally takes three or four men to handle.

Auleriano eventually recovered from his burns, but Firmino was left crippled and cannot work any more. The men could not remember what happened, not even when they were put under hypnosis by Dr Silvio Lago, a physician and former medical professor from Niteroi who at that time had used hypnosis in his practice for more than forty-five years.

The police investigated, of course, but were never able to determine what happened, although they were convinced the three survivors were telling the truth. There was no fire on the boat nor on the river bank, neither was there evidence of a fight, nor of the use of alcohol or drugs.

The dead man had no marks on him. By the time the boat arrived back in São Luis, his body had decomposed badly and no autopsy was done. The doctor who signed his death certificate listed the cause of death as an 'emotional shock'.

There is no strong UFO connection in this case. However, the incident occurred not far from Pinheiro during the four-month period of almost nightly UFO sightings that I mentioned earlier. Sightings and close encounters were taking place throughout the area.

The only real suggestion that a UFO might have been involved came from Firmino while he was in a hospital. He was in the hospital for a month and was semi-conscious the first six days. While he was delirious, a doctor who was highly sceptical of all UFO reports heard Firmino mumble something about 'o fogo', which means a light or fire and is a very common term for a UFO. However, Firmino consciously remembers nothing about a UFO.

That was a complex and very interesting case, and I spent a month in São Luis and Pinheiro working on it. It became doubly fascinating when I returned to São Luis in 1986 and learned that virtually the same thing had happened again on Crab Island.

This time, on 28 April 1986, almost exactly nine years later, four other men sailed in a similar wooden boat to Crab Island for the same purpose. They spent two days cutting more than 300 poles and stacking them on the bank next to the boat. On 30 April, they quit working about 6 p.m. and at about 8 p.m. one of the men, Juvencio, twenty-two, began to cook their supper. Suddenly, he complained about feeling dizzy and fell on the deck unconscious. Then the others began to feel dizzy and two of them, Anselmo and Lazaro, both in their forties, passed out.

None of these three know what happened to the fourth man, 21-year-old Verissimo. Lazaro, who was the first to wake up, regained consciousness at noon the next day – sixteen hours later – and he found Verissimo dead. There were no marks on him, although a little blood had trickled from his mouth. The other two men revived several hours later. All three were very sick and nauseated. In addition, Juvencio's head was also burned on the right side and was swollen.

Anselmo and Lazaro tried to load the wood on to the boat, but quit after getting less than thirty pieces on board. Then, with difficulty, they sailed the boat back to São Luis. This time, the port authorities investigated. When I interviewed port officials five months later, they still had not been able to determine what happened.

Of the three survivors, I was able to locate only Juvencio. Lazaro was somewhere near Alcântara, across the bay, and Anselmo had gone into the interior and no one knew exactly where he was. Just as in the first Crab Island case, none of the three survivors knows what happened to them. The authorities believe they are telling the truth. The men are certain that food poisoning was not to blame, and the authorities do not believe any kind of poisonous gas could have been the cause. No autopsy was performed on Verissimo. As happened with Cachope, by the time the boat reached São Luis, Verissimo's body was badly decomposed. His death certificate simply lists the cause of death as 'undetermined'.

Again, as in the first Crab Island case, the UFO connection is tenuous. One unusual thing did happen that night, however. Shortly before 8 p.m., when the men passed out, they heard a loud crashing sound in the darkness somewhere near the boat. They do not know what caused it.

Juvencio and Lazaro no longer will go aboard a boat. Furthermore, because of these two incidents the captain of the port has forbidden anyone to go to Crab Island to gather wood any more.

When we interviewed Juvencio at his home in São Luis, many

neighbours crowded around to listen. One man told us he had had a UFO encounter on a similar boat one night in 1983. The boat was in a stream between Alcântara and Itauna, both of which are across the bay from São Luis, and a big bright light came down, hovered overhead and shined a beam of light on the boat. This man and his companions dived overboard and hid in bushes until the UFO went away. He said people in several other boats in that area had similar experiences that year.

The UFO connection in both cases can be questioned. However, if UFOs were not involved then we seem to have some other phenomenon just as bizarre to deal with. Either way, it is a mystery that cannot be ignored.

The last death I investigated occurred near Parnarama, a small town on the west bank of the Parnaíba River eighty kilometres south of Teresina. Late in 1981, magazines in both Brazil and the United States published stories claiming four hunters had been killed by UFOs near Parnarama in October of that year.

I did not know how truthful these magazines were, so one of my main purposes in coming to Brazil in September 1986 was to go to Parnarama and find out if these men really had been killed by UFOs. I went there with Jean Alencar and four young men from a UFO group in Teresina.

The magazines had quoted both the mayor and the sheriff of Parnarama, but unfortunately neither was in office any more and they were no longer in Parnarama. We nevertheless went to the City Hall and started asking questions. At first, no one knew anything about the four hunters, but suddenly we began to get swamped with people who had seen or encountered UFOs – and one man, a landowner, confirmed that at least one of the hunters did die. He said the hunter and a companion saw a UFO one night in October 1981 and the companion ran and hid. When he returned, he found the other man dead. No one knew the cause of his death.

The man who told us this, the landowner, said he himself made the mistake of trying to shoot at a UFO one night. He said he was 'zapped', receiving a jolt that felt like an electric shock. As for the other three hunters who reportedly died, no one knew anything about them. However, the villages mentioned in the magazines were some distance from Parnarama, and we did not have time to go any further, although we did learn that UFOs had been reported fairly often around Parnarama. The new mayor told us there had been at least 100 sightings in the previous twelve months, and there had been a sighting as recently as ten days before our visit.

I think it is very possible the other three hunters did die. There is no doubt in my mind that UFOs can be hazardous to one's health. People are justified in fearing UFOs. People do get hurt, and some lose their lives.

*   *   *

Whatever UFOs are, they are real and should not be taken lightly. When individuals and entire villages are afraid to go out at night because of UFOs, that is a serious matter. UFOs may or may not be significant to mankind in the long run, but until we find out we should treat them with the greatest of caution.

Editor's Note

Further evidence for the UFO-related injuries and deaths in north-east Brazil is contained in Jacques Vallee's latest book, *Confrontations*, published by Ballantine Books, New York (1990). Like Bob Pratt, Vallee has visited Brazil and spoken with a number of victims, and is convinced of their sincerity.

Readers will also be interested in *Night Siege: The Hudson Valley UFO Sightings*, co-authored by Bob Pratt, together with Dr J. Allen Hynek and Philip J. Imbrogno, also published by Ballantine Books.

6

China Establishes UFO Observation Stations

PAUL DONG

Paul Dong was born in Canton, China, in 1928, but now lives in Oakland, California. He has been studying the UFO phenomenon for many years and has written many articles for newspapers and journals in China, and a number of books, including *The Four Major Mysteries of Mainland China* and *UFOs over Modern China*.

In 1981 Paul Dong lectured on UFOs throughout China, speaking to packed audiences at the Peking Ching Hua University Students Union, Canton Science Museum, and Canton Jinan University, etc.

He is an editor of the Chinese language magazine *Journal of UFO Research*.

Owing to the tragic collapse of the democratic movement in June 1989, resulting in a restriction on the flow of information from China, only two sighting reports are included here.

Wang Yongkuan, an engineer for the Weather Satellite Centre of the National Meteorological Service in Beijing, is a UFO researcher who has done much work in the observation of UFO phenomena. On 12 July 1986, he wrote a letter to the chairman of the Chinese Association for Science and Technology, Dr Qian Xuesen (formerly spelled Tsien Hsue Shen while living in America), requesting his ideas on establishing a UFO observation network. 'I have taken an interest in UFOs in connection with my work,' he wrote. 'My comrades and I have developed a video system for weather observations capable of taking in the entire sky from the earth's surface over a prolonged period. I wonder if it would be possible to use this equipment to observe UFOs at the same time . . .'

On 15 July, he received Dr Qian Xuesen's reply. 'UFOs are an objective phenomenon existing in nature,' he wrote. 'We must study them, and you should figure out a way to monitor them . . .

As for the talk of extraterrestrial beings and similar UFO tales, I do not believe any of that. I lean more toward the idea that the earth and atmosphere themselves produce this phenomenon and it would be a fitting subject for geological research.'

Dr Qian's brief opinion generated a great deal of publicity and mainland China immediately established two observation stations devoted entirely to UFO observation, including one at Changchun.

Who is Dr Qian and why is he so important? In fact, he is not just the chairman of the Chinese Association for Science and Technology; this is merely his official title. More importantly, he has made a name for himself in China as the 'Father of the Missile'. Since his return from the USA to China in 1955, he has done a great deal of scientific work for China, building rockets and missiles for military and scientific purposes. The Chinese people revere him as others do Einstein.

Not only is he famous in China; Dr Qian has also won international acclaim, sharing the 1989 Willard F. Rockwell Jr Medal of America's International Technology Institute (ITI) with Dr Edward Teller (America's 'Father of the H-Bomb') and Robert Klapisch, a French physicist. This prestigious medal recognized Dr Qian's high place in the international scientific community and his pioneering work in rocket and missile technology, space technology, and systems science and engineering. ITI, an organization for international science and technology exchange and development for the good of all mankind, has awarded this medal since 1982, the first winner being Willard F. Rockwell Jr himself, a major figure in the aerospace industry. No more than three individuals can win the medal each year, and only those of the highest degree of accomplishment, worthy of the World Level of the Hall of Fame for Engineering, Science and Technology, may receive this medal.

In 1955, when Dr Qian tried to leave the USA to return to China, he was detained by US security authorities and prevented from leaving the country because of his knowledge of defence technology. He was only allowed to return to China after Chinese Premier Zhou Enlai personally intervened and arranged a compromise deal with the USA. However, as a high-ranking official in the US Department of Defense described the deal: 'Giving up Qian Xuesen was equivalent to handing over four army divisions to the Chinese'.

Dr Qian's interests are wide-ranging. After retiring from his scientific duties, he has taken an interest in both psychic and UFO phenomena. On 21 April 1984, he wrote a letter to the *Journal of UFO Research*, the journal with the largest circulation in the world, calling for serious scientific investigation of UFOs and an end to the practice of passing off science fiction as science:

Recently, on reading your first and second 1984 issues, I became aware of the *Journal of UFO Research* as a scientific publication. Thus, I wish to offer a few suggestions for your consideration:

(1) Given that this is scientific research, it should be conducted in a serious and dignified manner and should not commit the error of treating the subject as science fiction.

(2) It is an objective fact that many people in most countries are interested in UFOs, and UFOs are a controversial issue. This means that UFOs are a social problem and should be studied as a sociological phenomenon. An article in the issue of the British publication *New Scientist* of 11 October 1989 discussed this topic. It seems to me that the author has made a fair appraisal of why UFO research has not been able to become a modern science.

(3) Assuming that so-called 'flying saucers' are an objective reality (that is, there are real ones in addition to the optical illusions), how should they be studied? The above-mentioned British publication, *New Scientist*, on 10 February 1983 (Vol. 97, No. 1344, page 380) and on 1 September 1983 (Vol. 99, No. 1373, page 627), proposed some concrete possibilities, suggesting that they are very possibly not extraterrestrial in origin but rather products of the earth's interior, brought about by fissures in the geological strata. From this, we could proceed to collect material, conduct an analysis, and even do laboratory experiments for true UFO research.

If this line of inquiry leads anywhere, UFO research may contribute to a matter of great importance: earthquake prediction. This would be something major.

(4) I respect your publication and believe you can contribute much to our country's socialist modernization. This is why I suggest that in the Editorial Department you have someone translate the three above-mentioned articles and publish them, in order to truly set out on the path of scientific research.

> Respectfully,
> QIAN XUESEN
> 21 April 1984

We published his letter in 1984, along with the articles from Britain's *New Scientist* for our readers' reference.[1]

Regardless of whether Qian Xuesen believed in UFOs or in 'earthquake lights' (light emitted by fissures in the Earth's strata), in other words, even though he believed that UFOs could be explained as a natural phenomenon, the very fact that he expressed an interest in them was enough to promote the expansion of UFO research and increase the layman's interest in UFOs in China.

In fact, in the past decade, UFOs themselves seemed to be doing their best to stimulate UFO research. Since the beginning of China's open door policy, China has been astir with UFO sightings. On one occasion, a giant UFO was even seen by people in seven provinces. Rather than dwelling on past incidents, let us look at a few UFO cases that occurred in 1989–90.

1989 Sighting

On 12 May 1989, a husband and wife were working in the mountains in Hubei Province. The sun had not come out yet, and they were working and chatting together. Suddenly, the land below was covered with a red glow. They thought it was the sun coming out, but they wondered why the sun would rise so early. While puzzling over this, they looked up to see a large red 'plate' hovering in the sky. They were so scared that they felt like running away but were too paralysed to run.

The red plate was really big, and it was emitting a powerful red glow, making a terrifying sight; the red glow made their legs feel too weak to run. They were not sure whether this was a psychological reaction or whether they were really physically unable to run. All they could do was stand there in shock, awaiting events. The UFO seemed to be mocking them, neither flying away, making any sound, spinning, nor changing colour. All it did was to emit a red glow.

About twenty minutes passed this way. The object was still there, but no other people were around besides the husband and wife. They hoped there would be others nearby who also could have seen the object and confirm their story, but unfortunately it was too early in the morning and the nearest village was too far from that hillside, so no other witnesses were to be found. They did not know how long they waited in this state of shock mixed with anxiety (villagers do not own watches).

Finally, the object began to glide. They could tell this because the red glow on the ground was moving. They looked up, and indeed, the object was gliding upwards very slowly, rotating slightly. When it reached the height of about a thirty-storey building, it flew away about three times faster than a jet plane.

Because there were no other witnesses, the couple were afraid nobody would believe their story, and that they might be accused of rumour mongering by village officials. So they kept it to themselves. One month later, however, they had a chance to go to town, where they visited members of the Hubei Province UFO Research Association to report their story.

Army Personnel chased by a UFO, 1990

In a previous case in Xinjiang province, a People's Liberation Army soldier rode a motorcycle in pursuit of a UFO.[2]

Now let us look at a recent incident which occurred out side Taiyuan City, Shanxi Province, in which a UFO chased a car.

At 9.10 p.m. on 10 January 1990, two men from a unit of the People's Liberation Army stationed at Taiyuan City were speeding along in a jeep about five miles outside the city, when one of them became aware of an object which seemed to be following them. Looking up, he saw that in fact there was a black, disk-shaped UFO 'monitoring' them from the air.

They started driving faster, hoping to shake off their pursuer, but after about fifteen minutes the object was still right above them. Overcome with fright, the driver, Cao Yongnian, suddenly recalled that there were things called UFOs which could go so fast that even modern jets could not keep up with them. So he realized it would be difficult to try to run away from it, and a better idea would be to slow down deliberately and wait to see how the situation developed. Thus, he started driving at only fifty miles per hour, but after thirteen or twenty minutes more, the black object was still in the sky. Since they were unable to escape, the driver and the soldier riding with him talked it over and agreed that they might as well stop.

Amusingly, the object also stopped in the air, but rose more than twice as high. The 'round black plate' began to give off blue light. Even though it was standing still in the air (and did not seem to be spinning, either), the light was constantly changing colour, now green, now yellow, now red. After watching for some time, they became less frightened, and even began to enjoy the show. Then the two Liberation Army men talked it over and decided to take a shot at the object to see what would happen, but they never got up the nerve to do it.

Finally, they decided to try shouting at the object. They moved over and stood at the side of the road, waving and shouting, 'Come down, come down, let's have a talk!' for a few minutes. There was no response, but then something strange happened. The UFO flew around in a circle and then zoomed off. They thought their shouting had been effective, and they reported their experience to a UFO enthusiast in the army, saying that shouting was the only way to deal with similar situations, in case they should occur in the future! But it would only work if the shouters were brave, and not afraid to be carried away or killed.

Incidents similar to the above have plagued China for the past ten years. However, nobody has yet offered a satisfactory explanation for the phenomena, which must still await further research into more incidents.

UFO Observation Station at Changchun

In order to expand the scope of such research, the Chinese UFO Research Society now has its own observation station devoted entirely to observing UFO phenomena – the Changchun Observation Station – located in the Balibao area to the north of Changchun. The observation station, which is China's second (the first being created by Wang Yongkuan in 1987), is equipped with an astrograph with a 130-mm field of vision, an 80-mm refractor telescope, a 150-mm Newtonian reflector telescope, as well as a wireless receiving set.

Hong Kong's Limited Viewpoint Association and the Hong Kong Hall of Space provided support throughout the process of building the observation station, which was completed at the end of 1988. The Chief of UNESCO's Asian branch as well as Vice-Mayor Zhang Mingyuan of Changchun have visited the staff of the observation post. There has also been material support.

With regard to the recent UFO phenomena around Changchun, the staff of the observation station provided newspapermen with scientific explanations for the layman. This has been highly effective in helping the Changchun City UFO Research Association in the task of popularizing UFO knowledge, and has won the praise of leaders of the city's Science Association.[3]

CHINA ESTABLISHES UFO OBSERVATION STATIONS

REFERENCES
1. *Journal of UFO Research*, 1984/4. (For details of this Chinese-language journal, please contact Paul Dong: P.O. Box 2011, Oakland, California 94604, USA.)
2. Stevens, Wendelle C., and Dong, Paul: *UFOs over Modern China*, UFO Photo Archives (1983), P.O. Box 17206, Tucson, Arizona 85710, USA.
3. *Journal of UFO Research*, 1989/3.

7

The Report on Operation Majestic 12

STANTON FRIEDMAN

An American nuclear physicist, Stanton T. Friedman has many years of industrial experience in the design, development and testing of a wide variety of advanced nuclear and space systems, including nuclear aircraft, fission and fusion rockets, and nuclear reactor and radioisotope systems for space and mobile terrestrial applications. He has been employed by General Electric, Westinghouse, General Motors, Aerojet-General Nucleonics, and TRW.

He received his B.Sc. and M.Sc. in physics from the University of Chicago in 1955 and 1956, and belongs to the American Physical Society, the American Nuclear Society, the Canadian Nuclear Society, the American Institute of Aeronautics & Astronautics, the American Association for the Advancement of Science, the Air & Waste Management Association, the American Association of Radon Scientists & Technologists, MENSA, and was a Fellow of the British Interplanetary Society.

Stanton Friedman is well known throughout the USA and Canada for his hundreds of lectures, TV and radio broadcasts, as well as articles on the subject of UFOs, which he has been studying for thirty-two years.

I have condensed the following from the report of his five-year study of the MJ–12 affair, which was completed with the aid of a grant of $16,000 from the Fund for UFO Research in May 1990.

There is no question that *if* the TOP SECRET/MAJIC/EYES ONLY briefing document for President-Elect Eisenhower of 18 November 1952 is genuine, it is one of the most important US Government documents ever leaked to the public.

The story told in the eight pages of the briefing that are available is deceptively simple. The wreckage of a flying saucer was allegedly recovered seventy-five miles north-west of Roswell, New Mexico, in July 1947. Four alien bodies were also recovered, apparently having been ejected from the vehicle two miles east of the main wreckage site. The government took into its possession the wreckage and the bodies and established a group called Operation Majestic 12, or MJ–12 or Majic–12 to deal with the problem. The report (allegedly prepared by Admiral Hillenkoetter, the first Director of the CIA) notes:

that the characteristics of the human-like bodies were different from those of *homo sapiens*,
that there were strange symbols on portions of the wreckage which had not yet been interpreted,
that there had been an increase in UFO activity in 1952,
that there had been another crashed saucer recovery in December 1950,

and

that it was strongly recommended that Operation Majestic 12 still be kept accountable only to the President of the United States.

Page 6 is a listing of Attachments A to H. Page 7 is a kind of sub-title page saying 'Attachment A', and Attachment A, itself, is page 8. This is a brief memo from President Truman to Secretary of Defense James Forrestal dated 24 September 1947, classified Top Secret/Eyes Only, and authorizing Forrestal to proceed with Operation Majestic 12. Attachments B to H were not included in the material that was received.

The question, of course, is whether or not the documents are genuine. The same applies to a third document known as the Cutler–Twining memo, dated 14 July 1954. (All these documents are reproduced in Figures 7:2 to 7:5.) There are many complications involved in trying to assess the validity of these documents. The evaluation story is much more complex, in a sense, than the original crash/retrieval story – an event which almost certainly occurred.

The purpose of this report is to review a substantial amount of research that I have done since becoming involved with the MJ–12 documents. In many ways the chase has been frustrating as well as fascinating. It is complicated by the simple fact that, if the documents are genuine, they deal with very highly classified matter. Of particular interest is the fact that the MJ–12 document names the twelve original members of Operation Majestic 12 and also the thirteenth member, who replaced Secretary of Defense Forrestal who died in 1949. All members were dead when the document was received (Figure 7:1).

It is certainly possible that all three documents (the Briefing, the Truman–Forrestal (TF) memo, and Cutler–Twining (CT) memo) are totally fraudulent. It is also possible that all three are genuine, or that only one, or two are genuine, or that there is a mixture of truth and fiction. A great deal of information is available which, with limited resources, can be investigated. To begin at the beginning, we need to look at the background of how these documents were received, the events that led up to this, and then deal specifically with the research that has been performed.

Background

In February 1978 I was put in touch with Jesse Marcel, who had been an intelligence officer at Roswell Army Air Force Base in Roswell at the time of the saucer crash. He was unsure of the date, he told me, but it was in the late 1940s. The local sheriff telephoned to report that some rancher had come in with pieces of strange wreckage and thought the base might be interested. Marcel met with the sheriff, talked to the base commander, Colonel William Blanchard, and then went out with a Counter Intelligence Corps agent named Cavitt. The rancher showed them the wreckage the following day. They brought back an army carry-all and an old Buick full of fragments, while leaving most of the wreckage out on the ranch.

There were several kinds of very strange material which were brought back to the base. Marcel was instructed to put it on a B-29 and to fly with it to Wright Field in Ohio. They were to make a stop at the headquarters of the 8th Army Air Force, of which his group, the 509th Composite Bomb Wing, was a part, in Fort Worth, Texas. When they arrived, General Roger Ramey, head of the 8th Air Force, instructed him not to say anything, told the press it was just the wreckage of a weather balloon radar reflector, and they went back to Roswell.

This conversation was the beginning of a long effort to dig out the truth about what happened at Roswell, a search which is described in other publications.[1-7] In October 1978 Bill Moore visited me and we discussed the possibility of working together on a project dealing with stories of crashed saucers. There had been a

Lloyd Berkner (1905–1967)   Scientist, explorer, space pioneer; first Executive Director, Joint Research & Development Board.

Detlev Bronk (1897–1975)   Aviation physiologist; Chairman, National Research Council & National Academy of Sciences; President, Johns Hopkins & Rockefeller Universities.

Vannevar Bush (1890–1974)   Outstanding Research & Development leader at MIT then Carnegie Institution; head of Office of Scientific Research & Development, Joint Research & Development Board and the National Advisory Committee on Aeronautics.

James Forrestal (1892–1949)   Secretary of Navy, First Secretary of Defense.

Gordon Gray (1909–1982)   Intelligence background; Secretary of the Army; many high security positions for Truman and Eisenhower.

Roscoe Hillenkoetter (1897–1982)   Admiral; Naval Intelligence; Director, CIA, 1947–1950.

Jerome Hunsaker (1886–1984)   Aeronautical engineer, MIT; head of NACA after Bush.

Donald Menzel (1901–1976)   Harvard astronomer; expert on cryptanalysis, eclipses and radio propagation; involvement with CIA and NSA.

Robert Montague (1899–1958)   Army general; head of Armed Forces Special Weapons Center, Sandia, New Mexico.

Walter Smith (1895–1961)   General; Eisenhower's WWII Chief of Staff; Ambassador to USSR; fourth Director of Central Intelligence.

Sidney Souers (1892–1973)   Admiral, Navy Reserve; first Director of Central Intelligence; first Executive Secretary of National Security Council; intelligence consultant.

Nathan Twining (1897–1982)   General; head of Air Matériel Command; Chief of Staff, USAF; Chairman, Joint Chiefs of Staff.

Hoyt Vandenberg (1899–1954)   General; second Chief of Staff, USAF; second Director of Central Intelligence.

Figure 7:1. The alleged members of Majestic 12

TOP SECRET / MAJIC
EYES ONLY

001

NATIONAL SECURITY INFORMATION

****
* TOP SECRET *
****

EYES ONLY

COPY ONE OF ONE.

BRIEFING DOCUMENT: OPERATION MAJESTIC 12

PREPARED FOR PRESIDENT-ELECT DWIGHT D. EISENHOWER: (EYES ONLY)

18 NOVEMBER, 1952

WARNING! This is a TOP SECRET - EYES ONLY document containing compartmentalized information essential to the national security of the United States. EYES ONLY ACCESS to the material herein is strictly limited to those possessing Majestic-12 clearance level. Reproduction in any form or the taking of written or mechanically transcribed notes is strictly forbidden.

****
* TOP SECRET *
****

TOP SECRET / MAJIC
EYES ONLY

T52-EXEMPT (E)

EYES ONLY

001

Figure 7:2. Reproductions of eight pages (001–008) of the alleged briefing document for President-Elect Eisenhower.

COPY ONE OF ONE.

SUBJECT: OPERATION MAJESTIC-12 PRELIMINARY BRIEFING FOR PRESIDENT-ELECT EISENHOWER.

DOCUMENT PREPARED 18 NOVEMBER, 1952.

BRIEFING OFFICER: ADM. ROSCOE H. HILLENKOETTER (MJ-1)

NOTE: This document has been prepared as a preliminary briefing only. It should be regarded as introductory to a full operations briefing intended to follow.

* * * * * *

OPERATION MAJESTIC-12 is a TOP SECRET Research and Development/ Intelligence operation responsible directly and only to the President of the United States. Operations of the project are carried out under control of the Majestic-12 (Majic-12) Group which was established by special classified executive order of President Truman on 24 September, 1947, upon recommendation by Dr. Vannevar Bush and Secretary James Forrestal. (See Attachment "A".) Members of the Majestic-12 Group were designated as follows:

> Adm. Roscoe H. Hillenkoetter
> Dr. Vannevar Bush
> Secy. James V. Forrestal*
> Gen. Nathan F. Twining
> Gen. Hoyt S. Vandenberg
> Dr. Detlev Bronk
> Dr. Jerome Hunsaker
> Mr. Sidney W. Souers
> Mr. Gordon Gray
> Dr. Donald Menzel
> Gen. Robert M. Montague
> Dr. Lloyd V. Berkner

The death of Secretary Forrestal on 22 May, 1949, created a vacancy which remained unfilled until 01 August, 1950, upon which date Gen. Walter B. Smith was designated as permanent replacement.

Figure 7:2 continued

COPY <u>ONE</u> OF <u>ONE</u>.

On 24 June, 1947, a civilian pilot flying over the Cascade
Mountains in the State of Washington observed nine flying
disc-shaped aircraft traveling in formation at a high rate
of speed. Although this was not the first known sighting
of such objects, it was the first to gain widespread attention
in the public media. Hundreds of reports of sightings of
similar objects followed. Many of these came from highly
credible military and civilian sources. These reports resulted in independent efforts by several different elements
of the military to ascertain the nature and purpose of these
objects in the interests of national defense. A number of
witnesses were interviewed and there were several unsuccessful
attempts to utilize aircraft in efforts to pursue reported
discs in flight. Public reaction bordered on near hysteria
at times.

In spite of these efforts, little of substance was learned
about the objects until a local rancher reported that one
had crashed in a remote region of New Mexico located approximately seventy-five miles northwest of Roswell Army Air
Base (now Walker Field).

On 07 July, 1947, a secret operation was begun to assure
recovery of the wreckage of this object for scientific study.
During the course of this operation, aerial reconnaissance
discovered that four small human-like beings had apparently
ejected from the craft at some point before it exploded.
These had fallen to earth about two miles east of the wreckage
site. All four were dead and badly decomposed due to action
by predators and exposure to the elements during the approximately one week time period which had elapsed before their
discovery. A special scientific team took charge of removing
these bodies for study. (See Attachment "C".) The wreckage
of the craft was also removed to several different locations.
(See Attachment "B".) Civilian and military witnesses in
the area were debriefed, and news reporters were given the
effective cover story that the object had been a misguided
weather research balloon.

T52-EXEMPT (E)

Figure 7:2 continued

EYES ONLY   COPY <u>ONE</u> OF <u>ONE</u>.

A covert analytical effort organized by Gen. Twining and
Dr. Bush acting on the direct orders of the President, resulted in a preliminary concensus (19 September, 1947) that
the disc was most likely a short range reconnaissance craft.
This conclusion was based for the most part on the craft's
size and the apparent lack of any identifiable provisioning.
(See Attachment "D".) A similar analysis of the four dead
occupants was arranged by Dr. Bronk. It was the tentative
conclusion of this group (30 November, 1947) that although
these creatures are human-like in appearance, the biological
and evolutionary processes responsible for their development
has apparently been quite different from those observed or
postulated in homo-sapiens. Dr. Bronk's team has suggested
the term "Extra-terrestrial Biological Entities", or "EBEs",
be adopted as the standard term of reference for these
creatures until such time as a more definitive designation
can be agreed upon.

Since it is virtually certain that these craft do not origin-
ate in any country on earth, considerable speculation has
centered around what their point of origin might be and how
they get here. Mars was and remains a possibility, although
some scientists, most notably Dr. Menzel, consider it more
likely that we are dealing with beings from another solar
system entirely.

Numerous examples of what appear to be a form of writing
were found in the wreckage. Efforts to decipher these have
remained largely unsuccessful. (See Attachment "E".)
Equally unsuccessful have been efforts to determine the
method of propulsion or the nature or method of transmission
of the power source involved. Research along these lines
has been complicated by the complete absence of identifiable
wings, propellers, jets, or other conventional methods of
propulsion and guidance, as well as a total lack of metallic
wiring, vacuum tubes, or similar recognizable electronic
components. (See Attachment "F".) It is assumed that the
propulsion unit was completely destroyed by the explosion
which caused the crash.

Figure 7:2 continued

• • • • • • • • • • • • • •
* TOP SECRET *
• • • • • • • • • • • • • •

A need for as much additional information as possible about
these craft, their performance characteristics and their
purpose led to the undertaking known as U.S. Air Force Project
SIGN in December, 1947. In order to preserve security, liason
between SIGN and Majestic-12 was limited to two individuals
within the Intelligence Division of Air Materiel Command whose
role was to pass along certain types of information through
channels. SIGN evolved into Project GRUDGE in December, 1948.
The operation is currently being conducted under the code name
BLUE BOOK, with liason maintained through the Air Force officer
who is head of the project.

On 06 December, 1950, a second object, probably of similar
origin, impacted the earth at high speed in the El Indio –
Guerrero area of the Texas – Mexican boder after following
a long trajectory through the atmosphere. By the time a
search team arrived, what remained of the object had been almost
totally incinerated. Such material as could be recovered was
transported to the A.E.C. facility at Sandia, New Mexico, for
study.

Implications for the National Security are of continuing importance in that the motives and ultimate intentions of these
visitors remain completely unknown. In addition, a significant
upsurge in the surveillance activity of these craft beginning
in May and continuing through the autumn of this year has caused
considerable concern that new developments may be imminent.
It is for these reasons, as well as the obvious international
and technological considerations and the ultimate need to
avoid a public panic at all costs, that the Majestic-12 Group
remains of the unanimous opinion that imposition of the
strictest security precautions should continue without inter-
ruption into the new administration. At the same time, contingency plan MJ-1949-04P/78 (Top Secret – Eyes Only) should
be held in continued readiness should the need to make a
public announcement present itself. (See Attachment "G".)

Figure 7:2 continued

```
* * * * * * * * * * * * * *
* TOP SECRET *
* * * * * * * * * * * * * *
```

COPY <u>ONE</u> OF <u>ONE</u>.

ENUMERATION OF ATTACHMENTS:

*ATTACHMENT "A"........Special Classified Executive
                    Order #092447. (TS/EO)

*ATTACHMENT "B"........Operation Majestic-12 Status
                    Report #1, Part A. 30 NOV '47.
                    (TS-MAJIC/EO)

*ATTACHMENT "C"........Operation Majestic-12 Status
                    Report #1, Part B. 30 NOV '47.
                    (TS-MAJIC/EO)

*ATTACHMENT "D"........Operation Majestic-12 Preliminary
                    Analytical Report. 19 SEP '47.
                    (TS-MAJIC/EO)

*ATTACHMENT "E"........Operation Majestic-12 Blue Team
                    Report #5. 30 JUN '52.
                    (TS-MAJIC/EO)

*ATTACHMENT "F"........Operation Majestic-12 Status
                    Report #2. 31 JAN '48.
                    (TS-MAJIC/EO)

*ATTACHMENT "G"........Operation Majestic-12 Contingency
                    Plan MJ-1949-04P/78: 31 JAN '49.
                    (TS-MAJIC/EO)

*ATTACHMENT "H"........Operation Majestic-12, Maps and
                    Photographs Folio (Extractions).
                    (TS-MAJIC/EO)

```
* * * * * * * * * * * * *
* TOP SECRET *
```
TOP SECRET / MAJIC
EYES ONLY
EYES ONLY

T52-EXEMPT (E)
006

Figure 7:2 continued

```
**************
*  TOP SECRET  *
**************
```

COPY ONE OF ONE.

ATTACHMENT "A"

```
**************
*  TOP SECRET  *
**************
```

EYES ONLY TOP SECRET / MAJIC

T52-EXEMPT (E)

EYES ONLY

007

Figure 7:2 continued

TOP SECRET
EYES ONLY
THE WHITE HOUSE
WASHINGTON

September 24, 1947.

MEMORANDUM FOR THE SECRETARY OF DEFENSE

Dear Secretary Forrestal:

As per our recent conversation on this matter, you are hereby authorized to proceed with all due speed and caution upon your undertaking. Hereafter this matter shall be referred to only as Operation Majestic Twelve.

It continues to be my feeling that any future considerations relative to the ultimate disposition of this matter should rest solely with the Office of the President following appropriate discussions with yourself, Dr. Bush and the Director of Central Intelligence.

Harry Truman

TOP SECRET
EYES ONLY

Figure 7:2 continued

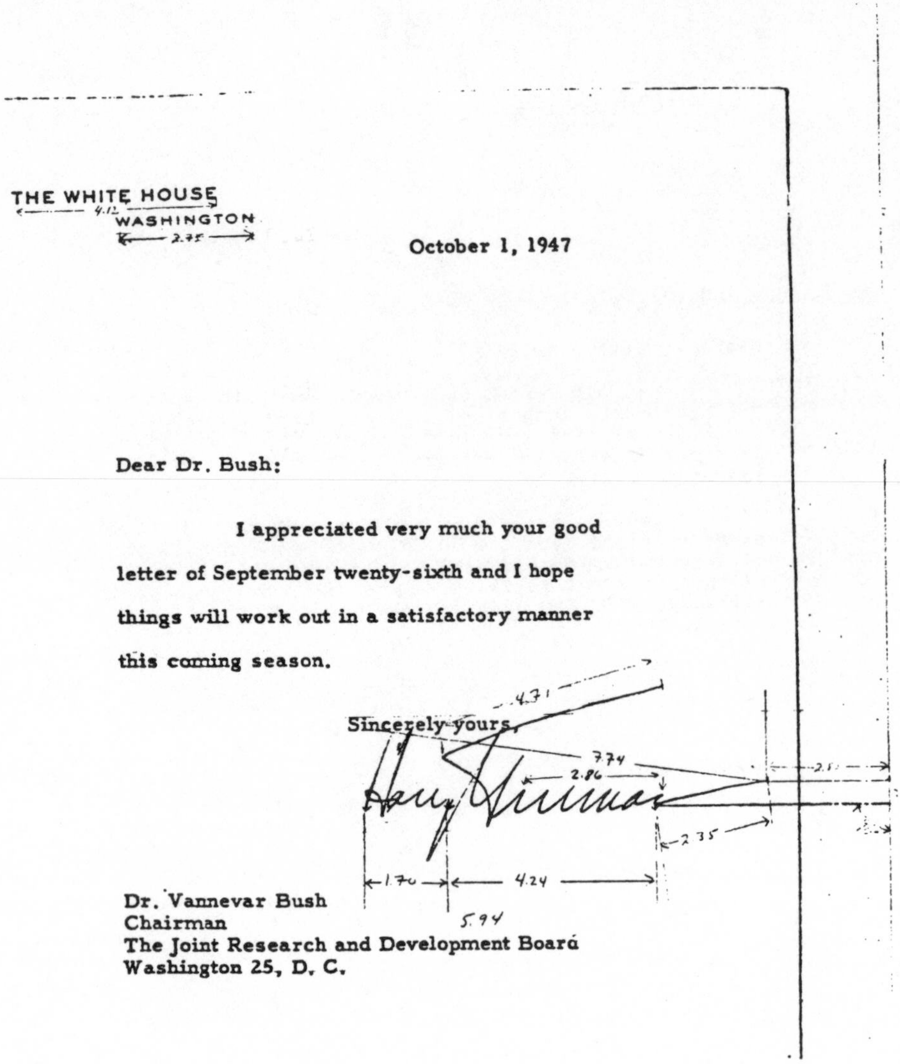

THE WHITE HOUSE
WASHINGTON

October 1, 1947

Dear Dr. Bush:

      I appreciated very much your good
letter of September twenty-sixth and I hope
things will work out in a satisfactory manner
this coming season.

      Sincerely yours,

Dr. Vannevar Bush
Chairman
The Joint Research and Development Board
Washington 25, D. C.

Figure 7:3. Comparison of the Truman signature of October 1, 1947 (above) with that of September 24 (opposite) shows a marked similarity, although there are differences in ratio.

144

TOP SECRET
EYES ONLY

THE WHITE HOUSE
WASHINGTON

008

September 24, 1947.

MEMORANDUM FOR THE SECRETARY OF DEFENSE

Dear Secretary Forrestal:

As per our recent conversation on this matter, you are hereby authorized to proceed with all due speed and caution upon your undertaking. Hereafter this matter shall be referred to only as Operation Majestic Twelve.

It continues to be my feeling that any future considerations relative to the ultimate disposition of this matter should rest solely with the Office of the President following appropriate discussions with yourself, Dr. Bush and the Director of Central Intelligence.

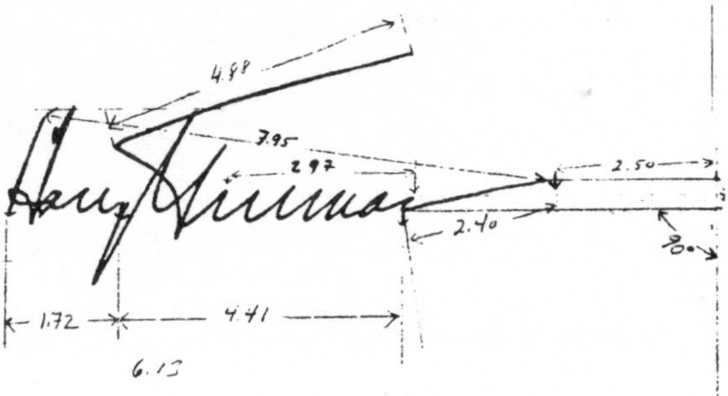

3.2% longer than signature on Truman-Bush.

TOP SECRET
EYES ONLY

Figure 7:4.

July 14, 1954

MEMORANDUM FOR GENERAL TWINING

SUBJECT: NSC/MJ-12 Special Studies Project

The President has decided that the MJ-12 SSP briefing should take place during the already scheduled White House meeting of July 16, rather than following it as previously intended. More precise arrangements will be explained to you upon arrival. Please alter your plans accordingly.

Your concurrence in the above change of arrangements is assumed.

ROBERT CUTLER
Special Assistant
to the President

DECLASSIFIED
Authority *ND 857013*
BY ___ *S DTH* NARS. Date *1/12/87*

COPY

from

NATIONAL ARCHIVES
rd Group No. **RG 341,** Records of the Headquarters United
States Air Force

Figure 7:5. The Cutler–Twining memo. (National Archives, USA)

lot of publicity about 'Hangar 18' at Wright Field (later Wright-Patterson AFB), supposedly containing twelve alien bodies, but unfortunately little in the way of hard evidence.

Then, in late October 1978, I met Vern and Gene Maltais, who told me that an old friend of theirs named Barney Barnett had in July 1947 come across a saucer stuck in the ground with four strange bodies around it, and that the military had come along and told him and a nearby archaeological expedition never to say anything under any circumstances.

As of 1980, when the book *The Roswell Incident*[1] (by Moore and Charles Berlitz) came out, Bill and I had talked to about sixty people in conjunction with the event. Having done ninety-eight per cent of the Roswell research, we were both shocked when the proofs of the book included extraneous material and left out important material that would have helped in evaluating the reliability of the witnesses. The book was a success from a writer's viewpoint because of the advance royalties paid by publishers in eleven different countries, but the critics panned the extraneous inaccurate material that was in the book (and there was plenty of that), ignoring the solid information.

When Bill was promoting the book, on radio and television, he was approached by an 'insider' who showed some credentials and indicated that he worked for the government (Air Force Intelligence, apparently) and was interested in getting the information out, and would try and help in any way he could.

In August 1980 I had moved from California to Fredericton, New Brunswick, Canada, a distance of 3,500 miles by road. Earlier that year I had been called by a company that was considering doing a fictional movie about UFOs. The director would be a man named Jaime Shandera. They also wanted somebody to help out with the script writing. Naturally, I thought of Bill, who by that time had moved to Arizona. We did have several sessions, and did shoot a little film, but project funding fell apart. Bill, after his contacts with the 'insiders', and with me living so far away, finally decided he had to bring Jaime into the picture.

The Briefing and the Truman–Forrestal memo were received in the form of a roll of undeveloped 35-mm film, on which there were two sets of eight negatives each. The roll was received in the mail by Jaime Shandera at his Burbank home in a double-wrapped plain brown envelope that arrived in early December 1984, with no return address.

Shandera had by this time been working quite closely with Bill

Moore and had many contacts with a group of 'insiders', some of whom were connected with the Air Force Office of Special Investigations (AFOSI) in Albuquerque, New Mexico. These insiders had given the impression that they were interested in having the facts about flying saucers released to the public, but in such a manner that would protect their identity and status, although there were occasional indications that they were willing to go public without that protection.

The Investigation Begins

Bill printed the film and notified me about it. The problem was, of course, were the eight pages legitimate or not? There were specific concerns:

(1) that they could be complete disinformation;

(2) that they might contain a lot of truth mixed with some phoney material that would lead us in the wrong direction; or

(3) that they could be entirely legitimate.

The most worrisome fact, when Bill and Jaime read me the list of members of Operation Majestic 12, was the presence of Harvard astronomer Donald H. Menzel. The other eleven names we had already picked up in our continuing research on the Roswell incident. It is of considerable interest that the last survivor of MJ–12 was Dr Jerome Hunsaker, who died on 10 September 1984, just three months before the document was received. If anybody was paying attention to when these people would no longer be available for questioning, he would have been waiting for Hunsaker's death.

By the time the film was received, we had contacted ninety-two people concerned with the incident, and had been checking on who was doing what in the government in early July 1947. If there indeed had been the recovery of a crashed flying saucer, one would have expected some kind of activity to reflect such an extraordinary event. We already had been looking at White House logs of visitors with Truman, newspaper articles around that would mention government officials, and cross-contacts between those who one would expect to be involved. We had re-examined a letter of 23 September 1947 from General Nathan Twining describing a number of government organizations which were to be notified of what was happening on the UFO scene.

In 1979 I obtained a copy of the hitherto Top Secret Canadian Government (Department of Transport, 1950) memo from Wilbert Smith, part of which states:

> . . . I made discreet enquiries through the Canadian Embassy staff in Washington who were able to obtain from me the following information:
>
> (a) The matter is the most highly classified subject in the United States Government, rating higher even than the H-bomb.
>
> (b) Flying saucers exist.
>
> (c) Their modus operandi is unknown but concentrated effort is being made by a small group headed by Doctor Vannevar Bush.
>
> (d) The entire matter is considered by the United States authorities to be of tremendous significance . . .

Because of the mention of Dr Bush, I had been delving in considerable detail into who he was, and who his contacts were. It transpired that he was the common factor in the organizations named by General Twining, so that all the names on the MJ–12 list made sense to us except that of Donald Menzel.

General (later Four-star) Nathan F. Twining was certainly no surprise as a member of MJ–12. A very important formerly Secret letter from him to Brigadier General Schulgen at Air Force Headquarters was first published in the 1969 Condon report. But I had missed two of the most important aspects of the letter besides its implications of the reality of intelligently controlled flying disks. One was the statement: '. . . The lack of physical evidence in the shape of crash recovered exhibits which would undeniably prove the existence of these objects.' Since the letter dated 23 September 1947 (interestingly, the day before the Truman–Forrestal memo) was only classified Secret, it could *not* discuss information that was Top Secret, which clearly the recovered wreckage would have been.

It was well after 1979 when I finally appreciated the importance of item 'a' in the recommendations listing the groups to which complete sets of all data should be made available: '. . . the Army, Navy, Atomic Energy Commission [AEC], JRDB, the Air Force Scientific Advisory Group (AFSAG), NACA, and the RAND and NEPA projects . . .' What forced me to re-examine this letter was my information on Dr Vannevar Bush. First of all, the last six groups were all concerned with sophisticated technology, *not* with ongoing defence work. Second, the common link seemed to be Vannevar Bush. Back in 1982 (well before the receipt of the MJ–12 documents) I had noted that Bush had been pre-war chairman of NACA (National Advisory Committee on Aeronautics), had established and was the first chairman of the Joint Research and Development Board (JRDB), the post-war successor to the Office of Scientific Research and Development (OSRD) which had been headed by him during the war and which had established the post-war AEC as well. JRDB had also had a say in establishing the Nuclear Energy for Propulsion Applications (NEPA) programme. Bush had been a professor at MIT for about twenty years before being named Chairman of the Carnegie Institution in 1939.

As a result of reviewing a number of NACA documents at the Truman and other libraries, I also had noted that Twining had served on NACA and that the NACA was expanded in 1948 from fifteen to seventeen members, with the two new members being Dr Detlev Bronk, an aviation physiologist (listed as an MJ–12 member) and Dr James H. Doolittle, one of the world's great flyers and also one of the first recipients of a Ph.D. in Aeronautics (from MIT, when Bush was dean). Doolittle eventually became chairman of NACA in 1956, was chairman of the AFSAG and was involved in a host of very classified intelligence-related activities throughout the post-war era, including chairing a committee which evaluated the CIA for President Eisenhower, and organizing the super-secret Operation Solarium in 1953.

Once the MJ–12 member listing was received, other links fell into place. For example, Jerome Hunsaker of MIT had succeeded Bush as NACA chairman; Vandenberg had served on NACA; Bronk became vice-chairman of NACA and had headed an OSRD biology committee under Bush.

General Twining

The reader by now will not be surprised that Twining was an early target of my research. He was actually alive when I started my quest, but according to his family was suffering from Alzheimer's disease. I did find out that his papers had been donated to the Library of Congress Manuscript Division and managed to get approval from his son to view the papers. Unfortunately, the great bulk were still classified. I put in requests for classification review of a number of boxes, based on the Finders Aid which covered about 40,000 pages. It was in one of these folders that a couple of discoveries were made in a folder labelled 'Eyes Only'. These were two memos from Cutler, noted earlier, relating to Operation Solarium. Interesting information was also discovered in Twining's correspondence files.

Twining had planned a visit to the Boeing company in Seattle on 16 July 1947, both to review the new B-50 bomber and to do some fishing with old friends. The trip to the West Coast had clearly been planned for a long time but was suddenly cancelled. Earl Schaefer, Vice President of Boeing-Wichita (Kansas), had written on 10 July 1947 asking Twining to stop by to see the prototype XL-15 plane on his way to the West Coast. In his response of 17 July, Twining said, '. . . with deepest regrets we had to cancel our trip to the Boeing factory due to *a very important and sudden matter* that developed here . . . I have been away quite a bit the last couple of weeks so have not had a chance to . . .' [Author's italics.]

Newspaper articles quoting Twining about flying saucers clearly established that he was in New Mexico around 9 July. This strongly suggested that the travelling referred to in the letter and 'the very important and sudden matter' were connected with New Mexico. Several years later, one of Twining's children gave me the name of his pilot whom I managed to locate and eventually meet in person and to copy many pages from his pilot log book. There was a 6.5 hour flight on 7 July (Wright Field to Alamogordo, New Mexico) and a return flight, with two stops, of eight hours and forty minutes on 11 July. The flight on 7 July was from Wright Field (Twining's base) to Alamogordo Army Air Field. For 11 July, the log notes flights from Alamogordo to White Sands (New Mexico), to Albuquerque (N.M.) – probably Kirtland A A F B – and back to Wright Field in Dayton, Ohio. This was the only trip to New Mexico for several months preceding July.

A key point that must be made here is that Twining left Dayton on Monday, 7 July, but the fuss about Roswell (the press release about the recovery of a flying disk) went out the next day, on 8 July. How could this be? A growing body of evidence indicates that there was actually a crash west of Socorro (the Barnett story as mentioned earlier) on about 3 July, which got *no* press coverage and which may well have been tracked by radar at the White Sands Missile Range, since the radar certainly would have been active, in preparation for a rocket launch that day. Newspaper articles say the launch did not take place because there had been an accident which injured several people with a toxic substance. If the radar had tracked the UFO down, that would explain the prompt appearance of the military at the location of civil engineer Barney Barnett and the archaeology group. Surely, if something had been tracked down, there would have been subsequent aerial reconnaissance from Alamogordo, as well as troops sent out as quickly as possible. Roswell was a good deal east of there. Alamogordo was the home of numerous rocket scientists, including the German contingent under Wernher von Braun.

It must have been quite a shock when Colonel Blanchard ordered First Lt. Walter Haut to put out his press release about the wreckage found on the Foster ranch by 'Mac' Brazel. Probably the recovery near Horse Springs, New Mexico, at the edge of the Plains of San Augustin, would have stimulated careful monitoring of all press wire service transmissions to assure that no story went out. It is very likely no coincidence that the newspapers noted that President Truman met with New Mexico Senator Chavez on 9 July with no good reason being given, and radio people from Roswell have stated that they were called to discontinue coverage of the crashed disk story or lose their licence.

It is important to remember that Roswell Army Air Force Base was basically a Strategic Air Command base whose primary purpose was not research and development, but rather the training of a powerful force of heavy bombers in the new tactics of atom-bombing, which were quite different from standard bombing tactics. It had very high security but with an entirely different mission from that at White Sands Missile Range and Holloman and Kirtland AAFB not far away.

The Menzel Story

Doctor Donald H. Menzel was a Harvard professor of astrophysics, a well-known astronomer who was an expert on eclipses, for example. He led a number of eclipse expeditions around the world, including one to the Soviet Union in 1936. His first quite negative book on UFOs was published in 1953 and he published two more after that. He proclaimed that he could explain every sighting. I had read his first book during my initial review of such books in the late 1950s and was astonished at how, in order to make explanations fit, he had to adjust the data. If one changes all the witnesses' testimony, then anyone can explain a sighting. I was terribly disappointed in his work. He seemed to take every public opportunity to take pot shots at UFOs. All sightings had explanations!

I had only one direct encounter with Dr Menzel. I was giving a lecture at Harvard University, sponsored by an engineering alumni group, and called him earlier that day in order to invite him to the lecture just so that nobody would think I was trying to avoid him. His response rather startled me. He said, 'Oh, I know who you are,' when I gave him my name. 'Oh, you read my paper next to yours in the Congressional Hearings Document of 1968?' I said. 'No, I've seen letters and memos about you.' I still do not know what that statement meant. He went on to say, 'You can't be a scientist and believe in UFOs.' At this point I laughed at such a strange remark. He got angry and started to rant and rave. 'Look, Dr Menzel,' I said, 'I just called out of politeness to invite you to my talk. I didn't call to argue with you.' 'OK. Of course I won't be there,' he responded. So I told the story that night.

I had been aware that Menzel had an enormous correspondence about UFOs, which is at the American Philosophical Society Library in Philadelphia, which I had visited. He gave testimony at the 1968 Congressional hearings, in writing, as I had. He was also a participant in a 1969 UFO conference in Boston, sponsored by the American Association for the Advancement of Science. Somebody else read his paper, but he was there. Menzel was a favourite target of Dr James E. MacDonald, one of the world's premier Ufologists, prior to his untimely death. Jim's speciality was upper atmosphere physics, and he dissected Menzel's explanations. It was clear that Menzel had got away with 'scientific murder', so to speak, in trying to supposedly use science to explain cases.

In any event, it was difficult to understand how an astronomer at Harvard, a total debunker, could be part of a committee that included such outstanding people, all with high level security clearances, all heavily involved in the Washington classified information scene. My initial reaction when I was told that Menzel's name was on the MJ–12 list was, 'That's all we need! Obviously the document must be a fraud.' But I persisted with my inquiries because some of the other information clearly reflected reality, as it was then known by us. I obtained a listing of his correspondence file folders at the American Philosophical Society Library and also found out that a number of his papers were at the University of Denver, where he had been an undergraduate student. I also determined that a considerable portion of his files were at the archives at Harvard University Library. I corresponded with all three places and found that I needed permission from the head of the Astronomy Department and from the head of the Smithsonian Observatory at Harvard to view the papers. In addition, it turned out that some of the material in his files required additional approval from Mrs Menzel. I arranged to spend a couple of days at the Harvard Archives with the assistance of grants from the Fund for UFO Research and the Fair Witness Project, with the other half of the week being spent reviewing the Forrestal papers at Princeton University (which required approval from Forrestal's heirs).

Looking at the finder's guide from Harvard, I did not see any obvious place to start. There was no big listing under 'UFOs', which is hardly surprising since his UFO correspondence was at the American Philosophical Society Library. So, because I could find nothing more exciting, I started with his correspondence with John F. Kennedy. It surprised me that there was any such correspondence, but I immediately found a number of 'bombshells', as follows:

From Dr Donald Menzel to Senator John F. Kennedy, 13 August 1960:

> I am sending you a copy of a letter sent to me by Oswald Jacoby. He and I served in the Navy together, in what is now the National Security Agency. I have been associated with this activity for almost thirty years, and probably have the longest continuous record of association of any person in the country. I still keep my close association with them. Properly cleared to one another, I should be able to help in this sensitive area.

To Senator John F. Kennedy, 3 November 1960:

> . . . but there is one deeper and more complex area in which I may be of assistance. I have been associated since 1930 with a small organization that has now grown to the great National Security Agency. I served with them as a naval officer during World War II. I have been a consultant to that activity with Top Secret clearance, and have also had some association with C.I.A. Obviously, in an unclassified letter, I cannot go further into detail. But I wish to register that I have certain facts in my possession concerning certain actions by Eisenhower and his subordinates that have had a very adverse effect in these supersensitive areas. Matters were so bad that I wrote a Top Secret report, which eventually reached Eisenhower and had some beneficial effect, but the reaction was only temporary. This report can be made available to you and would serve to educate you on the shortcomings – and successes – in this area. Because of my length of service, I probably know more about what has gone on in this agency over the years than almost anyone now within it. I also know the people, many no longer associated with the agency, that can be relied on to contribute. [Copies to Prof. A. Cox, Prof. A. Chayes]

To Senator John F. Kennedy, 27 December 1960:

Dear Jack . . . May I suggest one word of caution, in strictest confidence. Many of the scientists have some concerns [regarding] the strong influence exerted by Dr Bronk in the space area. As President of the National Academy of Sciences, he is a powerful man. Somehow he manages to get on almost every committee of importance. I have served on a number of these with him and have not been impressed with his breadth of vision or his depth. He will undoubtedly urge you to put a great deal of power in his hands. I simply urge caution . . .

From an undated item (probably early 1970s) entitled 'Review by Donald H. Menzel of the History of the Loyalty Hearings (1950)':

April 13, 1950 marked the beginning of the unhappiest, most traumatic experience of my life. Although the war had been over for more than four years, I had continued as commanding officer of Communications Unit 1-1 of the U.S. Naval Reserve in Boston. I was a consultant with TOP SECRET ULTRA CLEARANCE to the National Security Agency, which had replaced the Naval Communications unit I had been associated with during the war . . .

It should be stressed that Menzel knew Kennedy because the latter was a member of the Board of Overseers at Harvard and had chosen astronomy as his particular area of interest. As I found out from Mrs Menzel, Dr Menzel was a great admirer of Jack Kennedy. In any event, a whole new side of Donald Menzel emerged, much to my surprise. The facts that he had a longer, continuous association with the National Security Agency, and its predecessor navy group than anyone else, that he had a Top Secret Ultra security clearance, that he had done work for the CIA, that Menzel had even written a letter concerning what was happening during the Eisenhower Administration to the NSA, that he was a world class expert on cryptanalysis, were all surprises. As a matter of fact, Menzel had taught cryptanalysis before the war, and after the war headed the Cambridge, Mass., Navy Communications Group Reserve Unit No. 1.

Menzel served during the war as a Navy Commander in Washington and worked with a group that was involved in many different areas of research, one of which was code-breaking, and he had learned some Japanese to help break the codes. He was also an expert on solar astronomy and worked on a number of radio wave propagation problems.

I visited Menzel's wife in the company of two Harvard people and found her very charming and co-operative. She knew nothing about his classified work, and I did not mention the subject of

UFOs. What I did discuss was a particularly intriguing event that I had never heard about elsewhere involving Menzel. As noted earlier, the worst experience of his life was a loyalty hearing, one of the bizarre McCarthy-type hearings that occurred in 1950, even though he had a Top Secret Ultra clearance with the Navy, which continued after the war. Partly because he was head of Communications Group No. 1 in Cambridge and was doing all kinds of classified consulting work for numerous companies, he had a small contract with the Air Force at Cambridge Research Labs. The work interested him and required only a Secret clearance. One day two men showed up at his door serving legal papers on him. The US Air Force had reason to believe that his clearance should be removed because of his disloyalty to the United States. Much to his credit, he fought it vigorously. There were two weeks of hearings. The charges were absurd and the people who made them failed to turn up at the hearings.

There was no record of the hearings in the *New York Times* or *Washington Post*, and my Freedom of Information requests led nowhere. Then I re-discovered an item that had been in my files from the Library of Congress Manuscript Division where Vannevar Bush's files are located. There was one letter from Menzel's attorney to Bush mentioning the loyalty hearings. This was in January 1951, thanking Bush in strong terms for his help and saying that Donald had been cleared. This established a previously unknown link between Bush and Menzel. I contacted the attorney's firm and found out that there were over a thousand pages of hearing transcripts and that they were actually in the Harvard Archives. When I dug into them, I found Bush's testimony which, interestingly, was not in the Menzel file in the Bush papers.

It was clear that there was a long and close connection between the two of them dating from 1934, that Bush was quite familiar with Menzel's wartime highly classified work, that Bush, as with everyone else who testified, strongly noted Menzel's ability to keep things secret and his great discretion with regard to classified matters. Witness after witness, including his Princeton professor, Dr Russell, testified that Menzel simply never mixed the classified and unclassified worlds.

While at Harvard, thanks to the help of Joan Thompson, I also talked to a number of people who knew Menzel. Some of them knew nothing about the loyalty hearing, and one was helpful in pointing out that when he had been visiting the Naval Research Lab., Menzel was there all the time. There was quite a dichotomy at Harvard between those who were in favour of classified research and those who were opposed – and Menzel was certainly in favour. Here again his discretion about classified matters was stressed. The following are some of Bush's comments to the Loyalty Board, on 22 May 1950:

I first knew Donald H. Menzel . . . in either 1934 or 1935 when I was engaged in designing and building a machine known as a differential analyzer at Massachusetts Institute of Technology, where I was then Vice President and Dean of Engineering. Dr Menzel, who was then an Assistant or Associate Professor in the Astronomy Department at Harvard University, was much interested in the possibility of applying the differential analyzer to the solution of certain astronomical and astrophysical problems. This mutual interest led to a technical association of some intimacy over a period of about a year. Thereafter, until I became associated with the Carnegie Institution in 1939, we met in connection with scientific or technical matters fairly frequently, usually in connection with the development of specialized machinery for astrophysical use. Subsequently, in about 1941, Dr Menzel undertook for the Office of Scientific Research and Development, of which I became Director in that year, a special study of sighting anti-aircraft guns into the sun . . .

As a Lieutenant Commander and subsequently Commander, United States Navy, assigned to Naval Communications in the Office of the Chief of Naval Operations, Dr Menzel had occasions to discuss other highly classified matters with me from time to time during the period 1943–1945 . . .

All of his responsibilities with which I am familiar in the course of his war-time services to the United States Navy and the Office of Scientific Research and Development, Dr Menzel carried out faithfully, loyally, discreetly, and with a high degree of technical and scientific competence. I was, throughout my pre-war and war-time relations with him, entirely convinced of his complete loyalty to our country, his entire trustworthiness with respect to matters of the highest classification and his discretion, care and conscientiousness in all matters involving security . . .

Since Dr Menzel's return to civilian status in the latter part of 1945, my personal relations with him have included meetings and conversations on technical subjects . . . I am acquainted with many persons who have been associated with Dr Menzel in one or more of his various activities in scholarship, in service, in administration and in his country's service . . . his reputation among these associates is that of a loyal citizen of the United States and its Armed Services, deeply interested in the national security, and discreet, careful, conscientious and trustworthy in all matters relating thereto.

Coming from Bush, the above is high praise indeed.

I also discovered that Menzel was a close associate of Dr Lloyd Berkner, another member of MJ–12, and that he obviously was well acquainted with Dr Bronk even though as of 1960 he did not much approve of Bronk's views about space and other matters. He also considered Dr Robert Oppenheimer a close friend. In addition, I noted that Menzel's travel expense book for 1947 and 1948 included numerous trips to Colorado and then down to New Mexico, the ostensible reason being the establishment of an Air Force observatory for solar research. Obviously, he could have been doing other things in New Mexico: this was on a government, not a Harvard expense account.

I have more recently obtained further information on Menzel. A MUFON member told me that he had heard that while Menzel was consulting at Engineering Research Associates (ERA – established in the Minnesota area by his former Navy associates) one summer in the late 1940s, he supposedly got a phone call and had to leave to work on something very classified which he could not discuss. I made contacts with some members of the Minnesota MUFON group and also had a call from a John Dingley, one of whose neighbours was one of the old ERA team. ERA was a forerunner of a number of computer firms and was an outstanding organization. One of the reasons for its formation was a push by the then Secretary of the Navy, James Forrestal (listed as an MJ–12 member), who did not want the code-breaking capability lost to the Navy. ERA became the most successful post-war computer company and eventually became the enormous Control Data Corporation. Howard Engstrom, Menzel's war-time boss and later first assistant director of the NSA, was one of the company's founders.

At the Hadley Library in Wilmington, Delaware, I found further surprises, including the fact that Menzel not only owned 1,000 shares of stock, but also that his consulting fee was $18,000 a year – a very high fee at that time. Obviously, his services were highly valued. There is another item with Menzel's name next to it, entitled 'Diffractive Jewellery'. I have yet to find anyone who knows what that means, but it sounds like a cover title to me, since everything at ERA was classified. Also, in talking to a number of former consultants and managers, I found someone who recalled one summer when Menzel was at ERA for a very short time and left in a hurry. I asked him what year that was. He thought for a moment. 'That was 1947, I think,' he replied.

Menzel could very well have been involved in Operation Majestic 12. He had the right clearances, the right kind of background to deal with at least two aspects of the problem posed by the recovery of a crashed alien saucer – his astronomical background and his familiarity with another symbolic language, Japanese, coupled with his ability for code breaking (since there were definitely strange symbols on the wreckage at Roswell). He had an existing high-level clearance and was well known to some of the key people like Bush, whose testimony at the loyalty hearings clearly indicated he knew what Menzel was doing during the war, even though it was unclassified testimony.

What had seemed an irrational, crazy bit of disinformation – namely the inclusion of Donald Menzel's name on a list of high-level people with high-level security clearances – now did not seem strange at all. I have not been able to prove that Menzel was a part of MJ–12, but what I have shown beyond any reasonable doubt is that he very well could have been. I checked a number of biographies of Menzel, and while a number of sources mentioned his US Navy work during the war, not one even hints at his post-war involvement at a high level with intelligence activities. This, alone, establishes his discretion.

There was quite a violent reaction in the ufological community to my suggestion that Menzel could have been a part of MJ–12, mostly from people who do not understand how security works. For example, his close friend Dr Ernest Taves, a psychiatrist who writes science fiction and co-authored Menzel's last book, while admitting that Menzel would have been called in on such a project had there been one, felt that he, as a close friend, would have been told about it when they were working on that last book in the 1970s, and that there would have been no need of security past the first several months of involvement! In the first place, people who work on highly classified matters do not even discuss them with their families. I say this having had a clearance myself for fourteen years, and having talked to dozens of old-timers, especially from World War II. Obviously, one reason for this, besides the notion that 'loose lips sink ships', is that if the enemy thinks he can get secrets from the family, he will try to do so. It should also be noted that Nobel Prize-winning scientists involved in the Manhattan Project at Los Alamos Scientific Laboratory during World War II often travelled under aliases, and their mail went to a post office box in Santa Fe.

Taves' notion that there would be no need for security after several months is absurd. Clearly, the determination of the means of propulsion for the crashed saucer was a project that might require decades or centuries, not months. In 1947, it was certainly expected that the US would have a monopoly on the A-bomb for several years. There was great concern about the Cold War, about the build-up by Stalin of his military forces and the demobilization of the USA and the fact that the Soviets managed to obtain the services of numerous German rocket and aircraft technicians. If we did not have solid information about either the propulsion system or the motivation of the aliens, how could we dare to go public?

Taves has given no indication that Menzel ever broke his security oath. Certainly, Mrs Menzel insisted that her husband never spoke about classified matters to her. It was quite satisfying to me to have one of Menzel's long-term colleagues (to whom I eventually sent a copy of my paper about Menzel and the MJ–12 papers) say that he thought Menzel would have enjoyed playing the game of knowing there was the wreckage of an alien saucer at hand and throwing out phoney explanations for case after case and getting away with it. Interestingly, he had not known that Menzel had learned Japanese nor that he was involved with cryptanalysis, the CIA and NSA.

The Cutler–Twining Memo

Determining that Donald Menzel could indeed have been part of Operation Majestic 12 – if there was one – gave me full confidence to proceed in trying to dig out the truth about the documents. One problem with the briefing document and Truman–Forrestal memo is that because they came on film, there is no paper and there is no ink. Typewriter analysts have told us that it is much better to work from an original, rather than a Xeroxed copy of a photograph taken from a blow-up from a 35-mm negative. The Cutler–Twining memo, however, is an original piece of paper. So there is paper and ink, and the type is the original size, etc.

The history of the discovery of this memo is rather unusual. I was visiting Washington, DC, in March 1985 to participate in a scientific conference. I had some spare time and checked in with the National Archives and was told that they were 'classification-reviewing' US Air Force Headquarters Intelligence files. Since it had already been determined that UFO information was normally handled by the intelligence departments of various government agencies, it seemed logical to expect that in this material, dating back to the earliest days of the Air Force, there would be some UFO-related matter. I was given the original information by Edward Reese, an experienced archivist at the National Archives, who referred me to the classification division at the Archives, headed by a Mr Thompson, and I eventually spoke with Jo Ann

Plate 1:11.   105-ft Circle near Beckhampton, Wiltshire, where a BBC TV crew recorded a peculiar 'trilling' noise and experienced interference problems. (© Timothy Good)

Plate 1:12.   Ed Walters beside the Circle at Gulf Breeze, Florida, 17 November 1989. (© Duane Cook)

Plate 1:13.   Ed and Frances Walters, whose unique series of UFO photographs taken in Gulf Breeze, Florida, can be seen in their book, The Gulf Breeze Sightings. *(© Timothy Good)*

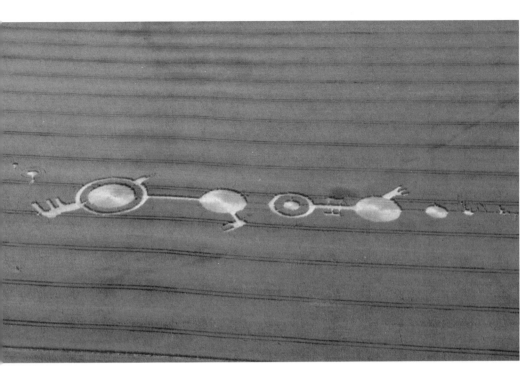

*Plate 1:14.   The extraordinary pictogram at Alton Barnes, Wiltshire, July 1990.
(© Timothy Good)*

*Plate 1:15.   Pictogram, Longwood Estate, Hampshire, June 1990. (© Timothy
Good)*

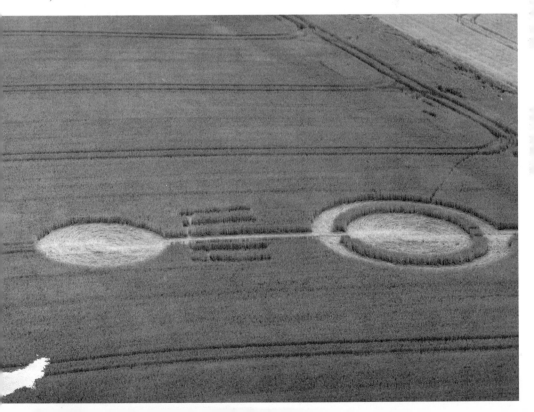

Plate 2:1. Sergeant Hubert Von Montigny, who together with another police officer twice observed a hovering, triangular object with powerful 'searchlights' which emitted a low humming sound, in the vicinity of Eupen, Belgium, on 29 November 1989. Many other witnesses reported the same object. (© Patrick Van Tuyne)

Plate 8:1. From left to right: Manuel Mercado, Wilson Sosa and Edgardo Plaza, who witnessed the Puerto Rico UFO/jet aircraft abduction on 28 December 1988. (© Enigma!)

Plate 8:2. Yesenia Velázquez, (of San Germán, Puerto Rico) one of the witnesses to the UFO/jet fighters incident on 16 November 1988. (© Enigma!)

Plate 9:1. Nounan, Idaho, 9 October 1989. Upper and lower jaw hide removed from cow. (© Bear Lake County Sheriff's Office)

Plate 9:2. Nounan, Idaho, 9 October 1989. Four teats cleanly removed from udder. (© Bear Lake County Sheriff's Office)

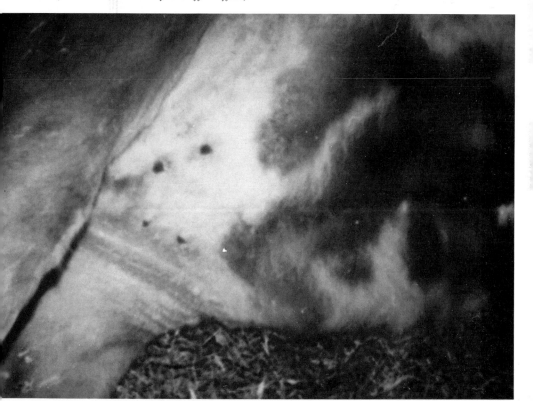

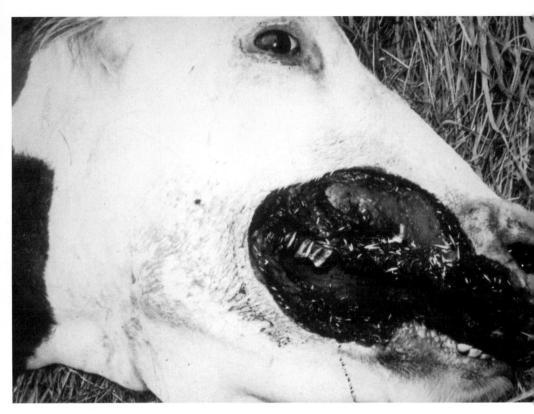

Plate 9:3. Maple Valley, Washington, 17 July 1989. Head of six-year-old cow showing oval excision of mouth tissue, jaw, teeth and tongue. (© William Veenhuizen)

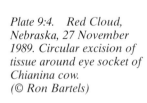

Plate 9:4. Red Cloud, Nebraska, 27 November 1989. Circular excision of tissue around eye socket of Chianina cow. (© Ron Bartels)

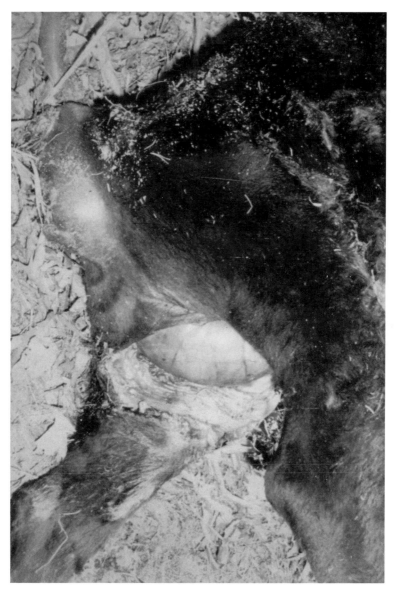

Plate 9:5.   Hope, Arkansas, 10 March 1989. Close-up of cow's bloodless cut belly, showing 18 × 18 ins excision on one of five pregnant cows found dead and mutilated. (© Jim Williamson)

*Plate 10:1.   Enlargement of photograph taken by Peter Woolaway at Bartley Green
Reservoir, Birmingham, 27 February 1990. Mr Woolaway has co-operated with the
Editor and Quest International in an endeavour to authenticate the photograph. See
also p238. (© Peter Woolaway)*

Williamson who now is Mr Reese's boss. Jo Ann told me that the reviewing should be finished in about a month or so.

I checked back with her at the end of the month and found that it was going to take more time. There were a number of phone calls, and a number of months passed. Finally, it was determined that this particular collection of papers (Entry 267), from Air Force Record Group 341, had indeed been completely reviewed. It should be stressed that reviewing does not mean total declassification. It means every document is examined by people with an appropriate clearance and need-to-know, who follow guidelines laid down by the originating agencies, and then decide what can be released at a particular time, versus what must remain classified. There is some grey area here where a document can be declassified with small deletions (e.g. names) where these are only a small part of the document. So it is a painstaking procedure, and, especially with intelligence files, one deals with a wide variety of subject matter.

I finally determined at the end of June that Entry 267 had been reviewed. I notified Bill Moore and Jaime Shandera, who meanwhile had received postcards with provocative riddles on them. One mentioned 'Reese's Pieces', a type of candy. It mentioned 'Suitland', which I had also visited in March and is a repository for government files and a kind of annexe of the National Archives itself. There were a number of things in the message that pointed toward it being a good idea for somebody to go to Washington. It should be stressed that the postcards were rather peculiar, with an off-beat sense of humour. One had an address, 'Box 189, Addis Ababa, Ethiopia', and was apparently mailed from New Zealand. This does not mean that somebody actually travelled to either Ethiopia or New Zealand. Obviously, a postcard can be put in a letter which is sent to somebody who is told to drop it in a mailbox. 'Box 189', as it turned out, was significant.

In early July 1985, Bill Moore and Jaime Shandera flew to Washington and started going through the boxes of Entry 267 that had just been reviewed. Much of this material was still classified but they found about seventy-five pages in the first 120 boxes that looked worth copying. The procedure is to make a list of the pages for copying, to put in a special sheet marking the place, and eventually the Archives mails the copies (at a price of 35c a page). It should be stressed that original documents cannot be removed from the Archives, nor can they be damaged or destroyed. They do not get borrowed. In one of the boxes Shandera discovered a piece

of paper between file folders which turned out to be the Cutler–
Twining memo.

The message, from Robert Cutler, Special Assistant to the
President, is straightforward: it refers to an NSC/MJ–12 Special
Studies Project briefing. If genuine, it would suggest that there was
indeed an MJ–12. But it does not say what MJ–12 dealt with. The
paper is old, there is a watermark, and it is clearly a carbon with
blue ink. There is a slanted red pencil mark through the security
marking in the upper right-hand corner. The memo is clearly a
simple administrative matter that a briefing will take place *during*
an already scheduled meeting, rather than after it, as originally
scheduled. Moore telephoned that evening and read it to me,
describing the circumstances of its discovery. Obviously, it had no
relation to anything else in the box. Believe it or not, it was found
in Box 189 – the same as on the postcard! This gave much greater
confidence (even though in retrospect) that this was what they
were looking for.

The memo has caused a great deal of controversy, partly from
the manner of its discovery, partly from the fact that many people
have no idea how archives operate, partly from people misrep-
resenting what it says or smearing it at all costs, and partly because
Moore and Shandera have chosen to withhold the postcards,
although at least two researchers have seen them. The obvious
checks that could be done with the memo have been done. There is
a watermark and the name of the company that manufactured the
paper. Photographing it gives one the opportunity to get a permanent record of both the colour of the paper, the memo, and the
watermark. Moore contacted Fox Paper and talked to their watermark expert, who determined that this onion-skin paper was made
only in bid lots and only between 1953 and the early 1970s. The
government bought a great deal of the paper, but the bid lots
limitation meant that it would not show up in all kinds of stores. So
at least this did not rule the paper out. Obviously, if the paper had
been manufactured in 1983 it could not have been a carbon copy of
something typed in 1954. There is also aging around the edge of the
paper. There is no signature, nor even a '/s/' next to the name on
the memo.

One objection to the memo is that Moore and Shandera planted
it in the box and then 'discovered' it. While there is a remote
possibility that they could have brought such a piece into the
Archives, certainly they could not have planted it in a box in its
own home grounds because that is totally inaccessible to them. The

boxes at the National Archives are stored in vaults, and only approved people can go into those vaults. It must also be stressed that the authorities are very careful about allowing one to bring in materials, and even more careful about what one takes out, since briefcases, etc., are checked.

The Cutler–Twining memo language, in its last sentence, reminded me immediately of the memo we had found in late 1981 in the papers of General Twining at the Library of Congress Manuscript Division. The only reason we found it was that it was in a folder labelled 'Eyes Only' – which should be the most classified material. The materials in the box had been declassified. There were two memos that dealt with Project Solarium, both from Cutler; one to the Secretary of Defense and then apparently to General Twining (as Chief of Staff of the Air Force). The other went directly to Twining. The 1954 memo contained language similar to that of the last sentence of the Cutler–Twining memo dealing with the 13 July 1953 memo from Cutler. The memorandum to General Twining includes this language in a 'Top Secret Eyes Only' document:

> . . . In order to avoid communication on this subject, it is understood that in the absence of contrary word your concurrence in the above arrangements is assumed.

The last sentence in the 14 July 1954 Cutler–Twining memo reads:

> . . . Your concurrence in the above change of arrangements is assumed.

Another clear-cut comparison is that the 13 July 1953 memo, even though 'Top Secret Eyes Only', gives no clue as to what the subject is of the extraordinary meeting of the National Security Council that was to be held from 9.00 a.m. to 6.00 p.m. at the White House. It is evident that it was a highly secret meeting since the statement is made that 'it is necessary to take special security precautions and to maintain absolute secrecy regarding participation in as well as the substance of the meeting . . .' There is not the slightest hint as to what the NSC/MJ–12 Special Studies Project is, as referred to in the 1954 memo. I have seen many formerly highly classified memos (now declassified) that have no clue as to the subject, and have determined that it is standard government practice. So long as the recipient knows what is being discussed, then secretaries and others need not be made aware of what is being discussed, even though they have appropriate clearances.

Absence of Signature

A peculiar aspect of the Cutler–Twining memo is the absence of a signature or the '/s/'. The 13 July 1953 memo does have a signature, and a Top Secret memo of 25 June 1953, for the Secretary of Defense, which is clearly referring to the same extraordinary all-day meeting on 16 July 1953, mentions Project Solarium (again, without the slightest clue as to what this dealt with). In this case there is the '/s/' next to the name. Clearly this was a copy of a memo, not an original, and it was to the Secretary of Defense even though we found it in the General Twining files. There was obviously a slight mistake here. The Top Secret Eyes Only memo is more highly classified than a Top Secret memo, yet the Top Secret one mentions Project Solarium and the Top Secret Eyes Only memo, eighteen days later, does not mention Solarium by name. (It turns out that Project Solarium was extraordinarily important in determining the foreign policy of the entire Eisenhower administration. Three different task forces were established, each looking at different means of containment of the Soviet Union, and each involving very important inside people.)

The fact of the matter is that the absence of a signature on the Cutler–Twining memo is highly significant. Researcher Robert Todd, who has written well over a thousand Freedom of Information requests over the years, wrote for more information about Cutler's activities, and from the Eisenhower Library learned that Cutler was out of the country on the date of the memo! Thus, if there had been a signature or even a '/s/' to indicate that he had signed the original, there would be a real problem, since Cutler could not possibly have been in Europe and Washington at the same time.

The absence of the signature, however, suggests another possibility, because Todd also turned up a memo from Cutler to James Lay, the executive secretary of the National Security Council, to keep things moving out of his basket. Lay and Cutler worked very closely together, and sat next to each other at the weekly meetings of the NSC, handled paperwork together, and seemed each to get copies of the other's memos. My suggestion, since there were specific instructions to keep things moving out of Cutler's basket, was that Lay sent the memo to Twining in Cutler's name. I also was able to determine that Lay had met with President Eisenhower at 2.30 p.m. on 14 July 1954, the date of the Cutler–Twining memo, and that, according to the phone logs, there was a brief phone conversation between Eisenhower and James Lay at about 4.35 p.m.

It should be further stressed that there was regular courier service between the White House and the Pentagon, not far away. For classified matters there was a regular flow of information back and forth. My own hypothesis is that Ike asked Lay to notify Twining that there was a slight change in plans which would influence Twining's schedule, since a briefing was to take place *during* an already scheduled meeting, rather than after it as originally planned.

Typeface

The question of the type on the Cutler–Twining memo is also interesting. Dr Bruce Maccabee and Robert Swiatek of the Fund for UFO Research spent some time going through the relatively small amount of declassified National Security Council material from the Eisenhower era that is available at the National Archives. They were able to determine that three different typewriters were in use there, and probably more. But even from that small sample of material there were two different larger pica type styles, as well as an élite type. The question of the type style was brought to a head by the well-known debunker Philip J. Klass, former senior avionics editor of *Aviation Week & Space Technology*, and now a head of the UFO sub-committee of the Committee for the Scientific Investigation of Claims of the Paranormal (CSICOP). At the beginning of 1989, Klass finally realized that the Cutler–Twining memo was done in large pica type and wrote to me as follows:

> I challenge you to produce known-to-be-authentic White House/business letters/memoranda written by Cutler or Lay during the 1953–55 time period which used a typeface identical in size and style to that used in the *alleged* Cutler/Twining memo of July 14, 1954. To provide motivation for your prompt response . . . I herewith offer to pay you $100 for each such letter you provide in the next sixty days, with an upward limit of $1,000 if you can supply ten different letters that meet the above conditions.

I was able to supply more than ten such examples and Klass sent me a cheque for $1,000! He was obviously convinced that the samples I provided were done in the same size and type style as the Cutler–Twining memo. The strange thing is that Klass had provided me with just nine examples of élite type in his attempt to prove me wrong. He was presumably unaware that at the

Eisenhower Library alone there are about 250,000 pages of NSC material!

It certainly appears that the one original MJ–12 document that we have passes muster with regard to the paper being manufactured in the right time frame, the language being appropriate, and the type style. Obviously, that does not prove the document *is* genuine. Somebody could have obtained an old typewriter as well as old paper, and somebody from the government could have been aware of Cutler's propensity for uses of certain phrases and could have typed the document recently, or as a cover document way back then. Furthermore, it certainly is possible that there was indeed an NSC/MJ–12 Special Studies Project but that it had nothing whatsoever to do with the recovery of a crashed flying saucer.

Further Objections

Another objection to the Cutler–Twining memo is that neither Ike's nor Twining's calendar for 16 July 1954, the date on which this briefing was to take place, says anything about an MJ–12 briefing. For some reason, others have also assumed that this was an NSC meeting or that the briefing would take place at a meeting of the NSC. Clearly, that is not the case. It was an 'already scheduled meeting': it does not say that it is an NSC meeting. Furthermore, it is not even clear that Ike would be present at the meeting. Does the absence of a mention in Twining's schedule establish that there was no such meeting? Of course not. It establishes that there was nothing listed. The schedules for Twining were unclassified. I have a record of Twining attending a meeting at the White House, ducking out to meet with Eisenhower for perhaps twenty minutes, then going back to his originally scheduled meeting.

Also, we know that there are often several versions of important officials' calendars. For example, I discovered at the Truman Library that there was a pre- and post-August 1, 1950, listing for President Truman. That date is significant in terms of the Operation Majestic 12 briefing document, but what was interesting was that when I asked for the calendar for that date I was given the pre-listing. When I actually visited the library, I discovered the post-listing, which includes five meetings between Truman and others that were not on the original sheet! The two were done in different type styles and different formats. Any conclusion based on one might have been invalidated by what was found on the other.

It is important to realize that both Eisenhower and Twining were in town on 16 July, that the time to get from the Pentagon to the White House is very short, and that Eisenhower's docket included a meeting of his cabinet from 9.30 a.m. to noon. Furthermore, Ike was often known *not* to be there all the time for those cabinet meetings. As a matter of fact, many people at such meetings were present only for portions of the meeting that directly concerned them – especially with regard to highly classified matters requiring a special clearance. In addition, Twining had a meeting of the Joint Chiefs of Staff from 11.00 a.m. to 11.55 a.m. and from 2.00 p.m. to 4.15 p.m. We do not have a record of what went on at that meeting, although we know who was supposed to be present, but it would have taken place in a vault at the Pentagon. Twining could have started the meeting, gone away, and come back later. We simply do not know. Contrary to what Klass has claimed, we cannot say that there was no such meeting because none is listed on Twining's calendar.

It should be also emphasized that Eisenhower was famous for putting as little down on paper as possible, was very much concerned about security, and often committed a lot of information to memory.

Another comment that must be made is that it is very difficult to accept the notion that the sentence about 'concurrence' was seen in a very obscure memo, which would mean that a forger was aware of both the security markings on that memo and the signature on the other Top Secret memo in the same box, as well as the '/s/', and could conjure up rubber stamps for the Truman memo, but would not worry about using the unusual typed marking, 'Top Secret Restricted Security Information'.

It was claimed by the National Security Council to the National Archives that this latter security classification was not used until the Nixon administration, which began in 1969. One must question this statement on several grounds. There were, for example, a number of 1953 documents that I looked at that were stamped 'Restricted Security Information'. There was one that had an additional 'Secret' on it; another one had 'Confidential Restricted Security Information'. Normally, when there is 'Confidential' and 'Secret' prior to a subsequent designator such as 'Restricted Data' (which is used for nuclear information), there will also at some point be 'Top Secret Restricted Security Information'. In addition, in going through the files, I noted that there were occasional security markings that I would only see once, such as 'Top Secret

Control' and 'Cosmic' (the latter being a NATO security marking).

Some idea of the difficulty in gaining access to official files can be gleaned from an April 1990 experience I had at the National Archives with regard to Record Group 341, the 'mother lode' in which the Cutler–Twining memo was found. The only listing is a *Preliminary Inventory of the Records of Headquarters United States Air Force*, compiled in 1963. It is 56 pages long and lists a total of 512 entries. The total volume of the records is 9,787 cubic feet, covering the period 1939–55. The size of the individual entries ranges from 1 inch to 1,743 feet! Unfortunately, there are no finder's aids for any of the entries and most have not been classification reviewed. Entry 23, for example, includes 51 feet of Top Secret incoming and outgoing messages.

One last-minute benefit of all the delays in my research was that finally, on 6 March 1990, I received the first response to my Mandatory Classification Review requests of February 1988. One document was acted upon: a message from James Lay to Robert Cutler dated – of all dates – 16 July 1954 (which of course is the reason I requested it). This was transmitted electronically by General Paul Carroll, White House Secretary, to Cutler in Europe, and is a brief review of the activities at the 15 July 1954 NSC meeting, as originally instructed by Cutler to Lay in his memo, which had also instructed Lay and J. Patrick Coyne to keep things moving out of his basket.

The last two lines are of particular interest for those who claim forgery, because they could find nothing else handled by Lay for Cutler: 'Hope you will recuperate, rest and enjoy yourself for a few days before returning. Will try to have everything tidy and not too much pressure upon you when you return.' According to the Eisenhower Library in response to my request, the message was a blue carbon on onion skin without a watermark, and there is no heading on the stationery. As with the Cutler–Twining memo, it reproduces poorly because of the blue ink and onion skin. Clearly, Lay was handling things for Cutler.

The Truman–Forrestal Memorandum

Regarding authenticity of this memo, which is dated 24 September 1947, I quote from a letter to me from the Harry S. Truman Library (23 June 1987). While declining to comment on the 'authenticity or handwriting', owing to regulations, they nevertheless confirmed the following:

> . . . President Truman's appointment records indicate that his only meeting with Dr Vannevar Bush between May and December 31, 1947, was on September 24, 1947. Dr Bush was accompanied at that meeting by Secretary of Defense James Forrestal. There is no indication in the files as to what was discussed at the meeting.

In addition, I was able to discover from both Bush's and Forrestal's files that Bush and Forrestal met for half-an-hour prior to their meeting with Truman, and left the White House together. There are unclassified notes in their files about the meeting. They were observed by reporters as they left the White House, so presumably there had to be some kind of cover story. One of the things that apparently took place at the meeting was Bush's acceptance of the appointment by Truman to be head of the newly formed Joint Research and Development Board (JRDB). It certainly is conceivable that the two men prepared a memo for Truman's signature. In any event, the date is unique. No other date for that eight-month time period would have the same significance, since that was the only day when Bush met with Truman at the White House, and Forrestal was there.

It should be stressed that Forrestal and Bush met quite often, sometimes more than once a week during 1947–48. So their meeting was not unique. They even played tennis together on occasions, and judging by their correspondence, it is perfectly clear that they knew and trusted each other very well. It is certainly true, however, that Bush, years later, mentioned that in a sense Forrestal (who had been Secretary of the Navy) was the wrong man for the job as Secretary of Defense because he was not really a believer in service unification.

The Signature Problem

One of the most serious charges made by Klass is that the signature on the Truman–Forrestal (TF) memo is *identical* to that on a brief letter from Truman to Bush (TB) on 1 October 1947 (Figure 7:6). The reasoning here is that no two signatures are identical, since if they are, one is a forgery of the other. In some of his writings, Klass admits that the TF signature is 3.2 per cent longer (hardly identical) than that on the TB memo, but explains it away on the basis that it would have taken three xeroxings to get the fake done. In one article,[8] Klass shows part of each memo,

(A)

Sincerely yours,

(B)

Figure 7:6 (A and B). Enlargements of both signatures.

even including the measurements of the lengths of different portions of the signature, as done by Bill Moore, but only for the Truman–Forrestal memo. He does not show the ones for Truman–Bush nor the top portions of either, which include the letterhead markings of the White House, Washington, and he also does not include the date on the TF memo.

If Klass had included the measurements on the TB memo and ratios of the lengths on the TF memo in comparison with those on the TB signatures, it would be evident that he had apparently misrepresented the facts, for the following reasons:

(1) The ratio of the lengths of the 'Harry' portions is only 1.012, while it is 1.032–1.04 for the 'Truman' portions and, most important, exactly 1.000 for the letterhead portions.

(2) Clearly, Xerox stretching has to be by the *same* ratio on all parts of a sheet of paper.

(3) Klass provides no comparisons or even a claim that a comparison had been made between other pairs of Truman signatures. Clearly, Truman would have signed a great many letters, memos, etc. If there are other pairs equally similar, then the similarity between the TF and TB signatures means nothing.

(4) Klass makes a big issue about the slip of Truman's fountain pen to create a little extra line at the upper right portion of the 'H' on both signatures, though of different thicknesses. He fails to point out that there are at least three other signatures in our possession showing the same kind of extra mark.

(5) Klass also claims that a forensics expert (a former CIA man at that) says the type is that of a Smith Corona typewriter not available until the mid-1960s. Not all examiners are agreed on this, however. There seems to be no doubt, however, that the typewriter used for the '24, 47.' portion of the date does pre-date 1947. Surely, if a forger had such an old typewriter, *why would he use it only for that portion of the date instead of for the whole memo?* This makes no sense at all.

Klass refers to the book, *Questioned Documents*, by Albert S. Osborn, from which he extracts this sentence:

> ... The fact that two signatures are very nearly alike is not alone necessarily an indication of forgery of one or both, but the question is whether they are *suspiciously alike*.

Klass fails to mention that the 1,000-page law book was actually written in 1910, with a second edition in 1929. The chapter from which the extract is quoted is titled 'Traced Forgeries'. The third sentence after the quoted one is, 'It should be understood that *suspicious identity* is that which suggests the tracing process and which is not inconsistent with the theory of tracing.' Tracing of signatures was, of course, a major legal problem before copying machines became common.

Klass also maintains that 'A person's hand-written signature is like a snowflake – no two are identical.' This sounds like a profound truth, until we learn what Osborn himself stated in the third sentence prior to the one quoted by Klass: '*In some cases such [identical] signatures can be found.*'

Let us assume for a moment that there was indeed an MJ–12 established by President Truman in September 1947, as described in the TF memo. Signatures might well have been signed on the original to Forrestal and possibly (though certainly not necessarily) on Bush's copy and a CIA copy. There might not have been a date either, since the exact date might not be set until later, depending on when certain things got done or a meeting would be arranged. If we take the memo at face value, then the date would seem to have been typed on at Bush's office because of the full-stop after the date, which was indeed typical of Bush's secretary. When it came time to put together the briefing for Ike in November 1952, there might well have been a serious problem. What happened to Forrestal's original? His sanity was rapidly slipping in the spring of 1949, shortly before he apparently jumped out of an eighteenth-story window at Bethesda Naval Medical Center. The FBI and Admiral Souers were certainly concerned about him, as was his friend (later Secretary of Defense) Robert Lovett. Bush was still around. His files would have had a copy and the signed letter from Truman of 1 October 1947. Truman himself might have added the signature, or perhaps Walter Bedell Smith (CIA director) had the file copy from Hillenkoetter's files and knew that Ike would want to see a signed copy or original. After all, we do have the following facts:

(1) We have some NSC memos from Lay where the date is done with one size type and the text with another. This certainly implies that the memos were put in two different typewriters. There is no reason to doubt the legitimacy of these memos.

(2) We have many examples of letters and memos from Bush's office with the full-stop after the date.

(3) We know that Smith had arranged four briefings for Ike after the election.

(4) We know that there were other classified briefings prepared 'for the President-Elect' on 18 November 1952.

(5) We know that both Bush and Truman and certainly Forrestal had been involved in matters so classified that there was a minimum of written record.

(6) We know, because of the serial numbers on the film of the Eisenhower briefing document, that the pictures were not taken until the 1983–84 time frame. So what was in the file might have been there for thirty-six or -seven years, or might have been replaced along the way with a slightly more official version.

(7) We do not know the whereabouts of Bush's highly classified files.

Further Discoveries

The Eisenhower briefing document refers to the date when Forrestal died, 22 May 1949, which is indeed correct. The next date given is much less well known – 1 August 1950, 'upon which date General Walter B. Smith was designated as permanent replacement' for Forrestal. It was difficult to imagine what was special about this date on initial perusal. But as I dug much more deeply into the role of Walter Bedell Smith, I found that this date is also special, and that to the best of my knowledge nobody else was previously aware of the fact. I checked appointments for Truman for that date and then asked for all the dates on which Smith met with Truman, since it would not be enough to establish that the two had met that day if they met once a week for many months before that, or many months afterwards. Then we could be reasonably certain, for example, that the two of them met every Thursday, so the date would not have any great significance. What I discovered was quite intriguing.

First of all, whereas Hillenkoetter, also an MJ–12 member and Smith's predecessor at the CIA, did not meet very often with Truman, Smith did, once he was fully installed as head of the CIA at the end of 1950. But 1 August 1950 was the *only* day prior to November (of 1950) when Smith met with Truman! It was a brief meeting, scheduled for less than fifteen minutes at the West Door of the White House. No subject was given and it was off the record. One person informed me that this is an area where they were not likely to have been seen. And there was certainly no press coverage of that meeting. It is interesting that later that same day, Truman met with another alleged member of MJ–12, Gordon Gray. That meeting is not on the advance calendar for that date. The location of the Smith meeting is the only location given for a meeting in the entire day's calendar. This does raise a question, of course. How did whoever wrote the document know that that meeting date would be of significance?

My hypothesis is that Truman had already decided that Walter Bedell Smith would replace Hillenkoetter. He certainly had full trust in Smith since Smith had been US Ambassador to Moscow from 1946–49, and had been Ike's chief of staff during World War II. Once Truman had decided that Smith would be the next Director of Central Intelligence (DCI) he probably also decided that Smith would now become a permanent member of MJ–12. It is interesting that the first three DCIs, namely Souers, Vandenberg, and Hillenkoetter, were also listed on the MJ–12 roster, so the choice of Smith would have been appropriate. In any event, although we have no specific record of what happened at that meeting, we do know that there was such a meeting and that the date was unique for a ten-month period. It would seem an incredible coincidence that a forger could pull such a date out of the air – especially an outsider. Also, the Truman Library archivist indicated that nobody else had asked him that question about dates of meetings between Smith and Truman.

Other Dates

Following a reference to the well-known sighting by a civilian pilot (Kenneth Arnold) on 24 June 1947, the next date referred to in the document is 7 July 1947, when, it states, 'a secret operation was begun to assure recovery' of the wreckage from the crash that had occurred 'approximately seventy-five miles north-west of Roswell Army Air Base'. Anybody studying the Roswell story would recognize that as the date when Major Jesse Marcel and Sheridan Cavitt (a Counter Intelligence Corps officer) went out to the Brazel ranch to bring back the first load of wreckage from the crash site. It is an obscure date, but certainly not one that would indicate inside information.

The next date mentioned, 19 September 1947, was supposedly when a preliminary consensus was released on the covert effort organized by General Twining and Bush, acting on the orders of the President. Here, again, we do not have a copy of that consensus, which apparently was Attachment D. According to the flight logs of both Twining and his pilot, they flew from Wright Field to Bolling AFB (DC) on 18 September, and returned the following day. Twining and Bush could easily have met in DC on that date. Twining's pilot, who became his aide and served him until 1957, said he often saw Bush and Twining together. It is interesting that the Twining memo to General Schulgen is dated 23 September 1947. It was only Secret, not Top Secret, but it certainly would indicate that there was a consensus reached about the legitimacy of flying saucers, and to gain further information thereon.

Supposedly, 30 November 1947 was the date of a report on the four alien bodies by Dr Bronk. I have been unable to find anything to establish this as a significant date. The next date mentioned, 6 December 1950, is allegedly when a second object impacted near the Texas–Mexico border. We do have considerable indication that *something* happened on that date with regard to UFOs. The FBI went on a red alert and there is mention in several books of great concern at the White House, and there were even newspaper reports about radar supposedly having picked up strange vehicles, an alert, and then the 'attack force' turning out to be a flock of geese, or other supposedly explainable objects.

The other dates given in the memo are the dates of Attachment E (30 June 1952), Attachment F (31 January 1948), and Attachment G (31 January 1949). Unfortunately, we have no way of verifying these since we have no other MJ–12 documents with which to establish their validity.

175

Format and Style Problems

Because the sceptics have been unable to come up with items of substance in their dealings with the MJ–12 affair, there has been a strong attack on various peculiar aspects of format and style. One constant objection is that the date format used in the Eisenhower briefing paper is wrong; that there is a consistent pattern of day-month-comma-year, rather than month-day-comma-year. In addition, there is a constant use of an '0' in front of a '1' digit date, e.g. '01 August, 1950'. This and the fact that William Moore sometimes uses a similar date format in his letters, and did in some of his letters to Philip Klass, led Klass to conclude that such a date format did not come into use until the computer era, and that the document was therefore fraudulent. He strongly implies that Moore was the forger. When Klass makes this argument, he never mentions the fact that he has letters from Bill Moore that do not use this date format.

Furthermore, Klass does not mention that many examples of a similar date format have turned up in a wide variety of places. For example, this had been apparently standard in NATO for many years, including the 1952 period. [*Editor's note*: Admiral of the Fleet, Lord Hill-Norton, the former Chief of the Defence Staff who wrote the foreword to *Above Top Secret*, told me that 'NATO documents always used the "0" in front of single date figures in my day', and this was additionally confirmed for me by another ex-Navy source.] I picked out a few examples from Timothy Good's book, from some of the older documents I went through, and from a number of Canadian documents, and found a whole host of different date formats. One has to remember that the briefing paper was done – if it is genuine – for a military man by a military man. Admiral Hillenkoetter had served in NATO and may have picked up the habit of using the '0' digit. Unfortunately, however, we have so far been unable to locate any known-to-be-authentic examples of Hillenkoetter's letters or memos where a similar date format is used.

One thing that becomes clear if one spends sufficient time in archives going through papers of a particular individual is that from the same office one can find many different date formats (including the day-month-comma-year format), many different letter formats, and many different style formats.

If Hillenkoetter did actually prepare the briefing document, where was it typed? Clearly, if genuine, this was at a very high security level. This led me to wonder whether or not Hillenkoetter would have been able to get it typed at the headquarters of the Third Naval District. Who, there, would have had a need-to-know for MJ–12 information if, as indicated in the document, this was considered to be something that was accountable only to the President? The obvious thought is that since Hillenkoetter was head of the CIA, 1947–50, while he was a member of MJ–12, he should have been able to have had it typed by somebody with a need-to-know within the CIA.

In 1952 that would have to mean that he would have been in touch with General Walter Bedell Smith, his successor at the CIA. But according to the briefing, Smith also became a member of MJ–12, replacing Forrestal and therefore in addition to Hillenkoetter. There should have been no problem in Hillenkoetter going to Smith and perhaps asking his advice about format for the briefing, what style Eisenhower liked, and so on, especially since Smith had worked closely with Ike during World War II and was also a general. Furthermore, in Ike's own book, *Mandate for Change*, he notes that at Truman's instruction, he was briefed on national security and defence matters by none other than Walter B. Smith.

Another objection to the documents, relating to the security markings, is that on the Cutler–Twining memo they are not rubber stamped, but merely typed and only in the upper right-hand portion of the memo. Some people have taken this to mean they are phoney, but if one goes through the NSC files one finds over and over again that there are variations on the normal. Sometimes the security markings are typed, sometimes stamped, or a mixture of both. Sometimes they are top and bottom, or only top, sometimes in the upper and lower right-hand corner, sometimes in the centre.

I must stress that the documents (if genuine) were prepared by people who never expected that they would serve any other purpose than to provide information to the recipients. They were highly classified with very limited distribution, with certainly no Freedom of Information Act in existence or even contemplated at that time. Format was of much less concern than today. For example, there are three different 1956 memos within a month from Allen Dulles (a former head of the CIA) to General Good-paster, who was Ike's aide. One can see that they are from different typewriters, and there are many differences between the

177

memos even though conveying basically the same type of information.

If one looks at the original of the Cutler–Twining memo, one is struck not only by the fact that it is in blue ink, apparently from carbon paper, but also that there is a short red pencil mark drawn on a slant through the security marking. Of course, on a Xerox copy it is hard to tell that it is pencil, and it is impossible to tell that it's red. During a visit to the Eisenhower Library I noted in a file consisting mostly of original documents that in a number of cases I found slant red pencil marks through the security markings. The archivist confirmed that this was standard practice when declassifying documents. This certainly suggests that the Cutler–Twining memo was found in a legitimate file. Whoever planted it at the National Archives was apparently well aware of this rule. It would have been a perfectly natural thing for somebody who is accustomed to dealing with such matters to do, such as the members of the many four-man teams of declassifiers.

Klass and others have also tried to point to spellings of various words as proving that somehow the document was forged. One example he cites is the spelling of 'Materiel' in Air Matériel Command, which should be 'Material', he insisted. As it happens, the correct spelling is indeed Mater*iel*.

Yet another concern about format and style is the use of the term 'Special Classified Executive Order #092447'. People have checked a whole host of available executive orders, including those proclaiming various special days, and find that this number does not fit in that numbering order at all. Of course, the number is the *date* of the alleged executive order, which seems peculiar. The problem here is that if the briefing document is genuine and was done for 18 November 1952, then that could be the first use of the term 'Executive Order'. If the Truman–Forrestal memo is genuine – or at least its contents are genuine – then it is possible that when the memo was put out, it was not thought of as an executive order in the official sense. They had no idea of the scope of the activity, how long it would continue, how soon there would be a confrontation, if any, with aliens, or with the public with evidence. It appears to be the kind of thing that was done to provide Forrestal with an authorization, should one be necessary for use of government funds, people, etc., for the effort.

It should be noted that they would have to call it something, that it might well be that one administration, in passing the power on to another of a different party and different people, would try and justify things on a rather formal basis. Ike, after all, had been a military commander, was accustomed to dealing with orders of one kind or another, and they might have wanted to provide him with some kind of formal authorization.

A peculiarity about the Truman–Forrestal memo (from a style and format viewpoint) is that it is clear when examined on the original print that the date 'September 24, 1947.' has three aspects which are disturbing. Firstly, the '24, 1947.' has a slightly different line location than the word September. That is, if one draws a line under September it will come well below the day and year. The memo had to be in the typewriter at least twice. Secondly, it is a different type. If one compares the comma in the text, a different typewriter was used to type the '24, 1947.', implying that the date might have been added later or added somewhere else.

The 'somewhere else' is suggested by the period [full-stop] after the date. While there are occasional items from Truman's office with the period after the date, the great majority do not have such a period. One office which almost invariably used the period after the date was that of Dr Vannevar Bush. Almost invariably, his secretaries put a period after the date and a period after the typed-in closing name: Vannevar Bush. A third peculiarity is the very existence of a signature on the memo. If some kind of executive order (or whatever one wants to call it) was sent to Forrestal, then his original should have had Truman's signature, but the copy at the White House would not! It might have had a rubber-stamped original 'signed by Harry Truman' on it.

Then, as discussed earlier, is the signature genuine? And if it was not on the original, where did this copy come from and why is there a signature on it at all? This presents a real puzzle. There are several possibilities: one, that the memo was prepared and signed by Truman and kept by Forrestal, with copies perhaps made for Bush and for the head of the CIA, Admiral Hillenkoetter, since both are mentioned in the memo. Both were well known for their discretion. Forrestal remained in office until March 1949, then resigned, was soon hospitalized and committed suicide in May that year. There is a real question as to what happened to his files. Would he have had a copy of this in it and were those files simply turned over to his successor, Lewis Johnson? We simply do not know. We do know that Forrestal was mentally disturbed for months before his suicide. There was even an active investigation because he made requests of the FBI to check out that people were 'spying' on him, and that he was exhibiting signs of paranoia. One possibility is that Hillenkoetter or Walter B. Smith decided that there was a need to have a copy of the authorization with a signature. Smith would almost certainly have been consulted with regard to any highly classified briefing for President-Elect Eisenhower, as already noted.

Truman's signature is similar but not absolutely identical to that on a memo from Truman to Bush, dated 1 October 1947, as I have commented on earlier. To some, this proves that the whole thing is a fraud, especially when coupled with the false allegation that the typeface on the memo is that of a Smith Corona typewriter which did not come into use until the 1960s. However, closer examination indicates that both typewriters are of the proper vintage, as will be reported by William Moore in his report on the MJ–12 documents (see *Editor's Note*). One way to fake such a document, obviously, is to get a piece of White House stationery, Xerox the letterhead, type on it, and then Xerox the signature on to it as well. These are certainly possibilities, but surely, if a forger had access to one pre-1947 typewriter, he would have used it for the entire memo.

Overall Approach to Validation of Documents

Ideally, one should be able to take a document that is questionable to a professional document examiner who would test the paper, test the ink, compare the signature with other signatures by the same person, compare the typefaces with those from typewriters known to have been used in that person's office, and a decision could be reached on those bases alone, for indicating that the document was a fraud. However, if everything is proper, does that establish the document as genuine? The answer is 'No', because presumably a clever forger or government disinformation specialist would have access to all the appropriate ink, paper, typewriters, etc. Particularly with regard to the briefing document, which is on film, one is denied the possibility of evaluating the ink or paper, or evaluating *accurately* the typefaces. In addition, there is the serious possibility that some of the information is correct and some of it is disinformation.

There could have been an MJ–12. The first two pages say nothing about what MJ–12 is. It is the third, fourth, and fifth pages that give the contents. Almost certainly there was a recovery of a crashed flying saucer, but an entirely different group could have been established. Thus, the procedure has to be to dig as deep as possible to find things that are false in the document. Ideally, we need the other documents that relate to the same project and give the same information. For example, it would be very useful to have Attachments B to H, which would clearly, if genuine, include details of the alien bodies, details of the materials and structures, names of investigators, etc. It would also be ideal if we could find other documents that dealt with MJ–12, but done later. The 1952 briefing implies that the organization went on for at least five years. The items noted as attachments were all done well before 1952. One can check on the dates given in the document, and can check the events and people involved. I have tried to do all of these.

The most obvious question, of course, is: 'Was there a crashed flying saucer recovered with alien bodies outside Roswell, New Mexico, in July 1947?' My answer here would have to be, 'Yes'. As already mentioned, my research on Roswell began a long time ago. By the time of the publication of *The Roswell Incident*,[1] Bill Moore and I had located sixty persons connected to the event. By the time of publication of Bill's update,[5] our total had risen to ninety-two. As of 1 May 1990, the grand total of persons contacted in one way or another about Roswell is well over 160.

The Center for UFO Studies (CUFOS) started off as rather sceptical about Roswell. Don Schmitt, their director of investigations, intentionally selected Kevin Randle to work with him. Kevin, a former Air Force captain and intelligence officer, and a close associate of Philip Klass, was entirely sceptical at the beginning. However, after making several trips to New Mexico, talking to many of the old-timers and then locating other witnesses, there is no question that both Don and Kevin are absolutely convinced that there was indeed the recovery of a crashed flying saucer and an almost immediate cover-up by the government. Much new research has been done, including a number of leads resulting from the *Unsolved Mysteries* TV broadcast on 20 September 1989 and 24 January 1990.

The Roswell Material

If we were capable of producing large quantities of the very high strength, very light weight material found at the Roswell site, where is it? Why are we not using that technology today? The material had the weight of foil on a packet of cigarettes, could not be torn, could not be permanently creased, could not be broken with a sledgehammer, and when crumpled returned to its original shape. Such a material as a skin for aircraft, spacecraft, etc. would be of enormous utility. We very obviously are still unable to produce large quantities of such a material.

The 509th Composite Bomb Wing, based at Roswell Army Air Force Base, was the only atomic bomber base in the world at that time, and everyone had high security clearances. One of the key people involved in the recovery was Major Jesse Marcel, the base intelligence officer. He was familiar with the rockets that were being tested at the nearby White Sands Proving Grounds, he was familiar with all kinds of balloons, and later even wrote the press release for President Truman announcing that the Soviets had tested their first atomic bomb in 1949. It is unreasonable to expect that this high-level group of people, in terms of security, would not be told that 'It's ours. You don't have a need-to-know about the details. Please leave it alone', because they did have Top Secret clearances and because the government would not have wanted any publicity for such material. They would not then have had to deal with the question of invalidating, in effect, or withdrawing the announcement that was made and that appeared in many after-noon newspapers on 8 July 1947, about the recovery of a crashed flying disk.

Continued investigation now reveals a more complex picture than was previously available. Several more crews who flew wreckage out have been located by Leonard Stringfield, Kevin Randle and Don Schmitt. New evidence also indicates strongly that there were two separate crashes, each including aliens, some possibly severely injured and others possibly alive. Thus, while it is certain that the wreckage at Roswell was *not* a World War II Japanese balloon bomb made of rice paper, and not 'highly classified' flying wing technology adapted from the German Horten Brothers' work,[9] the picture presented in the MJ–12 briefing seems much too simplistic. Why, if this is a unique document, is there nothing about the other crash, and the involve-ment of Alamogordo Army Air Field (AAAF)?

Preliminary Briefing

Since there was nothing in the press about the AAAF activity, from a security viewpoint it may well have seemed appropriate for a Preliminary Briefing to discuss only the crash that attracted national publicity. It may well have been that Ike, as Army Chief of Staff in July 1947, had been informed of this one, although he had already decided in June 1947 to leave his position and become the president of Columbia University. One almost has to wonder, if the document is genuine and the attachments were as detailed as seemed to be the case, why was this only preliminary? What more would there have been to tell, especially in view of the mention of increased activities in 1952, as noted in the text? Let us suppose that there was a live alien with whom there had been communication, for example. It seems likely that this incredible and far-reaching interaction would have been considered extraordinarily compartmentalized, with details only to follow when Ike actually became president, two months later.

18 November 1952

There is no question that Eisenhower was briefed in the Vault at the Pentagon on this date, where almost anybody with the right clearance could have been present. There were no newsmen. It might be objected that somebody reading the *New York Times* would have picked up on that briefing, which is certainly possible. It is also of interest that in late 1989, during a visit to the National Archives, in the files of the Office of the Secretary of Defense (OSD), which I had not previously reviewed, I discovered evidence that there were other briefings for the President-Elect dated 18 November 1952. I have only obtained one of these. The other two are still classified and I have asked for their classification review.

The OSD files are in the form of 3 × 5-inch cards in a special kind of filing index. They are in alphabetical order and under 'Briefings', for example, on card No. 5a, is '18NOV52 memo from Nash to Secretary of Defense RE Briefings for the President-Elect'. This is one that is still unavailable.

So it does seem to have been appropriate that the Truman administration was responsible for making sure that there were all kinds of briefings for Ike and that they were dated 18 November 1952. According to Ed Reese at the National Archives, nobody else that he is aware of has called his attention to these 'Briefings' listings. Unfortunately, these file cards are classified from 1953 on. There were many boxes of these cards and I was unable to go through them because of the classification. So that date, at least, is appropriate. Of course, there may well have been other briefings from other departments in the Office of the Secretary of Defense. I have not yet found reference to them although I have written numerous letters to the Eisenhower and Truman libraries and have obtained considerable background information.

Linguistics

Since Admiral Roscoe Hillenkoetter is listed as the briefing officer, one might ask if there is any indication that he could have been a briefing officer on 18 November 1952, and if so, could he have used the language that is used in the briefing document?

With regard to the language, at the suggestion of lawyer Robert Bletchman, I obtained copies of more than twenty different notes, memos, etc., written by Hillenkoetter, during one of my visits to the Truman Library. Bob provided these and the briefing document to Dr Roger W. Wescott, a world-class expert who is Professor of Anthropology and Linguistics at Drew University, Madison, New Jersey. In a letter to Robert Bletchman, dated 7 April 1988, he stated as follows:

> . . . In my opinion, there is no compelling reason to regard any of these communications as fraudulent or to believe that any of them were written by anyone other than Hillenkoetter himself. This statement holds for the controversial presidential briefing memorandum of November 18, 1952, as well as for the letters, both official and personal.

Some people are disappointed that Wescott did not make a more positive statement that his work proves that Hillenkoetter wrote the briefing. Obviously, no such statement could be made. Somebody working for the CIA, for example, could have read Hillenkoetter's papers and simulated his style. I should stress that I located Mrs Hillenkoetter in the hope of gaining access to his papers, but she explained that he intentionally did not keep his papers, precisely because he did not want anyone going through his files!

Public Release of the Documents

There has been a great deal of confusion within the small but vocal ufological community with regard to the documents. A major reason for this has been the confused, unconventional and often incomplete method by which the information has been released. I think most people can understand that Moore, Shandera, and I could not immediately release the information on the documents. We could not be sure that they were legitimate, especially with the name of Menzel on the MJ–12 list, and with no back-up information. The Cutler–Twining memo, when discovered in 1985, was of course very interesting, but obviously it does not say that MJ–12 has anything to do with flying saucers, the Roswell incident, or any related matters.

Moore has admitted that one of his major inside contacts is Richard Doty, who used to work as a counter-intelligence specialist for the Air Office of Special Investigations. His name appears on a document from Kirtland AFB, Albuquerque, New Mexico, in connection with multiple-witness observations of a UFO landing and then later taking off from the nearby Manzano Nuclear Weapon Storage area. Many people have suggested that Doty must have provided the MJ–12 document in the first place. [*Editor's note:* A logical suggestion, since Linda Howe (author of Chapter 9 of this book) has signed a sworn affidavit testifying that Doty showed her another alleged presidential briefing paper at Kirtland AFB in 1983, while she was researching material for a TV documentary.] Moore and Shandera have claimed that nobody, including Doty, has admitted sending the document, although the postmark was indeed Albuquerque. Doty obviously knew about the document, but so far as I know, has never admitted sending it. Frankly, I doubt that he did.

The first brief details about MJ–12 were published by Barry Greenwood in the December 1985 issue of *Just Cause*. The article included some information on the members of MJ–12, but no copies of any of the pages from the document. The information had been supplied by Lee Graham, who works with an aerospace firm and has written many Freedom of Information requests. Graham had given them the correct list of members of MJ–12, but claims that he had been shown the document by a supposedly military source. He had not been allowed to copy it but had taken notes. As far as I know, the source was actually William Moore, who was not in the military and does not work for the government [although, on his own admission, he has collaborated with the Air Force Office of Special Investigations at times – *Ed.*] I have no idea why Moore showed the document to Graham, except that Bill is a great one for throwing pebbles in the water to see where the waves go.

On 31 May 1987 an article appeared on the front page of the *Observer* in England, showing a tiny portion of the MJ–12 briefing paper and giving details. [This was following receipt by journalist Martin Bailey of the proofs of *Above Top Secret*, in which the document was first published – *Ed.*] The British paper also mentioned the Cutler–Twining memo. The *Observer* article was picked up by Reuters news service and appeared in numerous

North American papers the following day. When I heard about it I called Jaime, who went out and bought copies of the papers. The Reuters account was somewhat briefer than the original. Bill and Jaime had already been talking to their people about the need to release information and immediately swung into action. They published an unfortunately very much censored version of the document in Bill's Fair Witness Project publication, *Focus*. Part of the problem was that the *Focus* version had many heavy 'censor's' lines through portions of the document, especially the security markings, without any explanation as to why the markings were there, or if that was the way the document was received.

According to Bill, the words that he used to describe the document, and what he left in of the briefing, were in accordance with instructions from his contacts in New Mexico. My feeling is that either these guys were trying to create confusion or they simply did not understand how to communicate with the outside world. The fact of the matter is that the eight pages of the document on film were clean. There were no deletions. Bill had taken one set of 8½ × 11 inch prints and had run a marker through the security markings, because getting caught with a Top Secret document didn't seem like such a good idea. Ostensibly, that was one of the reasons that I was not given or sent a copy earlier, because taking it or sending it over the US/Canada border could be dangerous. Obviously, from my own viewpoint, I would have been happy to have had the government arrest me for carrying a 'classified' document, thus verifying its legitimacy. The government is in a Catch-22 situation here. If they prosecute, then obviously they are admitting it's a legitimate document, and certainly they would have no case that I faked the document because there is no such evidence since I did not fake it. It should be noted here that Tim Good's copy came from the US and had censor lines through the security markings which are different from those Moore put on his.

Freedom of Information

Many people unfamiliar with how the Freedom of Information Act works and how the various archives work are shocked that we have not simply requested from various government agencies all their MJ–12 documents and not been able to obtain other documents. This is naïve. The Freedom of Information Act, contrary to what many people assume, is *not* a key that opens all the doors. In the first place, the intent of the FOIA was not that the government should act as a searching team for people curious about various and sundry topics. Quite the reverse. The purpose is to provide public access to certain classes of documents *if* they can be well defined and easily sought. There are numerous exclusions.

Clearly of greatest importance are those matters which affect the national security and intelligence activities. Some people think the government declassifies everything after a certain period. While it is true that in Britain the Official Secrets Act does have provisions relating to how many years before information is released, the United States does not. [Some records at the Public Record Office in the UK can be withheld for 100 years or longer. – *Ed.*] Certain documents are put under security with the proviso that they shall be periodically downgraded. Many do not have such a limitation. There is not an automatic provision that any classified document becomes declassified after a specified period of time.

Next, who do you ask? Here we have an 'Eyes Only' briefing document, 'Copy One of One'. That would imply that there is only one copy in the first place, probably kept in a vault at the White House. One of Roosevelt's and Truman's assistants told me that highly classified Manhattan Project materials were stored in the White House Map Room. How in the world would one expect to find another copy some place? There would not have been one. Requests have been made to the Truman and Eisenhower libraries and they did a quick check of their indices and found no listing for MJ–12. This was not a computerized check. There are eleven different finders' aids for different portions of the NSC files at the Eisenhower Library alone. Nobody went through all those.

There is an additional problem with regard to getting official confirmation or back-up on the reality of MJ–12. Since it was a highly classified programme, classified 'Top Secret Majic', the 'Majic' would be a need-to-know limitation, and with 'Eyes Only' and 'One of One' there would be very few people in the government who would know about it. And suppose a request happened to be made of somebody who did know of the group? If the very existence of the group was classified, then clearly that person could *not* admit as much. At the highest levels of government there is compartmentalization. An example of this is that in a many-page Top Secret listing of NSC documents was an item that said 'Title classified for security reasons'. And this is in a Top Secret listing! The very title of the report was classified above Top Secret.

Further Limitations

Despite the amount of time, effort, and money spent on this investigation, it is still incomplete. The main reason for this is the great difficulty in obtaining documents known to exist but still classified, coupled with the fact that so much documentation for the Truman–Eisenhower era is still classified, such as:

(1) Copies of the four briefings by CIA director Walter Bedell Smith for President-Elect Eisenhower during the period from 4 November 1952 to 9 January 1953. These dealt with national security and defence matters and would make excellent comparison items for the MJ–12 briefing paper. The CIA has been asked, but they tend to respond years later.

(2) The briefings noted in the index of the Office of the Secretary of Defense for the President-Elect, dated 18 November 1952. These have been requested for mandatory classification review, but have not yet been considered.

(3) Numerous NSC documents that might shed some light on the Cutler–Twining memo were submitted for mandatory classification review by the NSC in 1988 and 1989. Average response time for the NSC is about two-and-a-half years, with some requiring as much as six years. These were selected on the basis of limited information on withdrawal sheets at the Eisenhower Library.

There exist many open leads on the recovery of the wreckage of at least one crashed flying saucer in New Mexico in July 1947. Tracking these down at this time is not inexpensive nor easy, and getting people to go public with their information is much more difficult. Apparently, the initial intimidation by government people was so strong that it is still effective.

The evidence that there was indeed a crashed or exploded flying saucer (or two) recovered in New Mexico in 1947 is so overwhelming that, if there was no Operation Majestic 12, we would have to invent one. There is no question that the US Government and its advisors (so many of whom had worked so effectively together on classified projects in New Mexico) would have both covered up the stories and established an organization at the very highest level to deal with the most important aspects of the crashed disk problem.

These would include a substantial effort to determine the technology of the saucers, the motivation and origin of the aliens, and how this information might be handled.

Conclusions

In North American courts it is required that the prosecution establish the guilt of a defendant. It is not the job of the defendant to establish innocence. With regard to questioned documents, the burden of proof is on those who claim the documents are forgeries, as opposed to being on those who say they may be genuine. After several years of sometimes very intense research with regard to the Operation Majestic 12 documents, I have still been unable to find any argument that conclusively demonstrates that any of the three primary documents are fraudulent. I have certainly been able to demonstrate that there is a very great deal of information in them that was not known to an outsider at the time the documents were received. Therefore I am forced to conclude that the documents are genuine.

There are still a number of questions that have not been resolved. This is not surprising, given the vast quantities of government documents that are completely inaccessible, and the difficulty in getting prompt access to those whose existence can be established but were still classified at the time they were sought. Most Americans, whether citizens, journalists or scientists, seem unaware of the huge 'black' budgets for programmes that are not accountable to the Congress, the compartmentalization of highly classified information, and the difficulty of penetrating the silent and very high walls of secrecy surrounding the intelligence communities.

*   *   *

I feel apologetic to the Fund for UFO Research for their having been attacked by various Ufologists for having spent their money on this project, even though its funding was a direct result of an appeal for funds for this project in particular. I am grateful for their encouragement and understanding.

REFERENCES
1. Berlitz, Charles and Moore, William: *The Roswell Incident*, Grossett & Dunlap Inc., New York 1980.
2. Friedman, Stanton and Moore, William: 'The Roswell Incident: Beginning of the Cosmic Watergate', *MUFON UFO Symposium Proceedings*, July 1981.
3. Moore, William and Friedman, Stanton: 'The Roswell Investigation: New Evidence in the Search for a Crashed UFO', *1982 MUFON Symposium Proceedings*, July 1982, pp. 85–104.
4. Friedman, Stanton and Moore, William: 'UFOs: Uncovering the Ultimate Answer', *1983 MUFON Symposium Proceedings*, July 1983, pp. 83–100.
5. Moore, William: 'Crashed Saucers: Evidence in the Search for Proof', MUFON Conference, St Louis, Missouri, June 1985. Available from UFORI, P.O. Box 3584, Fredericton, New Brunswick, Canada E3A 5H1.
6. Moore, William: 'Phil Klass and the Roswell Incident: The Skeptics Deceived', 1986. Available from the Fair Witness Project, 4219 W. Olive, Suite 247, Burbank, California 91505.
7. Friedman, Stanton: 'Flying Saucers, Noisy Negativists and Truth', MUFON Conference, June 1985. Available from UFORI.
8. Klass, Philip J.: 'New Evidence of MJ–12 Hoax', *The Skeptical Inquirer*, Vol. 14, No. 2, Winter 1989, pp. 135–40. Available from Box 229, Central Park Station, Buffalo, NY 14215.
9. John Northrop, who invented the YB-49 flying wing, was convinced UFOs were alien spacecraft, and told me of a UFO sighting by his test pilot while flying that airplane. One of the Horten Brothers flying wings (from which the Northrop plane was developed) is at the Air and Space Museum. The wings consist of two layers of plywood with sawdust and carbon in between. They do have a low radar profile, but hardly match the Roswell wreckage.

Editor's Note

Readers are urged to obtain a copy of Mr Friedman's full report on MJ–12, which is available from the author at 79 Pembroke Crescent, Fredericton, New Brunswick, Canada, E3B 2V1. I had hoped to publish the exhaustive report on MJ–12 by William Moore and Jaime Shandera, which includes the results of their research into typefaces, stampings, etc., but unfortunately it was not ready at the time of going to press. Those interested should write to Mr Moore at 4219 W. Olive, Suite 247, Burbank, California 91505, USA.

In order to obtain a balanced perspective, articles expressing different viewpoints should also be read, including those by Barry Greenwood, available from CAUS (P.O. Box 218, Coventry, Connecticut 06238, USA); Philip Klass in *The Skeptical Inquirer* (address above); Joe Nickell and John Fischer in the *International UFO Reporter* (with rebuttals by Friedman and Moore), Vol. 15, No. 2, March/April 1990 (J. Allen Hynek Center for UFO Studies, 2457 West Peterson Avenue, Chicago, Illinois 60659, USA).

The MJ–12 documents (minus page 7, which is a sub-title for 'Attachment A', and without the separate Cutler–Twining memo) were first published in my book,

Above Top Secret (Sidgwick & Jackson 1987), in the conviction that they were genuine. The signature on the Truman–Forrestal memo, however, raises serious doubts about authenticity, as Stanton Friedman has pointed out. Although not absolutely identical to the known-to-be-authentic signature of 1 October 1947, the difference in lengths and ratios could easily have been affected by a skilled forger. In addition, there is some barely noticeable thinning at the top of the 'T' (more readily visible in the photographic prints) which Nickell and Fischer argue is due to removal of the 's' of 'yours' from the October 1947 letter. Furthermore, in the examples I have seen, Truman's signature invariably overlaps the typed text.

Even if the entire MJ–12 briefing document turns out to be fraudulent, I am convinced that the information contained therein, at least, is essentially factual. Moreover, I have learned from reliable sources that there was indeed an above Top Secret Majestic 12 group dealing with UFOs. I have also learned that there was a Top Secret (not above) 'Plan Majestic', drawn up during the Truman administration in about 1951 by the Joint Chiefs of Staff, in the event of attack by the Soviets.

8

US Jets Abducted by UFOs in Puerto Rico

JORGE MARTÍN

Jorge Martín is State Section Director for the Mutual UFO Network in Puerto Rico and Director of the UFO Information Center, based in Rio Piedras, Puerto Rico. He is also editor of the magazine *Enigma!*

Since 1987, the island of Puerto Rico has been the scenario of an important wave of UFO sightings and close encounters, which seems to have begun after a mysterious underground explosion and tremor in the municipalities of Lajas and Cabo Rojo, at the island's south-west corner (Figure 8:1).

28 December 1988

The night of 28 December 1988 was normal until 7.45 p.m., when many residents of the Maguayo, Betances, Olivares, and Sabana Yeguas communities of Lajas and Cabo Rojo witnessed something they will never forget. Among the witnesses were Mr and Mrs Wilson Sosa and family, Carlos Manuel Mercado and family, Edgardo Plaza (see Plate 8:1) and his wife Carmen, and many others who at that moment were at a store on Luis Munoz Marín Street in the Betances area of Cabo Rojo, and on Route 101 which goes from Lajas to Boquerón, Cabo Rojo, a coastal resort area.

All witnesses stated that the UFO they observed on the above date was triangular in shape and totally silent. Some of those who saw it from the Lajas area assured us that 'it seemed to have some kind of extended appendage in its frontal section with many brilliantly coloured lights constantly blinking on and off'.

Wilson Sosa, a resident of the Betances community, who is a

UFO investigator and a fine collaborator of ours, explained what he, his wife and children observed:

'Starting at 6.00 p.m., we saw jet fighters flying over the area. At 7.45 p.m. or so, we heard some other planes that were either from the Puerto Rico National Air Guard or from the US Navy. Even though they were very high you could still clearly hear their engines. I was paying close attention to their fly-over because about a week before, another one of those jets, an F-14 or F-15, chased another UFO – a small one – over the Sierra Bermeja [a small mountain ridge] and the Laguna Cartagena [a lagoon (see Figure 8:1); sites related to many of the UFO incidents that have been occurring in this area since 1987]. I

Figure 8:1. Map of south-west Puerto Rico. The ringed area shows where the UFO incident occurred on 28 December 1988.

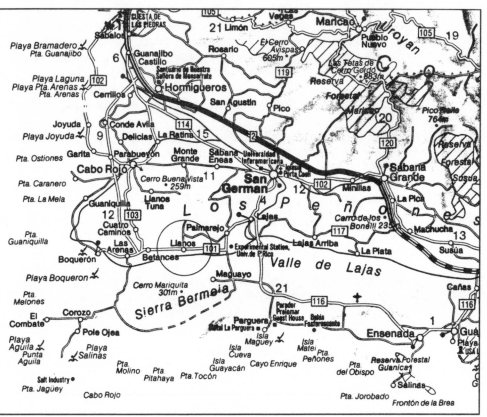

came out to watch them and then saw a big UFO flying over the Sierra Bermeja. It was enormous! It was blinking with many coloured lights. I ran and got my binoculars and could then clearly see that it was triangle-shaped and slightly curved at its rear side.

'It made a turn back and then came over lower, appearing much larger. It was then that we noticed two jet fighters right behind it. Then, when the UFO went [to the west], one of the planes tried to intercept it and passed in front of it, at which point the UFO veered to the left and made a turn back, reducing its speed. The jets tried to intercept it three times, and that's when the UFO slowed down and almost stopped in mid-air. It was incredible! How something that big could remain almost motionless was unbelievable. Considering its size, it must have been very heavy.

'The second jet remained at the right side of the UFO and the other one positioned itself at the left rear side. Then – I don't know exactly what happened – if the jet entered the UFO by the rear, by its upper side, or what. That was when we all yelled, because we were afraid there would be a collision and maybe an explosion. The jet in the back just disappeared on top or inside of the UFO, because I was observing everything through my binoculars and it didn't come out from the rear, the upper side or the other sides.

'The second jet remained very close to the right side of the UFO. It looked very small alongside that huge thing. As the UFO flew a little to the west, the jet disappeared, as well as its engine sound. This was exactly what happened when the first jet seemed to disappear inside the UFO.'

Wilson Sosa continued:

'That UFO was huge! I tell you that ship was bigger than this community's baseball park. You could observe its grey metallic structure and great central yellow light that was being emitted from a big, bulging luminous circular concave appendage. At the triangle's right "wing" tip it had brilliant yellow lights, and on the left side it had red ones.' (See Figures 8:2 and 8:3.)

'After "trapping" the jets, the UFO lowered its position and came very close to the ground [over the small Samán Lake]. It stood still in mid-air for a moment then straightened its corners and gave off a big flash of light from the central ball of yellow

194

light. It then divided itself in the middle into two separate and distinct triangular sections. It was just incredible! The triangle to the right was illuminated in yellow, and the other one in red. That's when they both shot away at great speed, one to the southeast and the other one toward the northeast, in the direction of Monte del Estado. You could see red sparks falling from it when it divided itself.

Figure 8:2. Drawing by Carlos Mercado of the UFO seen on 28 December 1988 over south-west Puerto Rico. Note similarity to the objects seen during the Belgian wave of sightings. (© Enigma!)

Carlos Manuel Mercado, another local resident, related his experience as follows.

'My wife Haydee yelled to me, "Manuel, come quickly! Look what's coming there!" As I came out to see, Wilson was calling me too. Then I saw that huge thing like a big light . . . At first I couldn't identify it. It had a very bright yellow light that almost blinded you – a great yellow light, like a giant searchlight.

'Suddenly, I saw two planes coming, each one at the side of that thing. When they got nearer to the ship, which I have drawn [see Figure 8:2], one of the jets came and crossed in front of the UFO to the left, and the other one crossed in front of it from left to right. Then, when they got next to it, we thought they would collide. The object stopped in mid-air . . . and the jets seemed to go inside it. And that was the last we saw of them. Then that thing – it must have been a craft because it was real – veered back, and that's when we noticed that it looked like a triangle. It had some lights on both sides and a great ball of light in the middle, from where the yellow light emitted. When it veered and stopped over there [the Samán lake], it divided itself, and one of the sections shot away at great speed to the east and the other one took off to the north. The jets seemed to be trying to intercept that thing, to force it to change its course, which they did on three occasions, until it stopped and trapped them. It grabbed them and took them both away! To me, that's what happened.

'I was really nervous because that thing was so big, and it was coming in our direction, and I shouted, "Those jets are going to collide!" But instead, they seemed to throw themselves into it, and just disappeared. At the same time, the noise of their engines stopped: we could no longer hear them.'

Mrs Eduviges Olmeda, a resident of the Finquitas de Betances residential area, said: 'It was like something out of science fiction. From our balcony we could see everything. Those planes were circling and getting in front of that thing with the big yellow light . . . It was beautiful . . . And suddenly it stopped and the planes seemed to disappear inside it.'

Edwin Olmeda, husband of Eduviges, recounted his observation. 'That certainly was a UFO, and it was really big,' he said. 'It was glowing with a large yellow light and didn't make a sound as it flew over the area, but the jets did. You know, we recently moved to this place, and this is the second occasion that we have seen UFOs over the area. The first occasion was about three weeks ago, and it was like a flying saucer, but shimmering with light. Something is going on around here.'

The details given by the Olmedes and their children are similar to those given by other witnesses.

Further Testimony

Iván Coté, a young resident in the Sabana Yeguas area of Lajas, explained what he saw.

'It was between 7.00 and 8.00 p.m. I was in the yard and all of a sudden I saw this huge thing like a triangle with big lights and many similar blinking coloured lights. Then some military jets arrived and began, I would say, to try and "corral" that thing, and there were other, smaller red luminous objects that were around the triangle and seemed to be trying to protect it from the planes. I really think that thing is what people call a UFO – a flying saucer. Suddenly, the planes seemed to enter or be sucked into it. I thought there would be an explosion – a collision – but they just disappeared. I couldn't see or hear them anymore.

'Then another jet came, but it flew away, apparently because they [the pilots] saw what happened to the other two jets, and got lost in some clouds while the smaller UFOs with red lights were chasing it. That is all I saw. Those jets did disappear. My grandmother, Josefina Polanco, saw it all too, because I called her out to watch.'

Later, we interviewed Mrs Polanco, and she verified everything that Iván said.

Iván's account was important, because it confirmed that the large UFO was apparently being escorted by a number of smaller UFOs which were trying to prevent the jets from getting too close to it. But whatever happened to the jet that escaped from the smaller UFOs? We have so far been unable to obtain any further information on this.

Youngsters Juan and Jeffrey Acosta, as well as their family, residents in the Vertedero section of Barrio Olivares in Lajas, also saw what happened, repeating the details given by all the others. They also made us a drawing of what they saw that night (Figure 8:3). Notice the similarity to the sketch by Carlos Mercado. [Notice, too, the similarity to the sketches made by Belgian witnesses, shown in Chapter 2. *Ed.*] 'That thing was much bigger than the jets,' said Juan. 'They seemed like mosquitoes next to it.'

Cover-Up

Immediately after the incident, some of the witnesses called to inform me about it. I contacted the Federal Aviation Administration office in Isla Verde, giving the time and details of the incident. My call was politely attended to by a supervisor, Ed Purcell. He stated that the FAA knew nothing about any UFO incident in the area, nor any incident similar to the one described, but that the FAA had been informed that 'there was some military movement down in the south-west region in Cabo Rojo and

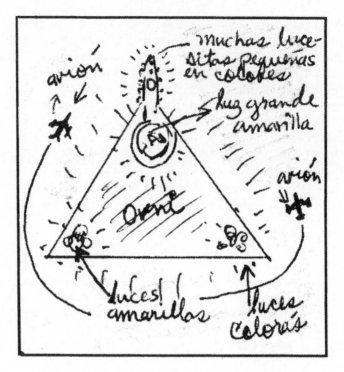

Figure 8:3. Drawing by Jeffrey Acosta. (© Enigma!)

operations manoeuvres were being made by personnel, apparently from the Roosevelt Roads Naval Base in Ceiba.'

At the Puerto Rico National Air Guard base in Muñiz, Isla Verde, we were informed that they knew nothing about the incident, but that if indeed it had happened, none of their interceptors had anything to do with it because none was flying that night. We later verified this information with an inside source. The same information was given to us from official sources at the Compamento Santiago National Air Guard base in Salinas, in the south of the island.

Representatives from a radar unit of FURA (Fast Action United Forces, a special air police force commissioned to fight against drug smuggling) at San German stated that they had no knowledge of such an incident, but showed considerable interest and told us that that night they had noticed a lot of combat planes overflying the western zone at low altitude, in areas where they do not normally fly. This information was corroborated for us by a high-ranking officer of the Criminal Investigations Corps of the Puerto Rico Police Department.

However, we received a surprise when we called the Roosevelt Roads US Naval Base the following day, informing the supervisor of air operations about the incident. 'That's absurd! It's not true,' he responded. 'What's more, to prove it, I can tell you that we did not have any personnel in that area yesterday or last night. Whoever said that is mistaken.'

We explained to the officer that many witnesses in the area who we personally knew as serious people had called us, giving the same details. But he insisted that they were mistaken. We therefore called the Federal Aviation Administration office at Isla Verde to check once more if they knew anything about such an incident or UFO report, although we knew that they have a rule not to say anything to the media about UFOs. An officer named Mirabal said he knew nothing about the incident but assured us that 'there were air exercises in that area in Cabo Rojo last night. Wednesdays are the official days for exercises in that sector, and the Administration is officially notified as such.' Mirabal was unable to explain why the Roosevelt Roads base denied having any jets in the area.

Later that day I called the FAA again, and another officer, who asked not to be named, commented: 'I don't know anything about the incident, but even so, whenever there is a UFO report we are not allowed to investigate it, since investigation is done by a special division of the FAA, based in Washington, DC.' This is the first time, as I recall, that an FAA officer has made such an admission.

There are obvious contradictions in the statements given to us by these authorities, leading to our conviction that someone wants to cover up this important incident.

Black Helicopters

On 29 December we went to Cabo Rojo/Lajas, accompanied by our friends José Reyes and his wife Damaris, in order to interview the aforementioned witnesses, as well as many others whose accounts were similar. So far we have traced over sixty witnesses.

Carlos Rocafort, supervisor of Air Operations at the El Mani airport in Mayaguez, near Cabo Rojo, told us (without knowing anything about the incident) that on Wednesday, 28 December, at 8.30 p.m. (the UFO incident occurred at 7.45 p.m.) a small military Cessna aircraft arrived at the airport with four individuals who, it was rumoured, were going to investigate 'something important that had happened in the area'.

Arístides Medina, a retired US Army veteran who lives in La Parguera, a resort area, reported what appeared to have been a search operation by military helicopters. 'At about 8.20 p.m.,' he told us, 'a bunch of black helicopters arrived, and for hours flew over the Sierra Bermeja and Laguna Cartagena areas without lights, until about midnight. They seemed to be searching for something in the area. Apparently they did not want to be seen and were flying low. Maybe they were looking for the planes that the UFO took away, or for some kind of trace. Apparently they were equipped with infrared detectors, and this might explain why they were not using any lights in the search.'

UFO Base?

At dawn, after the helicopters had left, five US Navy ships and one aircraft carrier positioned themselves some fifteen miles out in the Atlantic, just in front of the area known as the Cayo Margarita, where UFOs have constantly been seen entering or emerging from the sea by local fishermen as well as commercial and private pilots. The ships remained there for a considerable time.

Diego Segarra, who has been a fisherman in the Cabo Rojo area for more than twenty years, related some interesting information. He told us:

'Shortly before this happened, that aircraft carrier was stationed there for about a month and the area was restricted. The reason was that four mysterious huge metallic tubes apparently protruding from the bottom of the sea appeared in that area, where they had not been before, and just where those flying saucers are seen entering the water. They can tell us they are just manoeuvres, but to those of us who have seen all that is going on here, the truth is that they are searching and following up the UFO sightings there.

'On many nights, when we are fishing late at night, we can see the military overfly the area with huge aircraft equipped with searchlights, looking for something under water. On other occasions, a big AWACS plane has been seen flying over this area as well as the Laguna Cartagena and Sierra Bermeja, at low altitude, escorted by fighters. They are looking for something down there, and we think that "something" is probably a UFO base. After all we have seen here, that is the most plausible explanation for what is happening.'

Arístides Medina told us:

'Something abnormal is going on down here. Anyone in his right mind can see what all these events indicate. For some reason, the authorities don't want the people to know what is going on; the mysterious underground explosions that are felt here, and the UFOs that are constantly seen. I have seen them myself. On one occasion, I was fishing late at night near Cayo Margarita, and two of them passed under my boat, radiating a blue light. On other occasions, I have seen them when they emerge from the water and fly away at great speed, and I have also seen them plunge into the water – always in the same area where the Navy ships are now.'

16 November 1988

While investigating some important UFO sightings in the Guamá area, in the municipality of San Germán, in March 1990, I was informed about yet *another* incident involving two jet fighters that were abducted in mid-air by a huge luminous object.

José Pérez, a friend of mine who also investigates cases, spoke with Santiago Velázquez and his family, who claimed to have witnessed the incident. Velázquez, a civil engineer with good credentials, claims that he and his wife and family, as well as another witness who prefers to remain anonymous, were watching television at 9.00 p.m. on 16 November 1988, when daughter Yesenia (see Plate 8:2) suddenly rushed in the house. 'Daddy, come! It's a UFO! It's coming this way. Hurry!', she cried.

'We all ran, and then we saw this huge ball of yellow light that was flying over the area,' Velázquez related. 'It was coming from the south, as if from Guánica, I think, and it was noiseless, totally noiseless.'

We asked if he could specify any details:

'No. All we could see was that it was round and that it had a very bright, shiny yellow light all around it. It was really bright. You could not see any other details, only that it was round, oval-shaped, and that it had that yellow luminosity all over it. You couldn't hear anything. That is when I realized it was a UFO.

'Suddenly, two jet fighters appeared from the south, chasing the object. The UFO stopped in mid-air, next to the radio antenna on top of that mountain, and the jets began flying over it, under it, and all around it. Then, suddenly, they seemed to enter the object from underneath it, and disappeared! We couldn't see them anymore, and the sound of their engines couldn't be heard anymore. Then two smaller balls of light came out of the UFO and shot away at great speed. After that, the UFO also disappeared at high speed.'

Could there have been some confusion about the date? 'We are sure about the date this happened,' Velázquez' wife Rebecca stated, 'because on that day I had to work some overtime at the La Concepción Hospital in San Germán, and two days later – the 18th – a special commission came from the US to examine the hospital and certify it as a "bona-fide" health centre institution.'

The family is highly regarded in the community, I learned, and after checking all the details, I am satisfied that the witnesses are truthful.

Conclusions

The testimony of multiple witnesses, each independent of the other and from different areas in the Cajo Rojo/Lajas region, indicate that the UFO encounter and subsequent disappearance or abduction of the two US Navy jets *did* actually occur on the night of 28 December 1988, and that a similar incident took place on 16 November.

It is probable that, in the later incident, the jets came from the US Navy aircraft carrier that was stationed some twenty to twenty-five miles out to sea at the time. It is very possible that this carrier is the one which helped the *USS Iowa* after its unfortunate accident north of Puerto Rico. I have been able to verify that the jets involved in these incidents were of the F-14 (Tomcat) type.

A week after the December incident, I was able to talk with a Navy officer here on the island, whose name I cannot give for obvious reasons, who provided me with some sensational corroboration. He said:

'*There are radar tapes that show what happened,* and they were classified at once and sent to Washington, DC, to be analyzed. We were able to see what happened on the radar systems of the ships that were stationed nearby. We saw when the smaller targets on the radar, which represented the jets, merged with a bigger one [the UFO]. After that, the big target seemed to split [see Figure 8:4], and shot off at great speed. A lid has been placed on the whole incident. Many things like this have been happening, but we are not allowed to comment on anything we see. Many strange things are happening in the waters of Puerto Rico that should be known.'

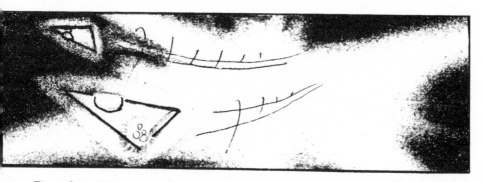

Figure 8:4. Artist's impression of the moment when the UFO divided itself. (© Enigma!)

There is a great deal of information on UFO incidents in Puerto Rico which seems to indicate that some kind of 'struggle' is currently going on between the US military and UFOs. The local government 'leased' the area at Sierra Bermeja and the Laguna Cartagena to the federal government, and another extension of the area is currently under control of the federal government, using the excuse that they are organizing a Voice of America radio station in the Sierra Bermeja region. But to the investigators and residents in the region, the real reason seems to be that they are controlling the area in order to maintain a constant follow-up on the UFO presence.

These are important cases, because if it can be officially proven that the jets disappeared, and some kind of official documentation on the incident can be found via the Freedom of Information Act, then the government would have to make a statement on the reality of UFOs. Somewhere in the United States, families were notified of the disappearance of the pilots, and some kind of documentation pertaining to these notifications must exist somewhere. It is more than likely that U S Naval Intelligence is involved in preliminary investigations, so this would be a promising agency to send F O I A requests.

These are solid cases, too, due to the fact that they were reported by so many reliable and independent witnesses. But for how long will they be denied?

9

1989 – The Harvest Continues

LINDA MOULTON HOWE

A graduate of Stanford University, Linda Howe has devoted her film and television career to documentary productions. She has received local, national and international awards for her documentaries about science, medicine and environmental issues, including *Fire in the Water* and *A Radioactive Water*. In 1979, as Director of Special Projects at CBS television station in Denver, Colorado, she began researching into the animal mutilation mystery. The result was an Emmy award-winning documentary, *A Strange Harvest*.

From 1983, Linda Howe began independent film productions and commenced her own research into government knowledge about alien life forms and the animal mutilations phenomenon. In April 1983 she was shown a 'Briefing Paper for the President of the United States' at Kirtland AFB in Albuquerque, New Mexico, which referred to on-going official communication with 'extraterrestrial biological entities' since the late 1940s. She was promised several thousand feet of official movie film documenting this sensational claim for inclusion in her documentary, but the promise was never fulfilled.

In 1989 Linda published her book, *An Alien Harvest*, which is a synthesis of ten years of research into the mysteries of animal mutilations, human abductions and government knowledge of these disturbing matters.

In September 1979 I began researching bizarre animal deaths that had periodically been making headlines for a decade. Much of my television work as Director of Special Projects for the CBS affiliate in Denver involved stories about environmental issues. I thought perhaps I was dealing with a contamination story; that maybe the government had accidentally released some kind of poison into the land and was randomly spot-checking tissue from grazing animals to monitor the spread of contamination. That was the context in which I began the investigation to produce the documentary, *A Strange Harvest*.[1]

I quickly learned from newspaper files, however, that the mutilations had been reported worldwide: beyond Canada and the United States, mutilated animals have been reported in Mexico, Panama, Puerto Rico, South America, parts of Europe, the Canary Islands, and Australia. Further, it did not make sense that the government would brazenly leave the carcasses to be discovered by a shocked public. Within a month, after talking with dozens of ranchers, law enforcement officials and fellow journalists who had investigated the intense mutilation activity in 1975–76, I heard one 'off-the-record' UFO story after another.

Reports of UFOs, mysterious helicopters, as well as orange or white glowing lights and/or beams of light shining down from something silently hovering above pastures, were common among people I interviewed. The documentary shifted from environmental contamination to an accumulation of human testimony that suggested the presence of extraterrestrial mutilators.

After *A Strange Harvest* was first broadcast in May 1980, I received hundreds of phone calls and letters from people with their own stories about encounters with strange lights and mutilated animals. This led to the publication in 1989 of *An Alien Harvest*,[2] which gives a detailed history of the mutilation phenomenon.

No one knows for certain how many animals have been mutilated over the years and around the world. In Colorado, Elbert County Sheriff George Yarnell's files contained sixty-four reports between April 1975 and September 1977. During that same period, the Logan County Sheriff's office in north-eastern Colorado had over a hundred mutilation reports in its files. Many mutilations go unreported because ranchers are either afraid or do not want public attention.

Hope, Arkansas

Early on the morning of 10 March 1989, five pregnant cows were found dead by L. C. Wyatt on his property near Hope, in Hempstead County, Arkansas. Mr Wyatt was amazed to find the cows laid out in a straight line in one of his pastures near an old abandoned logging road. He had seen them alive and well two days before with the rest of his herd. One cow had its legs drawn up 'as if it had been running and was zapped by something,' said Jim Williamson, editor of the *Little River News* in Ashdown.

Mr Wyatt contacted the Hempstead County Sheriff's Department and two deputies were dispatched to the farm. Their conclusion was that some kind of instrument was involved in the excisions, but there was no obvious sign of what had killed the cows.

That same day, at around 6 p.m., *Little River News* associate editor Juanita Stripling went to Mr Wyatt's farm to take black and white photographs. 'The first look at the scene gave the impression the cows were dropped dead in their tracks,' she reported. 'One cow was lying on her right side. There was a large, round cut out area with the calf lying just outside the cow and still in the embryo sac. The cut area was neat, precise, and approximately 1¾ to two inches deep. There was no blood on the ground or on the body of the cow or calf. There was also no dampness on the ground of water or body fluids.'

Four other cows were laid out in a straight line, all but one with their legs straight out. The rectal areas 'were distended and it seemed as if they had been bored around in approximately a ¼-inch deep smooth circle.'

After dark, when Juanita Stripling had left the farm, veterinarian Dr James Powell of Hope, and Hempstead County Sheriff Don Worthy went to the mutilation site. With the aid of flashlights, Dr Powell cut open some of the cows and took stomach and organ samples for analysis.

Little River News editor Jim Williamson contacted me and I called Dr John Altshuler, the pathologist and hematologist who had seen and taken samples from the mutilated horse 'Lady' in Colorado in 1967 (see later). Dr Altshuler instructed Jim to obtain a new straight razor and cut a rectangle of cowhide that would include the mutilator's cut in one corner, with normal cow tissue in the rest of the sample. Jim cut tissue from the belly and eye excisions and sent them in a 10 per cent formaldehyde solution to us in Denver for analysis. I was at Dr Altshuler's lab when he prepared the tissues for microscopic examination.

Dr Altshuler's comments and photomicrographs are published in *An Alien Harvest*. Briefly, he concluded as follows: '. . . Taking all the microscopic findings into account, one would have to conclude that the surgical procedure performed on these animals took place quickly, probably in a minute or two, and utilized high temperature heat (e.g. laser) as a cutting source applied in a fine probe or cutting instrument.'[3]

Nounan, Idaho

In 1989, there were so many cattle mutilations in Southern Idaho that Bear Lake County Sheriff Brent Bunn told me, 'We haven't seen anything like this since the 1970s.' The sheriff sent me sixteen neatly typed Investigation Reports about cattle mutilations in his county between May and December. Over half occurred in a remote valley called Nounan. Only eighty people live there. Ranching is their main source of income and cattle are precious. Disease and predators are old and well understood enemies. What descended on Nounan, Idaho in the summer and fall of 1989 was not understood – and it frightened people.

Bloodless and precise cuts are what baffle and worry ranchers the most. Plates 9:1 and 9:2 show the excision of hide from a cow's upper and lower jaws and the neat removal of four teats on the udder. The date was 9 October 1989. 'There were no visible signs of the cause of death,' wrote Officer Gregg Athay in his report. 'It appeared that only the soft tissues (nose, lips, and tongue) were gone off the head and four nipples off the bag. Again there was no blood on the hair or ground.'

No veterinarian report was made on that cow. But a month earlier, Dr Charles Merrell at the Bear Lake Animal Hospital examined a dead Hereford cow, and wrote: 'Some time between approximately 8 p.m. [31 August 1989] and 7 a.m., 1 September, the anus, vagina to include uterus and ovaries, and all four teats (one teat deeply incised, the others shallow cuts) were removed by knife cuts around these tissues. There were no other signs of injury and no blood to be found on the ground.'

A neighbour said that she saw unusual lights in that area at about 2 a.m. on 1 September.

The UFO Connection

Throughout the history of animal mutilations there have been numerous eyewitness accounts of large, glowing disks or 'silent helicopters' over pastures where dead animals are later found. In 1980, a Waco, Texas rancher encountered two four-foot tall 'creatures' with large, black, slanted eyes, carrying a calf which was later found dead and mutilated.[4] A Missouri couple in 1983 watched through binoculars as two small beings in tight-fitting silver suits worked on a cow in a nearby pasture. The alien heads were large and grey.

Several hypnosis sessions with various UFO abductees have produced information suggesting that the alien intruders are using the tissues and blood for genetic experimentation and sustenance. One woman in Missouri who has experienced repeated encounters with small grey beings (and large black eyes) claimed that the creatures told her, 'We use substances from cows in an essential biochemical process for our survival.'

Downey, Idaho

In the continuing harvest of 1989, over half of the Idaho mutilations were of young calves. On 24 December 1989, a steer calf was found north of Downey, Idaho, lying on its back with the rectum and genitals neatly cut out of the white belly. No blood could be seen anywhere. The animal was taken to Dr Chris Oats at the Hawthorne Animal Hospital for an autopsy. She checked all of the vital organs and was unable to determine the cause of death. During the autopsy, a sharp cut was found in the right chest and Dr Oats discovered that a main blood artery had been severed under the wound. She was surprised that though the steer had lost a large amount of blood, she could not understand where it went to, since there was no blood on the animal or on the ground. Dr Oats also determined that the steer had not been dragged by the neck or tied up around the feet.

Maple Valley, Washington

Southern Idaho was not alone in its fear and confusion about the mutilations. William Veenhuizen woke up on 17 July 1989 to find his finest cow mutilated about 200 yards from his farmhouse in Maple Valley, Washington, south-east of Seattle. The six-year-old animal was due to calve in about three weeks. But the mutilators had cut away a smooth oval section of the cow's mouth, removed a section of jaw with teeth, excised the tongue (Plate 9:3) and cut out the entire udder, vagina, and rectal area. The calf was still inside the belly.

Mr Veenhuizen recalls that around 1 a.m. on 17 July something woke him up. He even put his shoes on and went outside, but neither saw nor heard anything out of the ordinary. He was so upset after the mutilation that he started keeping the rest of his animals inside his barn. 'A neighbour said to me that coyotes did it,' he commented later, 'but I said the coyotes don't have that sharp a knife.'

Bill Veenhuizen was not the only farmer in Maple Valley, Washington, having mutilation problems. On Sunday, 11 November, two female sheep were found with their sexual organs removed. The Hicks-Raburn King County Police found small holes on the carcasses that they concluded might be gun pellet wounds, but no pellets were found.

Red Cloud, Nebraska

In November 1989 rancher Ron Bartels found a 1000-pound Chianina cow dead and mutilated in Red Cloud, Nebraska. The Franklin County Sheriff Department investigated and veterinarian Dr Carl Guthrie was asked to perform a necropsy.

In his report, Dr Guthrie stated that a four-inch straight incision had been made over the cervical trachea. Beyond that cut inside the animal, over eight inches of trachea and œsophagus had been surgically removed. 'The skin over the abdomen was removed in a clear, demarcated line – no musculature disturbed,' the veterinarian commented. And the rectum and vagina were cored out. 'There were definite signs of suspicious acts to the body of this cow – the nature in which the skin was severed and removed was not characteristic of a predator strike,' Dr Guthrie concluded.

In addition to those cuts described by Dr Guthrie, the neat circular patch of skin removed around the cow's eye, along with eyeball, is one of the hallmarks of animal mutilations since the 1970s (Plate 9:4).

Ron Bartels told me that 'after several days, there had been no predation, and with the number of coyotes we now have in this area, they [normally] completely strip a carcass very quickly.' But nothing had touched the strangely cut cow.

How are the Cuts made?

In my book *An Alien Harvest*, I show for the first time that tissue gathered from mutilator cuts in Arkansas on 11 March 1989, revealed the following characteristics under microscope examination:

(1)   The cut line is pinpoint thin.

(2)   The cut line was subjected to high heat, probably 300 degrees Fahrenheit or above, leaving a hard, darkened edge.

(3)   The cuts were made rapidly, probably in two minutes or less, because there is no inflammatory cell destruction which typically begins in a few minutes after any trauma to tissue.

Plate 9:5 shows the clean, bloodless 18 × 22 inches excision in a pregnant cow found on the L. C. Wyatt farm near Hope, Arkansas, on 10 March 1989. Colour photomicrographs (reproduced in my book) show a microscopic view of tissue cut from that cow's belly, and indicate that the blood was subjected to high heat which ruptured the blood cells.

These findings were made by Dr John Altshuler, Assistant Clinical Professor of Medicine (Hematology) and Pathology at the University of Colorado Health Sciences Center in Denver. Dr Altshuler has been keenly interested in the cattle mutilations ever since he witnessed UFO activity in Colorado in 1967 and shortly afterwards examined a horse ('Lady') which had been mutilated. His examination convinced him that we were dealing with highly advanced technology. He states in *An Alien Harvest*:

'. . . When I got close to the horse, I could also see that it was also cut from the neck down to the base of the chest in a vertical, clean incision. At the edge of the cut, there was a darkened colour as if the flesh had been opened and cauterized with a modern-day laser. But there was no surgical laser technology like that in 1967. Today when we use cauterizing to control bleeding, the flesh still has a soft, pliable feeling. But the edges of that horse-cut were stiff, leathery and a bit hardened . . .'[5]

The first significant laser use in medical surgery began in the late 1970s to early 1980s. In 1979–80, when I produced the film, *A Strange Harvest*, I asked a laser surgeon at Rose Medical Center in Denver to demonstrate laser cuts on poultry bodies for my camera. It took him about seventeen minutes to remove a two-inch diameter by one-eighth-inch deep circle of flesh *after* a team of experts took nearly a half hour to set up the bulky equipment. To make large cuts, I was told then and in 1989, surgeons still use scalpels or electric cauterizers.

In April 1989 a sales engineer reported that a laser required to make the type of cuts described in the mutilations at the L. C. Wyatt farm in Hope, Arkansas, would weigh 550 pounds and would be the size of an average office desk. The length of laser would be three feet. With the existing known laser equipment, surgery covering that large an area on just one cow would take about an hour in a hospital facility, the engineer said. He also stated that the equipment is expensive, with an average cost of about $20,000, not including the electrical generators required and special wiring. Safety precautions would also be needed to protect the eyes from the heat.[6]

The Mutilations Continue

In addition to the 1989 mutilation reports in Idaho, Washington, Nebraska, and Arkansas, there have been other cases in Colorado, Oklahoma, Missouri, and Florida. Furthermore, over 800 wild horses in Nevada have died mysteriously, about seventy domestic cats have been found dead and bloodlessly mutilated in Tustin, California, and thirty more cats in the East Bay of San Francisco. A city employee in Setauket, Long Island, New York, has reported to me that about a dozen racoons, opossums, dogs and cats have been found bloodlessly mutilated – with cuts similar to cows – in the Percy Rayner Park. I have also received calls about mutilations in Canada, but have no firm photographs or reports.

Alien Harvest

After *An Alien Harvest* was released in June 1989, I received a letter from a security guard in Denver, Colorado, who described a night in August 1987 when he was patrolling the grounds of a large corporation west of the city. From his truck he could see a large circle of lights in the dark sky. The lights remained stationary over a pasture a few hundred feet away. He was afraid to report the incident because UFOs meant ridicule and he did not want to lose his job. But he later regretted not having reported it because the following morning he watched a farmer gather up a couple of dead and mutilated cows from the pasture where the lights had hovered overhead. 'What kind of technology are we talking about?', he asked me. 'I never took my eyes off those lights. There was no beam, no sound – nothing. How did they do it?'

That is a question which has haunted ranchers and law enforcement officials since the first worldwide reported mutilation of a horse ('Lady') in 1967. Not only how, but why? If alien life forms are intruding on this planet and harvesting from animals and humans, are genetic experimentation and sustenance the answer? Or is this only *part* of a larger alien need?

Will the 1990s finally bring humans face to face with an alien intelligence that has secretly used Earth-life for aeons? As we become more conscious of its presence, will we learn that the alien intent is simply to survive, with or without human help? Or is there some larger and more complex alien scheme which could challenge the future of human existence?

REFERENCES
1. VHS copies of *A Strange Harvest* are available from Linda Moulton Howe Productions, P.O. Box 3130, Littleton, Colorado 80161, USA, and from Quest International Publications, 15 Pickard Court, Temple Newsam, Leeds, Yorkshire, LS15 9AY, UK.
2. Howe, Linda Moulton: *An Alien Harvest*, Linda Moulton Howe Productions, 1990.
3. Ibid. p. 101.
4. Ibid. p. 83.
5. Ibid. p. 4.
6. Williamson, Jim: 'Cattle Mutilations with Significant Evidence', *Little River News*, Ashdown, Arkansas, 20 April 1989.

10

World Round-up of Selected Reports

TIMOTHY GOOD

Although certain correlations can be made, no firm conclusions of a statistical nature should be drawn from the following reports, which I have selected from hundreds, covering the period of January 1989 to April 1990.

The preponderance of reports from the USA, Great Britain, and the USSR, for example, should not lead to the assumption that more sightings have occurred in these countries. The shortage or lack of reports from other countries is probably due to such factors as a reluctance to report, a dearth of researchers or journalists, and poor communications.

In addition to providing some interesting reports, my intention here is to emphasize the massive scale of the phenomenon, which is too frequently overlooked.

Those requiring further information should contact the reporters, researchers, newspapers, and journals concerned, since I am unable to vouch for the accuracy of all these necessarily condensed accounts.

---

18 January 1989: Somerville, Ohio, USA

At 3.57 a.m. a retired air force man, awakened by his barking dog, observed three oval-shaped objects fifty yards away. He woke his family and together they watched for most of two hours as the objects moved low over nearby farm buildings and land, displaying various bright colours which covered the surfaces from an apparent belt of light on each. At one point, the father and son chased the objects by car before losing sight of them. Shortly thereafter, two of the objects returned over an adjacent field before departing again. (Dick Seifried, *MUFON UFO Journal*, No. 259, Nov. 1989)

24 January 1989: Valliant, Oklahoma, USA

More than a dozen witnesses gave almost identical reports of an hour-long display of luminous objects. One family described two large objects, diamond or triangular in shape, with red, blue, and white lights, at tree-top level, accompanied by four or five other smaller bright objects which made individual manoeuvres around the larger objects. (*McCurtain Daily Gazette*, Idabel, Oklahoma, 1 Feb. 1989)

30 January 1989: Benfleet, Essex, UK

At 9.40 p.m. a witness reported seeing a large object 'the size of a double-decker bus' moving slowly and silently across the sky at about 800–1,000 feet altitude. It had two sets of lights or windows along the centre and the length was estimated at 250–300 feet (Figure 10:1). (Ron West, East Anglian UFO & Paranormal Research Association)

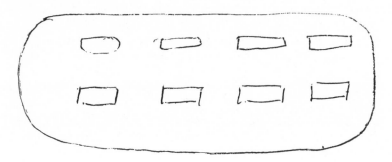

Figure 10:1. The description was of a black object with white lighted windows.

30 January 1989: Montauk, Long Island, NY, USA

A triangular- or diamond-shaped object was observed by Captain David Gaviola and two crew members of his fishing boat, just after leaving Montauk Harbour. The object, which appeared to be about 150 feet long, caused the boat's radar set to fail. It 'turned belly-up and then cruised west, then south, climbing higher until it disappeared,' reported the witnesses, after which the radar set became operational again. (Russell Drumm, *Star*, East Hampton, NY, 9 Feb. 1989)

8 February 1989: Stroud, Gloucestershire, UK

A policeman reported seeing a triangular-shaped flying object a mile away from the A46 road near Stroud. (*Swindon Star*, Wiltshire, 16 Feb. 89)

10 February 1989: Fyffe, Alabama, USA

Many witnesses reported seeing a 'banana-shaped' aircraft in DeKalb County [leading to some amusing comments in the British tabloids about 'Fyffe's bananas'! – *Ed.*] 'There was a red light on each end and a white line between them,' one witness in Grove Oak reported to the police. 'The top of the curve was outlined in green lights.' When the craft turned, the green lights splayed outwards 'like fireworks'.

Police chief Junior Garmany and assistant chief Fred Works were sent to investigate. 'It was completely silent,' said Garmany. 'We got out of the car and turned off the engine and the radio. When we started towards it, it began moving away.' The officers followed the object in their car for about twelve miles, then it suddenly reversed direction and silently flew over the heads of the startled officers at an estimated altitude of 1,000–1,500 feet. 'We figured it was going about three or four hundred miles an hour,' Garmany reported. 'It looked like an airplane at first, and it was moving fast,' added Works. Garmany said that the object was 'bigger than a jumbo-jet' and 'oval-shaped', while Works described it as 'triangular-shaped'. The object appeared to be metallic in hue, and had no wings, windows, or letterings, with flashing green, red, and white lights along the sides. White lights dotted the bottom, which appeared to be shining upward, illuminating the bottom of the strange aircraft.

The DeKalb County Sheriff's Office received over fifty telephone calls about the sightings. One terrified Lickskillet resident 'was about to have a heart attack and his wife was screaming,' an official said. 'He said it came over at tree-top level and that he had shot at it with a 12-gauge shotgun.'

Spokesmen at various airports and Air Force and Air National Guard bases said none of their aircraft was in the DeKalb County area on the night in question. (Elton Roberts, *Times Journal*, Fort Payne, Alabama, 14 Feb. 1989; *News Journal*, Pensacola, Florida, 23 Feb. 1989) [Numerous sightings were subsequently reported during the following weeks. – *Ed.*]

13 February 1989: Nalchik, Checheno-Ingush, USSR

At 21.30, Beslan A. Shogenov, a militia (police) lieutenant, claimed to have seen an extraordinary aerial craft. 'At first I thought it was a passenger jet crashing,' he said, 'but it seemed about ten times the size of a plane. It had a sharp nose, a tail at the back, and very short wings, from which sparks fell to the ground, and clusters of lights continually came out of the tail (see Figures 10:2, 3). I was particularly amazed by the huge portholes along the side of the machine, which were brightly illuminated. I counted ten of them. No people could be seen. All this took place in total silence. I was afraid the thing might explode, but it flew toward the Chegem forest, hovered for a few seconds, the light faded and it disappeared, as if dissolving in the air. The whole sighting lasted about five or six minutes.'

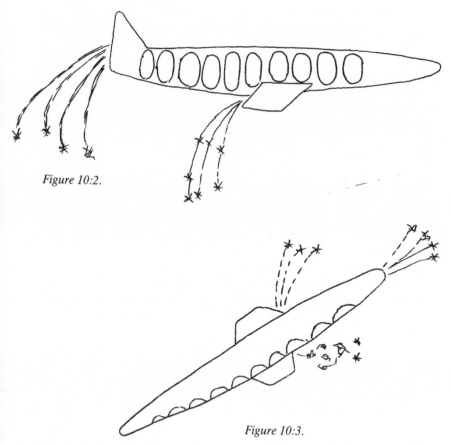

Figure 10:2.

Figure 10:3.

Two views of the object seen by police lieutenant Beslan Shogenov at Nalchik, Checheno-Ingush (USSR), on 13 February 1989. (Sketches by Nikolai Lebedev, copied from Nedelya, *No. 23, 1989)*

217

A junior sergeant, Artur Aiubov, observed the same (or similar) object at about 22.00: '. . . I saw something fantastic in the sky. My first impression was that this was an aircraft on fire, but it was moving so slowly and silently, and emitted bright lights like searchlights, trailing a tail as if from a bright red flame.'

Among hundreds of other witnesses who saw the object as it flew over large areas of Dagestan and Checheno-Ingush were doctors, militia personnel, and a *Nedelya* correspondent, Uri Gergokov. (*Nedelya*, No. 23, 1989, translated by Nikolai Lebedev)

20 February 1989: Basildon, Essex, UK

A motorist claimed to have been followed for ten minutes by a 12-inch metallic disk as he was driving along the A12 road from Brentwood. The disk was moving at about three feet above the road and twenty-five feet behind a car in front, which was seventy-five yards away. (*Southend Evening Echo*, 23 Feb. 1989; *Essex Chronicle*, 3 March 1989) [The witness was also interviewed by the East Anglian UFO & Paranormal Association who found him to be sincere. – *Ed.*]

20–23 February 1989: Russell, Kansas, USA

On 20 February, an object was said to have landed east and slightly north of Russell, Kansas. An unnamed woman described it as 'huge, about the size of a football field . . . a city of lights'. Frightened, she left the area. On 21 February, a 'prominent lady and a male friend' claimed to have sighted eleven objects, and twenty-two on 22 February. Also on that date, a motorist caught sight of a group of lights. Other witnesses gave matching descriptions. The objects manoeuvred soundlessly. At one stage, five of the UFOs joined into a formation and hovered above the town. The objects reportedly moved swiftly, 'coming to a sudden dead stop and hovering'. In the hover position, the lights blinked in a specific pattern. (Irene Jepsen, *Daily News*, Russell, Kansas, 24 Feb. 1980)

25 February 1989: Benayeo, Victoria, Australia

Mrs Nella Williams claimed to have observed a large oblong object which remained stationary in the sky for five minutes, at 7.30 a.m. She reported that the object was very bright and shiny, with a dome shape at the rear end, and it disappeared without any apparent movement. It was 'there one moment and gone the next', she said. (*Advocate*, Eden Hope, Victoria, 1 March 1989)

February–March 1989: Guatemala City, Guatemala

Hundreds of sightings were reported by witnesses, including doctors, lawyers, students, and government officials. Most of the sightings were made from forty miles north-east of Guatemala City. 'We saw two red lights far off in the distance,' reported Juan Carlos del Monte. 'They seemed to be playing around out in space. Then suddenly, one began to move. Within thirty seconds, it was flying over our heads. It was bigger than a jumbo jet, and it did not make a sound. It was circular in shape, with one red light and three amber lights.' (David Kirby, UPI, *Arizona Republic*, Phoenix, Arizona, 5 March 1989)

12 March 1989: Fyffe, Alabama, USA

Gary Coker observed an extremely large object with red and green flashing lights on the side and two white lights on the bottom. The object suddenly vanished. Five miles away, another witness, at exactly the same time (7.30 p.m.), said that an object the size of a football field hovered over his chicken house. It was a metallic blue, with two white lights underneath and red and green lights on the sides. (*Weekly Post*, Rainsville, Alabama, 16 March 1989)

14 March 1990: Over the French Polynesian Islands

At 6.30 a.m. (EST), radio ham Donald Ratsch, who had been monitoring the communications of the space shuttle *Discovery* from his home in Baltimore, Maryland, heard the following communication: 'Houston, Discovery, we have a problem. We have a fire'. Checking his recorder, he found that it had stopped, and inserted another tape. At 6.42 a.m., the following message was recorded: 'Uh, Houston, uh, this is Discovery. We still have the alien spacecraft under observance.'

Between 6.30 and 6.40 a.m., another radio ham in Baltimore, Ron Trump, reported hearing the transmission: 'Kicking in breakers. Houston, we have a problem . . . We have a fire.'

The communications of the *Discovery* (STS-29) astronauts were being retransmitted over several frequencies by the Goddard Amateur Radio Club (WA3NAN) at NASA's Goddard Space Flight Center in Greenbelt, Maryland. Only the unclassified channel or channels were being sent over the air. The two radio hams were receiving the broadcasts on 147.450mhz. Extensive investigation by Vincent DiPietro (whose report is available from the Fund for UFO Research) and former NASA mission specialist Bob Oechsler, revealed that the recorded voice was probably not that of any of the astronauts on board, according to Voice Identification Inc., a New Jersey company, for example, who concluded:

... the results of our analysis fall in the 'probable' range because of the limited number of words on the questioned recording ... With the additional samples that you sent us we were able to locate more repetitions of each word, giving us a better basis for determining the intraspeaker variability of [crew member] Dr Bagian's voice. From our preliminary analysis, his was the only one of the five astronauts whose voiceprints exhibited enough similarity to the questioned speaker to warrant further analysis. Upon further analysis ... we found that there was more dis-similarity than similarity, indicating that Dr Bagian was not the questioned speaker ... It is our opinion that in all probability, none of the five astronauts made the questioned transmission. This analysis carries a low degree of confidence due to the previously mentioned limitations.

Colonel John Blaha, the captain, whose voice was also considered a possibility, denied that the incident had ever occurred. Bob Oechsler has told me that none of the communications heard by the radio hams was located on the official *Discovery* tapes, and that the transmissions were made from the Fort Meade, Maryland, area – where the National Security Agency has its headquarters. He is also puzzled by the fact that a NASA source informed him that an incident involving a UFO, lasting eight hours, had in fact taken place, causing extensive electrical problems on board.

17 March 1989: Perm, Siberia, USSR
Many witnesses observed a flying object, with a diameter of thirty metres, moving at an estimated speed of 70 k.p.h. Suddenly it changed to a vertical trajectory, accelerating to an estimated 7,000 k.p.h. At one stage, a beam of light extended then retracted from the object. (*Soviet Youth*, July 1989)

17 March 1989: Gulf Breeze, Florida, USA
A retired F-4 [Phantom] pilot took three Polaroid photos of a UFO from the Garcon Point peninsula at about 3.45 p.m. 'I was able to snap three photos in rapid succession before the object departed to the west,' the witness said. 'I'm not sure what I photographed but it wasn't one of our local aircraft. This thing made no noise and climbed away like a rocket. I can't reveal my name because my co-workers would think I flipped out ...' (Figure 10:4) (*Sentinel*, Gulf Breeze, Florida, 30 March 1989)

21 March 1989: Longmont, Colorado, USA
According to a member of the National Air Traffic Controllers

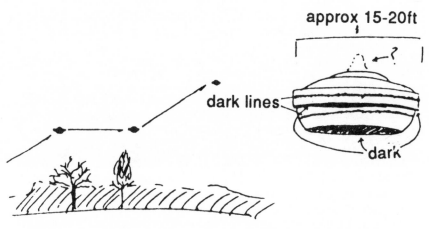

Figure 10:4. The whole craft was bronze or gold in colour with no visible windows.

Association, UFOs were tracked at the FAA's *en route* centre at Longmont, Colorado. 'Longmont air traffic controllers at several sectors were astonished to see numerous "UFOs" appearing on their radar displays,' said centre spokesman and safety chairman Kevin Cain. 'These unidentified targets looked like actual aircraft, with apparently normal speeds and altitudes', Cain's written statement said. 'Some controllers had a dozen or more of these targets over a half-hour period.' But Mitch Barker, an FAA spokesman at the regional office in Seattle, debunked the report. 'They were having a problem with the transponders that automatically send information from the aircraft to the centre,' he said. (*Coloradoan*, Fort Collins, Colorado, 26 March 1989). [*Editor's note*: Some military aircraft with sophisticated jamming equipment can generate dozens of false radar echoes, each aimed slightly differently, creating the impression of a whole squadron of planes arrayed at various intervals across the sky. It is highly unlikely that such equipment would be used in the vicinity of a civilian air traffic control centre without adequate warning, but the possibility cannot be overlooked.]

2(?) April 1989: Bogota, Colombia

Bogota's international airport was put on a state of alert after a UFO flew over it, forcing aircraft preparing to land to divert to another airport 500 kilometres away, according to several passengers. The soundless UFO was detected on radar and seen by a number of witnesses, including passenger Teresa Sanchez, who stated that the captain announced that he was changing course due to the presence of the UFO. (*Jornal Noticias*, Portugal, 3 April 1989)

21 April 1989: Haifa, Israel

At 2.20 a.m. a young Israeli couple, Alon Eilat and Ada Biderman, were driving along a beach in Haifa when they noticed a huge glowing light over the sea, emanating from an object. The couple got out of their car and saw the object begin to descend, appearing to change shape. The object fell noiselessly for about six seconds and came to rest on the beach about 300 metres away. The witnesses estimated the object at about twenty metres long and six metres wide.

On landing, the object suddenly burst into a huge pillar of flame and emitted white/blue sparks. Thinking an aircraft might have crashed, the couple ran towards the craft to help, but were prevented from doing so by the intense heat. After about ten minutes, however, they were able to get closer, and as they approached they noticed that within the flame was a lump of heated, elliptically shaped material. This material had some holes in it which gradually became larger until they formed a larger hole, from which sparks and flames continued to appear. The couple threw stones on to the fire in an attempt to stifle the flames, which only grew larger.

The couple summoned the police, who also made a vain attempt to put out the fire with stones. At 3.00 a.m. the police sent for Israeli UFO researcher Hadassah Arbel, who by the time she arrived found a formless lump of crispy white and extremely light material that was still hot. The object had come down on a dry, rocky part of the beach, surrounded on most sides by the sea, and within a radius of fifteen metres of the lump the sea was bubbling. It was still bubbling when Hadassah Arbel left at 5.00 a.m.

Samples of the remaining material were sent to various laboratories for analysis. Iron, zinc, niobium, indium, copper, arsenic, molybdenum, antimony, magnesium, chlorine, sodium, calcium, titanium, and manganese were among the substances found during a university analysis arranged by the Canadian UFO Research Network (CUFORN). 'Of great significance is the presence of technetium,' it was noted. 'If this can be confirmed, this element is not present in the crust of the Earth.' [Technetium is a fission product of uranium. – *Ed.*]

Quest International sent another sample to a university in England, and the results of their preliminary analysis were as follows:

> The material supplied consists of three aggregates of white grains. Examination of these under binocular microscope revealed that the material was composed of grain aggregates with a dust-like appearance.
>
> A small portion of the material was then ground/disaggregated to a fine powder and examined by X-ray diffraction [in order] to reveal the nature of the compound, not its chemistry. The mineral Periclase (MgO) [natural magnesium oxide] . . . Although this is a naturally occurring material it is rare and not found in this powdery form. No other phases were evident from the X-ray diffraction analysis; this means only that no other phase is present in over about 5% of the sample weight.
>
> Two of the smaller aggregates were mounted and coated for SEM [Scanning Electron Microscope] analysis. The samples were coated with gold so as to produce better images than would be possible from a carbon coat. SEM examination revealed that the substance is composed largely of a series of hollow spheres and plates with a large void space between the grains. This structure is not consistent with the sample being natural Periclase. EDX [Energy Dispersive X-ray] analysis showed as expected, that Magnesium is the dominant element together with minor and variable amounts of Ca [Calcium], Na [Sodium], Cl [Chlorine], S & K [Sulphur & Potassium].
>
> The remainder of the sample was prepared for XRF [X-ray Fluorescence]. This involved crushing the sample and pressing the powder into a 32-mm diameter pellet. The sample was then analysed qualitatively on a Philips PW 1400 XRF spectrometer for its trace element content. The results of this were: Bromine, Strontium, Rubidium, Iron, Thorium (radio-active), and Uranium. Elements present in larger amounts: Mg, Na, Cl, S, K.
>
> In conclusion, all I can say is that this sample is not a natural terrestrial sample of Periclase and that to the best of my knowledge Periclase is not known from meteorites. From your description of the origin of this material, my best guess is that it is the product of burning Magnesium, but has a different structure from the Periclase produced when I burnt a piece of Magnesium ribbon . . .

(Tony Dodd/Hadassah Arbel, *Quest International* (the journal of UFO investigation), Vol. 9, No. 3, 1989. Further details may be obtained from Tony Dodd: 18 Hardy Meadows, Grassington, Skipton, North Yorkshire, BD23 5DL.)

21 April 1989: Crestview, Florida, USA

At 9.15 p.m. a man, alerted by his barking dogs, saw a disk hovering overhead within a few hundred feet. The object, which made a humming sound, was estimated to be 90 feet in diameter, with window-like sections around the perimeter and a brilliant white light centred on the underneath. The witness grabbed a .22

calibre rifle and took aim, at which point a beam of light engulfed him and the weapon misfired. The object then sped away. (Allen Reynolds, *MUFON UFO Journal*, No. 259, November 1989).

24 April 1989: Cherepovetsk, Vologda, USSR

According to local inhabitant I. Veselova, a strange object, three times larger than a plane, flew over the city of Cherepovetsk. The UFO coasted at an altitude of 300 metres absolutely noiselessly, leaving a large radiant trail. (*Trud*, 24 June 1989)

1 May (?) 1989: Llandudno, North Wales, UK

Douglas Haig Hughes, a retired former RAF gunner, together with his wife, sighted a 'cylinder-shaped object' which approached from the Glan Conway area about 600 feet up and proceeded towards Llandudno. 'It was massive in diameter,' said Mr Hughes. 'It appeared at first to be moving at about 45 to 55 m.p.h. Then it slowed down and flashed a bright red light, like an infrared light, from the window of the cylinder on to us. We didn't feel anything. When the light went out, it travelled on towards Llandudno. It was definitely not from this earth . . . There was no noise at all.' (*North Wales Weekly News*, Conway, Wales, 4 May 1989)

2 May 1989: Southend-on-Sea, Essex, UK

At 9.00 p.m. several witnesses saw a very large, black, silent object shaped like a 'triangle or Manta-ray fish' with shimmering edges, which during the few minutes of observation 'changed its

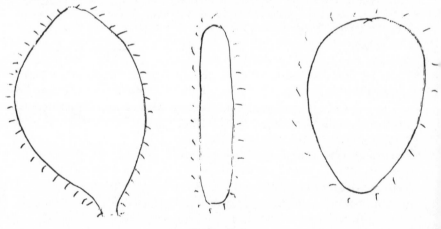

Figure 10:5.

form three times, appearing to revolve around itself before showing its true form'. (Figure 10:5) (G. & D. Dillon, East Anglian UFO & Paranormal Association)

10 May 1989: Bautista Canyon, Anza, California, USA

An elderly woman was driving from the Bautista Canyon area when she noticed a mushroom-shaped luminous craft, measuring an estimated thirty feet in diameter, that descended and hovered slightly above powerlines. She stopped her vehicle and observed about six to eight beings emerge from the craft and begin working on the outside. After approximately ten minutes they re-entered the object, which departed with a loud humming sound and a burst of blue flame. There were reports of TV and electrical interference at the time. (Debbie Steinberg, *Anza Valley Outlook*, Anza, California, 2 June 1989)

16 May 1989: Perm, Siberia, USSR

An object allegedly landed on the banks of the River Kama, leaving rectangular marks measuring 12 × 4 metres. (*Soviet Youth*, July 1989)

28 May 1989: Edmonton, Alberta, Canada

Witness Mr Gilmore claimed to have had a close encounter with a UFO shortly after 1.30 a.m. '. . . I could see depth and everything into it,' he reported. 'The bottom was shaped like the bow of a boat . . . It looked large to me but there was nothing to judge it against. I held up my index finger to get a relationship but it's hard to judge. I guess it was about 1,500 to 2,000 feet away and about 800 feet wide . . . It was shimmering and what looked like heat waves radiated from it, but there was no heat.' (Randy LaBoucane, *Examiner*, Edmonton, Alberta, 11 June 1989)

6 June 1989: Konantsevo, Vologda, USSR

A group of children outside the village of Konantsevo observed 'a fast-increasing luminous dot in the sky, which soon turned into a shining sphere', the official news agency TASS reported. 'The mysterious object reportedly landed in a meadow and rolled to a nearby river as the children looked on no more than half a kilometre away. They claim that they saw the sphere kind of split, and something resembling a headless person in dark garb appeared in the meadow. It struck them that the alien's hands hung lower than his knees. At that moment, however, the "flying craft" melted into the air, while the creature from it proceeded to the village.' TASS quoted 'eyewitness' accounts as saying that three more spheres later touched down in the same meadow. 'Just like the very first one, the rest of the spheres and their "passengers" quickly became invisible.' (*UPI*, Moscow, 24 June 1989)

4 July 1989: Kiev, USSR

Vera Prokofievna, Alexsandra Stepanona, and a young girl claimed to have had a bizarre encounter with three 'aliens' in a strange 'boat' on a canal, towards twilight. The beings wore silvery, collarless suits, and their faces were identical and pale, with long, golden hair and large, radiant eyes. 'Are you tourists? Where are you from?', the witnesses asked. The beings replied in Russian, but with a strange accent: 'We have flown from another planet. The whereabouts of this planet is beyond human understanding. If you come with us you will understand. Every day we take one person from Earth. We will show our ship to you.' At this point, the 'aliens' came out of their 'boat'.

One alien went in front of the women and the other two went to their side. The witnesses tried to run away but felt tingling sensations and were unable to move or shout. They explained to the strangers that they were unwilling to accompany them as they had families to look after. Through some trees could be seen a 'spaceship', which resembled a giant, silvery-white barrel with a round aerial at the top. 'Well, we will not take you with us. We will find others,' the strangers allegedly responded, then entered the craft by means of a step-ladder, and took off quickly and silently.

A local UFO researcher, A. F. Pugach, declared that in his opinion all the witnesses were truthful. In addition, the Iskuskovi family in Podgorczi, near Kiev, claimed to have seen a large, round flying object, together with people in silvery suits, which landed at 22.40. (Adapted from Nikolai Lebedev's translation of an article appearing in *Nedelya*, No. 33, 14–20 Aug. 1989)

7 July 1989: Kanazawa, Ishikawa Prefecture, Japan

A video film of a diamond-shaped UFO was taken as it first descended rapidly then suddenly changed directions and rose at a steep angle and at such a speed that it disappeared from several video frames. The photographer, Yasuhiko Hamazaki, also managed to get some close-up film of the object, which shows a Saturn-shaped white object with a prominent ring encircling it in the horizontal plane (Figures 10:6 and 10:7). Optical physicist Dr

Bruce Maccabee (whose report is available from the Fund for UFO Research) concluded that the object on the film could be acknowledged as a 'real UFO'. (Dr Richard Haines, *MUFON UFO Journal*, No. 263, March 1990; *Japan Times*, Tokyo, 23 Sept. 1989)

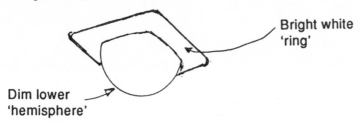

Bright white
'ring'

Dim lower
'hemisphere'

(Blue sky background)

Dim 'gap'

Bright spots

Figure 10:6. Two sketches of the object filmed by Yasuhiko Hamazaki.

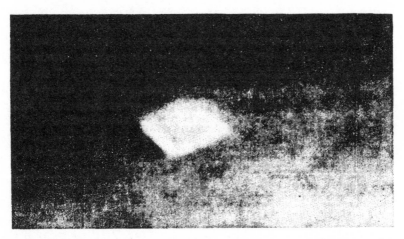

Figure 10:7. A frame from the Hamazaki video film. (Yasuhiko Hamazaki)

12 July 1989: Southend-on-Sea, Essex, UK

Two witnesses reported a cone-shaped object that kept pace with their car. It was 'lit up like a Christmas tree' with different colours and seemed to be rotating anticlockwise. When they stopped their car for a better look, the object shot off at fantastic speed. Four other witnesses reported sightings of the same object. (Figure 10:8) (Ron West, East Anglian UFO & Paranormal Research Association)

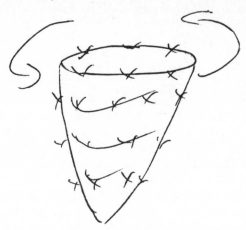

Figure 10:8. Crosses denote multi-coloured lights.

16 July 1989: Hilton Head Island, South Carolina, USA

A security supervisor claimed to have observed an illuminated oblong-shaped object, the length of a football field, with a large window on one side, at 1.30 a.m. The object had a greyish metallic back end and was moving at about 20 m.p.h. The witness got a good view of the object for nearly five minutes, and managed to alert his wife before it picked up speed and disappeared in a streak of light. (Greg Barrett, *Hilton Head News*, Hilton Head Island, South Carolina, 20 July 1989)

22 July 1989: Swans Island, Maine, USA

Two pilots flying over Blue Hill Bay claimed to have seen a UFO in the vicinity of Swans Island or Bass Harbor. 'I've got 4,500 hours flying time as a commercial pilot and I've never seen anything like this during the day,' said Randy Rhodes, who was flying with a lawyer friend, Bill Rieff, when the two sighted the object at about 3.00 p.m. They described it as a metallic, oblong-shaped disk which moved extremely quickly in one direction, stopped, then moved again. The object appeared to be about 25 miles away. No military or civilian planes were in the area at the time. (Polly Saltonstall, *Times*, Bar Harbor, Maine, 3 Aug. 1989)

8 August 1989: McGuire Nuclear Plant, North Carolina, USA

At about 2.30 p.m., Paul Moore observed a reddish-brown, triangular object at an estimated height of 1,000 feet, which then dived to about 300 feet above the ground and headed towards the McGuire nuclear sub-station. (*Lincolnton Times-News*, 6 Sept. 1989)

9/10 August 1989: Clacton-on-Sea/Leigh-on-Sea, Essex, and Margate, Kent, UK

At midnight, two witnesses saw a very large round object, about 200 feet in diameter, with blue, green, and red lights spinning in an anticlockwise direction, which seemed to be made of a dark metallic material. No noise could be discerned as the object hovered at a height of about 150 feet. Suddenly, it shot out to sea at tremendous speed.

A woman in Leigh-on-Sea, driving home at midnight, was astonished when 'this huge round object shot right across my view. It was approximately 200–250 feet across and the same distance up, and had blue, green, and red lights spinning anticlockwise'. The object crossed the Thames Estuary and headed towards Kent. Three other witnesses reported a similar object in Leigh-on-Sea at the same time.

At 1.30 a.m. on 10 August, two students near Margate, Kent, claimed to have witnessed a UFO descending into a cornfield, making a low humming sound, and to have found two circles in the corn. This incident now appears to have been a hoax. [See Chapter 1, and Plate 1:10.] (Ron West, East Anglian UFO & Paranormal Research Association)

23 August 1989: Gulf Breeze, Florida

Two women observed a 'silver or white' delta-shaped object (estimated 70 feet per side) pass low and almost directly overhead. On the leading apex was a globe or cluster of white lights, 12–16 feet in diameter. Globes or clusters of red were at the other apexes. Three lights – one white the others red – followed closely behind. After trying to follow the object in their car, the women drove to a friend's home, where they saw the same or similar object and lights pass by. (Carol and Rex Salisberry, *MUFON UFO Journal*, No. 260, Dec. 1989)

31 August 1989: Trumbull, Connecticut, USA

Two witnesses saw 'small white lights in what appeared to be a triangular shape, moving very slowly' and making a low humming sound. It stood motionless for about a minute, followed one witness's car, and then disappeared in an easterly direction. (Ellen Beveridge, *Times*, Trumbull, Connecticut, 7 Sept. 1989)

11 September 1989: Near Pickeral Lake, Kalamazoo County, Michigan, USA

Alerted by the barking of numerous dogs, two fishermen noticed a cross-shaped object, with four rows of red lights along with many tubes and pipes lining the underside. Its length was estimated at 250 feet, and it had broad stubby 'wings' near the front (c.f. with Figures 10:2). As it neared the witnesses at tree-top level, the vehicle halted and hovered, and a low hum/whistle could be heard. One of the men ran and stood directly under it for about forty seconds, sensing warmth. The object then glided away, and the witnesses followed in their truck. After a few miles, the object reversed and again approached. The men stopped and began flashing their headlights, at which point the object made a smooth turn and headed out of sight at high speed. (Shirley & George Coyne, *MUFON UFO Journal*, No. 262, Feb. 1990)

12 September 1989: Pensacola, Florida, USA

Thirty-five witnesses, including twelve investigators for the Mutual UFO network (MUFON) sighted an elliptical, red, glowing object in the sky, which hovered for several minutes and then began to ascend toward the east. The object entered cloud cover but could still be seen. Seven minutes into the sighting the red object was no longer visible, but a white object was then seen ten degrees further to the west which moved swiftly toward the west before disappearing. Ed Walters, the well-known witness who has photographed many UFOs in nearby Gulf Breeze, was the only person who had a camera, and he took two shots with a small 110 camera. (*Sentinel*, Gulf Breeze, Florida, 21 Sept. 1989)

21–29 September 1989: Voronezh, USSR

A series of extraordinary sightings, including landings by 'aliens', was reported worldwide. (See Chapter 3)

9 October 1989: Melbourne, Australia

At 9.15 p.m. two witnesses driving in Melbourne encountered an orange-red object, about twenty feet in diameter, at ground level near some power lines. From a hover position, the object climbed into the sky, flew over the car and disappeared from view over a hill. John Auchettl, of the Victorian UFO Research Society, noted unusual markings on the ground near where the UFO had been seen. Laboratory analysis of grass samples showed that the cells to the upper exposed side of the grass stems were dead, while those on the bottom side were still alive. Tests conducted at Monash University showed, for example, that yellowing of the grass and the surrounding organic material was caused by intense or massive amounts of ultraviolet radiation. (John Auchettl: 'The Churchill Park UFO Encounter/Ground Ring Summary', *The Australian UFO Bulletin*, Victorian UFO Research Society, March 1990)

9 October 1989: Near Tunica, Mississippi, USA

A crop-duster pilot was flying to an assignment at 5.45 p.m. when he spotted an aluminium-coloured sphere, estimated to be 300 feet or more in diameter, rapidly approaching from the distance. The object passed diagonally and below his plane at an estimated 800–900 m.p.h. at a half-mile or greater distance. (James Scarborough, *MUFON UFO Journal*, No. 264, April 1990)

10 October 1989: Memphis/Clarksdale, Tennessee, USA

Pilot Bill Kimmel reported that while flying between Clarksdale and Memphis he observed a round, metallic UFO which kept changing colours and was moving at 800–900 m.p.h., 3,000 feet off his left wing. 'There was no way it was a weather balloon because no balloon can travel that fast,' he commented. (*Commercial Appeal*, Memphis, Tennessee, 12 Oct. 1989)

13 October 1989: Near Langenburg, Saskatchewan, Canada

At 10.20 a.m. Rose Neumeier was surprised by a flash of light at her farm home. Looking out of the window she saw an oblong-shaped, silver object hovering soundlessly above the garage. The light she had seen had apparently come from a bright silver band around the middle of the object. The object then moved off to the north, paused and then returned to hover over the barn. After a few seconds it took off and disappeared in almost an instant. A number of other sightings were reported in the area in mid-October. (George Bentley, *Leader-Post*, Regina, Saskatchewan, 4 Nov. 1989)

14 October 1989: San Marcos, San Diego, California, USA

Toward dusk, Jerry and Janet Clark noticed some red lights in the sky in 'an oval pattern'. Shortly afterwards, together with six other witnesses, the Clarks watched as a dark object passed silently over their heads, its perimeter lights turned off. 'It looked like a boomerang, and it was massively huge, about the size of a football field,' Janet said. Twenty minutes later, a second, 'triangular' object passed over the Clark group, with six military jets in pursuit. Other sightings were reported in the immediate vicinity that night. (Brae Canlen, *Reader*, San Diego, California, 8 Feb. 1990)

23 October 1989: Delamere Forest, Cheshire, UK

At 7.15 p.m. an off-duty police officer and his family were driving past the forest, near the village of Alvenley, when they encountered a triangular object, covered with white, red, and blue lights, which hovered silently for two minutes then shot away. (Peter Hough, *Northern UFO News*, No. 142, April 1990)

24 October 1989: Northern Indiana, USA

A commercial airline crew in flight encountered a boomerang-shaped vehicle passing overhead at 6.15 a.m. A vertical beam of light shone downward from the underside of the object, which passed from view in thirty seconds. (Franklin Reams, *MUFON UFO Journal*, No. 264, April 1990)

26 October 1989: Mangotsfield, Bristol, UK

Simon Carter was walking along a main road at Mangotsfield at 12.45 a.m. when he suddenly became aware of two bright lights approaching, as bright as floodlights at a football ground. As they passed within 150 feet, Mr Carter was able to make out a triangular-shaped object, as large as five articulated lorries. Both lights were on the underside and pointed towards the ground. Although he could clearly see the object, the witness was amazed to observe that it was almost transparent. The UFO then moved away at less than 50 m.p.h., the lights suddenly increased in intensity until the whole structure was engulfed in the glow, and it suddenly disappeared. No sound could be heard throughout the observation. (Tony Dodd, *Quest International*, Vol. 9, No. 3, 1990)

Late October 1989: Kecskemet, Hungary

Hungarian Air Force pilots were followed during training flights by a 'strange, spherical, orange-coloured' object which did not show up on radar, the independent weekly *Del-Kelet* reported. Days later, two soldiers on duty at the airport there saw a figure of fluorescent green about four feet tall who 'passed around a plane, lifted one of his arms and created a cone-shaped light beam above his head, disappearing silently within seconds into a high-rising tunnel of light.' (Reuters, *The Independent*, London, 14 Nov. 1989)

2 November 1989: Cwmtillery, Gwent, South Wales, UK

Three boys, Lee Holt, Carl Jones, and Sidney McLoughlin, claimed to have seen a UFO over Cwmtillery Lake at 5.30 p.m. 'We saw a bright light coming down the hillside,' said Lee. 'It was really low in the sky, clipping the tops of the trees. It circled above our heads several times, then flew off really quickly. It was silver, disc-shaped, with a domed top and luminous lights, about the size of a car, and it made no noise.' Inspector Brian Heal, of the Abertillery police, was quoted as saying: 'We have to take any incident like this seriously and whatever it was the boys saw they were very scared by it.' (*South Wales Argus*, Newport, 7 Nov. 1989)

3 November 1989: Whitefield, Manchester, UK

Two retired professional people saw a luminous, golden-coloured, cigar-shaped object – described as like a 'test-tube' – with a domed nose but a flatter, less defined 'end', which seemed to have a type of flickering and moving 'fluid' inside. (Michael Cookson, *Northern UFO News*, No. 141, Feb. 1990)

9 November 1989: Leningrad, USSR

A shining rectangular-shaped object, apparently metallic, was seen flying swiftly at very low level above the Prospect Prosveshenia by P. A. Stibel. (Supplied by Nikolai Lebedev)

18 November 1989: Torquay, Devon, UK

A witness encountered a cylindrical-shaped, fluorescent object, possibly 100 feet in length, hovering about 200 feet above the sea, fifty yards from the beach, at 7.50 a.m. (*Torquay Herald Express*, 22 Nov. 1989)

20 November 1989: Tarnaszentmaria, Hungary

Following a number of strange occurrences at the Tarnas-zentmaria army barracks, beginning on 20 October, soldiers on guard duty noticed a cloud of red mist in the sky with curious flashing lights inside it, followed by a Saturn-shaped UFO, which floated over the barracks and disappeared over the forest. Two of the guards reported that they were illuminated briefly with a powerful beam of light which made them sick. Later that night Private Lajos Dioszegi reported seeing ten-foot-tall figures in the forest clearing facing the barracks. 'They were moving as if they were chess pieces,' he stated. 'All the animals in the barracks – pigs, sheep and dogs – became frantic.' (Gabriel Ronay, *The Times*, London, 19 April 1990)

24 November 1989: Papa, Hungary

Meteorologists sighted four large, spherical, bright orange objects, approximately fifty metres in diameter. Gyula Bazso, from a meteorological station in Papa, western Hungary, reported that one of the objects flew at 2,625 m.p.h. He contacted the local military airbase which sent up a pilot, who located four objects at an altitude of about four miles. All the objects disappeared shortly after 2.00 a.m. on 25 November. (*Shropshire Star*, Wellington, 27 Nov. 1989)

29 November 1989: Eupen, Belgium

On two occasions, Sergeant-Majors Heinrich Nicoll and Hubert von Montigny of the Belgian police observed a triangular-shaped object with beams of light illuminating a field. Many other witnesses reported sightings that evening. (See Chapter 2)

2 December 1989: Butgenbach, Luxembourg

A young boy reported that he came so close to a UFO that he panicked and jumped into a canal to hide. At precisely the same time, witnesses nearby claimed to have seen four or five objects. (See Chapter 2)

7 December 1989: Miami, Florida, USA

Tony Arias, a night watchman at the Colonial Palms Shopping Center, claimed to have encountered a strange being, seven feet five inches tall, bald, with a 'big head and cat eyes', in the parking lot. According to police, Arias called at 4.30 a.m. and officer Juan Santana responded. 'This sketch was provided by the reporter. We are not joking, this is what he drew . . . this is one of the weirdest reports I've ever read.' In his official report [a copy of which is in my possession. – *Ed.*] Santana wrote: 'Upon my arrival an extensive search was conducted for the described "thing", with negative results. Reporter thinks he saw two other "things" with the first one.' 'My first thought was that it was someone in some kind of scary costume,' said Sgt. Joe Wyche. 'But I just don't know. Whatever he saw shook him up enough to call us.' (Jon O'Neill, *Miami Herald*, 10 Dec. 1989)

8 December 1989: San Diego, California, USA

Two hospital secretaries saw unusual lights in the sky as they were driving southbound on Interstate 5. Pulling into a parking lot they watched the lights manoeuvring over San Diego for half an hour. Suddenly the lights approached the witnesses, and a silvery-blue object passed silently over their pick-up truck. 'It was so close, if I'd had a gun, I could have shot at it,' said Martha (last name withheld). She described the object as an octagon with a V-shaped appendage on the back. Under the 'V' were three bright pulsating lights. (Brae Canlen, *Reader*, San Diego, California, 8 Feb. 1990)

21 December 1989: Moscow, USSR

Many witnesses in Moscow reported seeing unexplainable glowing objects which suddenly appeared in the sky. Particularly interesting were reports from Arczimovich and Ostrovskiy streets, where for almost three and a half hours a giant glowing, rotating ellipse was seen. On its sides were sparkling red, green, and white small 'flames'. It was surrounded by a blurred, twinkling cloud, and a glowing column came down, like a searchlight. The object moved slowly over the streets, sometimes changing direction.

'We contacted the Cheremuskinskiy Internal Affairs district's department and asked them to help ascertain what was happening,' the *Trud* correspondent reported. 'At 18.15, deputy chiefs of the 27th Department of the Militia, R. Sadretdinov and I. Nosov, departed for the Beliaevo underground station. They were surprised to see, over the Moscow ring road, a bright red sphere in the sky, flying in the direction of the Domodedovo airport.

'Militia men tried to overtake the object in cars, but the UFO behaved as if it was aware of this, sometimes moving quickly to the left or right, sometimes remaining stationary. The pursuit continued until the village of Sosenki, approximately twenty kilometres from the ring road. Eventually the object disappeared. It will be left to the scientists to explain what it was . . .' (*Trud*, Moscow, 22 Dec. 1989, supplied and translated by Nikolai Lebedev)

22 December 1989: High Wycombe, Buckinghamshire, UK

Aviation expert Peter Halliday and his wife claimed to have seen a disk-shaped aircraft speed across the sky at 11.42 a.m. 'I know what I saw was no aircraft or weather balloon or a satellite . . . it was definitely a UFO,' he said. (*Bucks Free Press*, High Wycombe, 29 Dec. 1989)

8 January 1990: Gulf Breeze, Florida, USA

Brenda Pollak and eight other witnesses observed this black disk hovering for about fifteen minutes (Figure 10:9). (*Sentinel*, Gulf Breeze, Florida, 18 Jan. 1990)

Figure 10:9. A drawing of the black disk over Gulf Breeze. In the centre was a red circle with four or five very bright spots that seemed to 'boil'. The outer white dots show the approximate position of 'portholes'.

9 January 1990: Skipton, Yorkshire, UK

At 6.30 p.m. John Sharp was walking his dog along a country lane on the outskirts of Skipton when his attention was drawn to a pulsating, pale yellow light approaching from the south. As it came closer, Mr Sharp was able to clearly see that it was triangular in shape with a single tail-fin at the rear. He said the object was about twenty feet across at its widest point.

As it passed overhead it banked and turned, at an estimated speed of below 50 m.p.h. The object appeared to be black, and the only light visible was of the pale yellow colour, pulsating on half of the underside. The only noise was a 'swish', presumably from displaced air. The UFO then gained height as it approached nearby hills and eventually went out of sight (Figure 10:10). (Tony Dodd, *Quest International*, Vol. 9, No. 3, 1990)

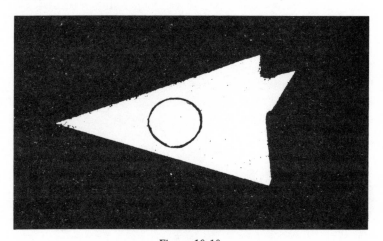

Figure 10:10.

10 January 1990: Near Taiyuan City, Shanxi Province, China

At 9.10 p.m., two People's Liberation Army soldiers encountered a black disk which followed them in their jeep for about half an hour. When the soldiers stopped, the object also stopped in the air, then circled and disappeared after the men shouted at it. (See Chapter 6)

20 January 1990: Boyle, Mississippi, USA

A man driving home observed a slow-moving silvery object at tree-top height. A crease in the surface near the rounded top was the only variation in an otherwise cone-shaped exterior. Two rows of numerous lights, each in a blue-blue-green pattern (see Figure 10:11), shone steadily. One row was situated near the base, the other along the perimeter of the flat bottom. The object picked up speed and paced just above and in front of the car for two to three miles, repeatedly moving left and right to avoid larger trees along the roadside. Abruptly the car's engine, lights, and instruments died. The witness pulled to a halt and watched as the object continued down the road, then executed a smooth turn and climbed out of sight. He was then able to restart the engine. (James Scarborough, *MUFON UFO Journal*, No. 264, April 1990)

Figure 10:11.

31 January 1990: Halifax, Pennsylvania, USA

Driving to Harrisburg at 6.30 p.m., Donna and Tom Rode encountered a strange object, shaped like a 'sting-ray' with three lights, one blinking. The object had no fuselage and Donna (who knows about aircraft) estimated that it was much larger than a Boeing 747 and flying at about 10–15,000 feet. Ten minutes later the object went out of sight in a northerly direction. (Lori Schoffstall, *Sentinel*, Dauphin, Pennsylvania, 20 Feb. 1990)

27 February 1990: Bartley Green Reservoir, Birmingham, UK

Two witnesses encountered a hovering UFO at about 3.00 p.m., and a photograph was taken (Plate 10:1). I have spoken and corresponded with the photographer, Peter Woolaway, who seems sincere.

4 March 1990: Provincetown, Massachusetts, USA

Captain Gerald Costa and three other crew members, returning home after a two-day trip aboard a scalloper, saw an unidentifiable spherical object next to the Wood End lighthouse at about 11.30 p.m. The object was described as 'completely round', grey in colour, 'about thirty feet high by thirty feet wide' with 'a lot of windows' that ringed the top half of the craft. Costa said that he then heard four booms and saw what he thought were four more objects taking off from Long Point, at an estimated speed of 1,000 m.p.h. (Peter Steele, *Advocate*, Provincetown, Massachusetts, 15 March 1990)

21 March 1990: Moscow, USSR

According to the Chief of the General Staff of Air Defence Forces, Colonel Igor Maltsev, a disk-like UFO with a diameter of 100–200 metres and a speed two or three times that of jet fighters, was seen and tracked on radar at a height of from 1,000–7,000 metres. Lt-Col A. Semenchuk approached and flew above the object in an interceptor jet. (Lt-Col M. Zaharchuk, *Workers Tribune*, 19 April 1990 translated by Nikolai Lebedev)

6 April 1990: Ulyanovsk, USSR

Soviet pilots, air-traffic controllers and hundreds of residents in the Volga city of Ulyanovsk saw a UFO hovering above the city between 8.30 and 9 p.m. The object reportedly looked like a blue-green ball, and seemed to be larger than the apparent size of the moon. (*Rocky Mountain News,* Denver, Colorado, 16 April 1990)

14 April 1990: Southend, Essex, UK

Eight people in the Southend area reported seeing a large, dull, red-coloured object which 'waggled' in flight, was saucer-shaped and about 40 feet in diameter, at an estimated height of 500 feet and speed of 1,000 m.p.h. (*Yellow Advertiser*, Colchester, 27 April 1990) (Further details available from the East Anglian UFO & Paranormal Association)

21–22 April 1990: Rome, Italy

Phone lines to police, radio and TV stations were jammed for two hours as hundreds of witnesses, including pilots, reported seeing a 'kind of luminous ball that left smoke in its trail' over Rome. Air force jets were sent in pursuit, but failed to catch the UFO, which vanished in a puff of smoke. (*Rocky Mountain News*, Denver, Colorado, 30 April and *Daily Star*, London, 23 April 1990)

Appendix

Some major UFO organizations
(Australia, Canada, UK and USA)

Australia

Australian Centre for UFO Studies, P.O. Box 728, Lane Grove, NSW 2066.

UFO Research Australia, P.O. Box 229, Prospect, South Australia 5082.

UFO Research Queensland, P.O. Box 111, North Quay, Queensland 4002.

Victorian UFO Research Society, P.O. Box 43, Moorabbin, Victoria 3189.

Canada

Canadian UFO Research Network, P.O. Box 15, Station 'A', Willowdale, Ontario, M2N 5S7.

Centrale de Compilation Ufologique de Quebec, CP 103, Drummondville, Quebec, J2B 2V6.

Manitoba Centre for UFO Studies

United Kingdom

British UFO Research Association, 16 Southway, Burgess Hill, Sussex, RH15 9ST.

Contact International (UK), 11 Ouseley Close, New Marston, Oxford, OX3 0JS.

East Anglian UFO & Paranormal Association, 95 Chilburn Road, Great Clacton, Essex, CO15 4PE.

Quest International, 18 Hardy Meadows, Grassington, Skipton, North Yorkshire, BD23 5DL.

United States of America

Citizens Against UFO Secrecy, 3518 Martha Custis Avenue, Alexandria, Virginia 22302.

Fund for UFO Research, P.O. Box 277, Mount Rainier, Maryland 20712.

J. Allen Hynek Center for UFO Studies, 2547 W. Peterson Avenue, Chicago, Illinois 60659.

Mutual UFO Network, 103 Oldtowne Road, Seguin, Texas 78155-4099.

UFO Reporting & Information Service, P.O. Box 832, Mercer Island, Washington 98040.

Pennsylvania Association for the Study of the Unexplained, 6 Oak Hill Avenue, Greensburg, Pennsylvania 15601.

The Crop Circles

Centre for Crop Circle Studies
The CCCS was founded in 1990, with Professor Archie Roy, BSc., PhD., F.R.A.S. as President. The main objective of CCCS is to conduct well organized research into the Crop Circle phenomenon, both in the UK and overseas, and to publish its data and findings in CCCS publications and other serious outlets. CCCS is very conscious of the fact that the Crop Circles occur almost invariably on private land owned or cultivated by the farming community, and encourages its members and affiliates to adhere to a strict Code of Practice, an agreement on which has been reached with the National Farmers Union.

For further details, send a stamped addressed envelope (UK only) to: CCCS, P.O. Box 146, Guildford, Surrey, GU2 5JY, UK.

Some UFO Journals

Flying Saucer Review
Edited by Gordon Creighton, M.A., F.R.G.S., F.R.A.S., with an international team of consultants, *FSR* is arguably the leading journal on the subject of UFOs, and is taken by many governmental bodies and institutions, including the Chinese Institute of Scientific & Technical Information and the USSR Academy of Sciences.

For subscription details, send a stamped addressed envelope to: The Editor, FSR Publications Ltd, P.O. Box 12, Snodland, Kent, ME6 5JZ, UK.

Fortean Times
A quarterly journal devoted to news, notes, reviews, and references on all manner of strange phenomena, continuing the work of Charles Fort (1874–1932). Write to: *Fortean Times*, SKS, 20 Paul Street, Frome, Somerset, BA11 1DX, UK.

International UFO Reporter
Edited by Jerome Clark and published by the J. Allen Hynek Center for UFO Studies, *IUR* is one of the two leading UFO journals in the USA. Address inquiries to: *International UFO Reporter*, 2457 W. Peterson Avenue, Chicago, Illinois 60659, USA.

241

Journal of UFO Research

A bi-monthly Chinese-language journal with the world's largest circulation, devoted to UFOs and Science. Write for details to: Paul Dong, P.O. Box 2011, Oakland, California 94604, USA.

Just Cause

Edited by Barry Greenwood and published by Lawrence Fawcett (authors of *Clear Intent*), this journal is essential reading for those interested in the US Government cover-up. Write to: CAUS, P.O. Box 218, Coventry, Connecticut 06238, USA.

MUFON UFO Journal

Published by the Mutual UFO Network, with a staff of reporters and columnists second to none, the *MUFON UFO Journal* has established itself as one of the finest magazines on the subject in the world. Write for details to: MUFON, 103 Oldtowne Road, Seguin, Texas 78155-4099, USA.

Northern UFO News

Edited by Jenny Randles, this journal is always packed with fascinating reports that are seldom published elsewhere. Write to: *Northern UFO News*, 37 Heathbank Road, Cheadle Heath, Stockport, Cheshire, SK3 0UP, UK.

Quest International

Edited by Graham Birdsall, *Quest International* is a highly popular journal, featuring articles by a wide variety of international contributors. Slides, audio and video tapes, etc., are also available from this organization (formerly the Yorkshire UFO Society). Send a stamped addressed envelope to: Quest Publications International Ltd, 15 Pickard Court, Temple Newsam, Leeds, Yorkshire, LS15 9AY, UK.

Services

Books on UFOs

Those requiring books on UFOs which are not currently available in the bookshops should write, enclosing a large stamped addressed envelope, to: Susanne Stebbing, 41 Terminus Drive, Herne Bay, Kent, CT6 6PR, UK, or Arcturus Book Service, P.O. Box 831383, Stone Mountain, Georgia 30083-0023, USA.

UFO Newsclipping Service

The UFO Newsclipping Service will keep you informed of all the latest United States and worldwide reports, many of which are carried only in local newspapers. For subscription details, write to: Lucius Farish, UFO Newsclipping Service, Route 1, Box 220, Plumerville, Arkansas 72127, USA.

UK Newsclippings

For those requiring UK newsclippings only, a service is provided by CETI Publications in association with Quest International. For subscription details, write to: CETI Publications, 247 High Street, Beckenham, Kent BR3 1AB, UK, enclosing a stamped addressed envelope.

UFO Call

The British UFO Research Association and British Telecom run a 24-hour UFO news update service on (0898) 121886.

UFO Hotline

Quest International has a 24-hour UFO Hotline for reporting sightings in the UK: telephone (0756) 752216.

Computer UFO Network/UFO Reporting & Information Service

CUFON was established in the USA by Dale Goudie for the purpose of providing other UFO researchers with quick access to sighting data and locations, as well as documented Freedom of Information material.

Contact: Computer UFO Network, Computer line: (connect at 300 or 1200 bauds, eight data bits, no parity, one stop bit) (206) 721 5035, from 20.00–08.00 WST. The UFO Reporting & Information Service functions from 08.00–20.00, also on (206) 721 5035.

MUFON Amateur Radio Net

80 m – 3.990 MHz, Saturdays, 10.00 p.m.
40 m – 7.237 MHz, Saturdays, 8.00 a.m.
10 m – 28.460 MHz, Thursdays, 8.00 p.m.
10 m – 28.470 MHz, Sundays, 3.00 p.m.
All times are Eastern Standard or Daylight

Reporting Sightings

The majority of sightings turn out to have a mundane explanation, such as aircraft landing lights, balloons, planets, satellites, space debris, etc., but if you *really* think you may have seen something more exotic, do contact one or more of the organizations listed above. In addition, the police will investigate a sighting if it is considered sufficiently important, and they are required to submit a report to the Ministry of Defence, as are military bases and air traffic control officers (in the UK), but in most instances the report is simply filed away and neglected. If you approach the MoD directly, they will point out that they investigate cases solely for defence implications, and seldom notify witnesses of their findings.

I also recommend contacting your local newspaper or radio/TV station, so that someone else in the vicinity may be able to corroborate the sighting. The national press keep tabs on local papers, so there is also the possibility that they may decide to carry the story if it is sufficiently interesting; indeed, in this case you could telephone one of the national dailies immediately, thus ensuring that in the event of publication we all learn about it with the minimum delay.

Index

INDEX